Gender and Christianity
in Medieval Europe

THE MIDDLE AGES SERIES
Ruth Mazo Karras, Series Editor
Edward Peters, Founding Editor

A complete list of books in the series is available from the publisher.

Gender and Christianity in Medieval Europe

New Perspectives

EDITED BY LISA M. BITEL AND
FELICE LIFSHITZ

PENN

University of Pennsylvania Press

Philadelphia

Published by
University of Pennsylvania Press
Philadelphia, Pennsylvania 19104-4112

Printed in the United States of America on acid-free paper

10 9 8 7 6 5 4 3 2 1

Library of Congress Cataloging-in-Publication Data

Gender and Christianity in medieval Europe : new perspectives / edited by Lisa M. Bitel and Felice Lifshitz.
          p.   cm. — (The Middle Ages series)
    Includes bibliographical references.
    ISBN-13: 978-0-8122-4069-6 (hardcover : alk. paper)
    ISBN-10: 0-8122-4069-3 (hardcover : alk. paper)
1. Sex role—Religious aspects—Christianity.   2. Europe—Church history—600–1500.
I. Bitel, Lisa M.   II. Lifshitz, Felice.
    BT708.G45 2007
    274′.03082—dc22

                                                                              2007030143

To Jo Ann McNamara
magistra doctissima et mater omnium bonarum

Contents

Introduction

Convent Ruins and Christian Profession

Toward a Methodology for the History of Religion and Gender

Lisa M. Bitel

Near Tuam in the west of Ireland, a partial wall stands in an otherwise empty field (Figure 1). It forms an arch of big, rough rocks. A passerby who looks through the arch will see more fields marked by a recent low wall meant to keep in the cattle. If she looks through the other way, she will also glimpse fields. The farmer who owns the land has neither knocked down the arch nor preserved it. Cows graze around it. Nineteenth-century surveyors noted it on ordnance survey maps. Modern tourists who stray into the field to confront the arch—and there are not many—cannot possibly make much of it.

The broken arch is all that remains of the medieval convent of Cell Craobhnat, also known through the medieval centuries as Kilcreevanty, Saint Mary of Casta Silva, Kilcreunata, Cill-Craebhnat, and Kilcrevet.[1] Only a few written records marked the birth and death of the convent. Its foundation document from around 1200, along with a petition submitted to Pope Honorius III by the first generation of nuns, hint at the diverse devotional practices and spiritualities of women who once lived there. Cell Craobhnat's nuns began as Benedictines, decided to become Cistercians, and then, at the order of a local bishop, were forced to turn Arrouasian, a more restrained order of the Augustinians popular in Ireland. A brusque account of the convent's dissolution in the Tudor period three hundred-some years later reveals that Cell Craobhnat had by then become the mother house of at least fifteen more Arrouasian communities in western Ireland. When King Henry VIII emptied and expropriated Irish monasteries in the early sixteenth century, Cell Craobhnat still owned a thousand acres.[1] Together, however, the texts mention only four women who lived at Cell Craobhnat over the course of more than three centuries, all of whom were abbesses descended from the convent's founding family of O Conors.

Fig. 1: Cell Craobhnat, thirteenth-century Arrouasian convent near Tuam, County Galway. (Photograph by Pete Schermerhorn).

Only a few stones and written words suggest the generations of vowed women at Cell Craobhnat. The stones tell us that women and men to-gether once built and practiced religion in this now lonely field. The scant records of Cell Craobhnat hint at who these people might have been and what they did. Other longer documents from better preserved communities can help historians imagine life at Cell Craobhnat. Per-haps the nuns' prayers and processions were like those at richer con-vents or men's monasteries. Maybe their cloister resembled the fine enclosed courtyards of French or English houses. But modern travelers to the arch near Tuam who hear the name of Cell Craobhnat must also be struck by how much history—as well as whose history and what kind of history—has escaped professional historians. Nothing remains of the nuns' everyday tasks, desires, devotions, lifelong aims, friendships, superi-ors, confessors, families, servants, kings, and the mundane world that con-tained them all. Since that world disappeared, historians have learned more about Continental religious women than about Irish women. They discovered more about religious men than about religious women, more about Irish monasteries than about this particular convent, and much more about the religion of the well-read and well-bred than about the beliefs of the unlearned and powerless. Modern scholars still know almost nothing about how ordinary Europeans used to live as Christians.

Cell Craobhnat's ruins are a fitting metaphor for this book, which seeks to explain the convergence of religion and gender in medieval Christendom. All the chapters directly address the scanty, imbalanced nature of the evidence. Together, the chapters follow two main lines of inquiry. First, they seek to explain how Europeans identified themselves as women, men, and Christians both in thought and in everyday practice, and how these identities intersected with religious belief and practice. Second, the chapters extend the definition of religious profession to mean more than monastic vows or formal ecclesiastical ordination. In these chapters, the religiously mindful behavior of all medieval Christians counts as religious "profession."

The Lenses of Gender and Religion

In the beginning—after God created man and woman, and after the Middle Ages but before medievalist scholarship was infiltrated by archaeology, art history, social science, feminism, and gender theory—most historians studied only important men and their texts. These masculine subjects were mostly but not exclusively ecclesiastics or rulers. Academics at nineteenth- and early twentieth-century universities wrote footnoted tales of medieval institutions built by kings, knights, churchmen, and merchants. Then, close to 1900, a few female scholars inspired by suffragist movements in their own societies began to hunt for evidence about women's lives in the medieval past. Because nuns left proportionately more documents than other medieval women, many of the first major studies of women focused on convents. Even though other medievalists had begun to scour the archives for economic and religious evidence and to publish multivolume editions of sources, they tended to leave the charters and prayer books of convents behind in dusty boxes of manuscripts. Women's historians remained in the archives, seeking evidence for prosperous, well-established convents, which helped them map some medieval women's lives and devotional practices on the landscape of men's institutions and hierarchies. The women who had once inhabited these famous convents became explicable to scholars when their communities mimicked men's institutions and models and when the documents that recorded women's experience used the language of monks and monasteries.

The authors of such pioneering studies imagined medieval religious women to have been much like modern nuns in teaching and nursing orders who, protected by heavy veils and celibate vows, seemed like living relics of the Middle Ages.[2] Early twentieth-century medievalists thus applied modern social logic to medieval women's religious inspiration. It seemed to sympathetic scholars that a young girl would seek imprisonment in a convent only if she were fleeing an even worse situation, such as the burdens of marriage and childbearing. Women went to convents when they had no other options. For a progressive scholar such as Eileen Power (1889–1940), medieval spirituality was a delusion of independence driven by gender politics and patriarchal economies that denied women jobs and property.[3] She wrote in her 1924 *Medieval People* that Eglentyne, Geoffrey Chaucer's fourteenth-century fictional Prioress, "became a nun because her father did not want the trouble and expense of finding her a husband, and because being a nun was about the only career for a well-born lady who did not marry. Moreover, by this time, monks and nuns had grown more lazy, and did little work with their hands and still less with their heads, particularly in nunneries, where the early tradition of learning had died out and where many nuns could hardly understand the Latin in which their services were written."[4] In Power's view, sexual norms and religion together oppressed women who rarely engineered their own destinies. In the eyes of her German contemporary, Herbert Grundmann (1902–1970), women's medieval devotions resulted from a skewed sex ratio that set too many single girls loose in society; as a result, medieval fathers who lacked sufficient dowry funds, along with dismayed secular rulers and church leaders, tried to send extra daughters and widows into the cloister.[5]

Throughout the twentieth century, medievalists continued to peer at religious institutions and vowed women through blinkers of their own sexual politics. They also continued to engage Power and Grundmann. When feminist historians of the latter twentieth century came to study evidence for medieval nuns, their heightened gender consciousness led them to new but no more generous interpretations of religiosity. In the 1960s and 1970s, when demographic and economic historians were striving valiantly to include women in their studies of family and household, scholars began to emphasize the strategies and solidarities of medieval European women who chose religious careers as a conscious alternative to patriarchy and its institutions of marriage and motherhood.[6] Some argued that women's departure for the cloister brought them wide-ranging influence over kinship and clientage networks within and beyond convent walls.[7] Janet Nelson showed, for instance, how the moral criticism leveled at Frankish queens by Gregory of Tours and other ecclesiastical authors reflected the immense political power of Frankish abbesses.[8]

Toward the end of the twentieth century, historians of religious women became preoccupied with "silences" and "gaps" in the written record, by which they mean the lack of female-authored evidence. Where, they wondered, were women's own voices? The feminist campaign to recover women's literary output inspired literary scholars to rescue the writings of cloistered women, previously dismissed as personal and devotional rather than relevant to the mainstream development of Christianity.[9] Archaeologists dug up material evidence to fill the historical gaps between written words. Some pointed out the chronic poverty of convents compared to monasteries, consistent with a more general historical picture of female disinheritance, which reduced vowed women to dependence on male overseers and guardians or left them in abject poverty.[10] Others used archaeological evidence to free women's monastic communities from the impositions of men's history; Roberta Gilchrist, for example, showed how women in convents organized, located, and understood their spaces differently than men did, based on distinctly female religious aims.[11] Scholars used everything from postholes in the dirt of convent sites to hand-colored devotional pictures in order to trace the daily labors of women's lives. Material remains and economic records, examined together, revalued women's labors and revealed convents to be self-sufficient communities in which privileged females contributed to discretely feminine spiritual and artistic canons.[12] In the light of such success stories of medieval convents, scholars also debated which decades of the Middle Ages had been most receptive to religious women, searching for a golden age of nuns by examining the range of women's religious choices and the durability of religious communities.[13]

Even more recently, scholars have begun to return to the texts, using them to reframe the medieval past as a period inflected and even defined by gender. Historians no longer segregate the Middle Ages into histories of single sexes or of one sex strictly in relation to the other. Building on Joan Scott's 1986 admonition to use gender as a lens for looking backward, many medievalists have tried to understand the absence of female agents in historical documents by studying patterns of interactions among women and men. Some have closely examined men-as-a-group and probed the creation and meaning of masculinities. Others have sought to understand how gendered expectations of ordinary men and women guided their social and cultural performances.[14] Still other scholars have wondered whether, when medieval writers wrote of men, women, femininity, or masculinity, they were really writing about other problems—kings and subjects, bodies and souls, or Christians and non-Christians.[15] Jo Ann McNamara used gender to deconstruct the chronological definition of what we call the Middle Ages, arguing that the most powerful noblewomen and noblemen of the early medieval period shared the same gender status until a shift in family systems transformed gender ideologies and roles sometime in the twelfth century or so.[16] By the early twenty-first century, then, medievalists and scholars of other periods and places had finally learned how to spot vowed women as well as other sorts of (Christian) women in the past, how to revise traditional history to include women, and how to explicate both the gendered history and the history of gender in medieval Christendom.

What historians still sometimes forget, however, is that the lens of gender is but one of many glasses that help observers focus on the medieval past. Another equally essential tool for explicating the European Middle Ages is religion, specifically the dominant doctrines of Christianity. Just as sexual politics have channeled historians' understanding of gender in the medieval past, so the secularization of Western academe over the last two hundred years and the resulting tension between religious and non-religious interpretations of history have prevented historians from appreciating just how profoundly Christianity penetrated the lives of pre-modern Europeans. The distinctions that historians draw between secular and religious life or between religious professionals and laypeople are peculiarly modern markers born of much later European developments: the Reformation and Enlightenment, capitalism and industrialization, and the increasing dominance of scientific and social science discourses in public discussion of the past. Except for some self-identified religious and intellectual historians, too many scholars assume that Christianity was a feature of the medieval background that needs no direct reference in relation to topics of social, political, or economic history. Just as medievalists once could not imagine the importance of gender for the study of politics or trade, most still fail to examine these phenomena through the lens of religious belief and practice. The few exceptions have tended to treat either comparative medieval cultures or historical situations where people of different religions came into contact or conflict.[17]

Medievalists seem unable to achieve true binocularity with their lenses of gender and religion. Monographs and essay collections purporting to take the double perspective still concentrate mostly on three areas: beliefs and practices of self-identified religious women, Christian gender ideologies and discrete feminine spiritualities; and issues of masculinity. Studies of women's spirituality tend to focus on women who defied norms and practiced subversive forms of Christianity, usually under the disapproving if not hostile scrutiny of male overseers. Dyan Elliott has shown how female confessants of the twelfth and thirteenth centuries forced their interpretations of Christianity on their religion's leaders and ideologues.[18] A few historians have also found examples of women's direct, positive influence on the ecclesiastical mainstream. Caroline Walker

Bynum famously showed in her work of the 1980s how monastic men and holy women both manipulated concepts of gender to express new religious ideals and debut devotional practices. For example, the abbot Bernard of Clairvaux (1090–1153), whose authorial voice was often sternly masculine, promoted the cult of the Virgin Mary and developed an interpretation of the Christian savior as a nurturing mother to his Cistercian monks; as abbot, Bernard himself practiced the same maternal role. Bynum also showed how the bodily oriented spirituality of such mystics as Gertrude of Helfta and Catherine of Siena pervaded mainstream Christian spirituality.[19]

Only a very few medievalists have been able to step outside the march of historiographical fads and maintain a broad, unblinkered focus on the mutual operations of gender and religion in the medieval centuries. As Jo Ann McNamara observed in a 1973 article, historians then were still working to fit medieval women into the traditional and "generally respected" parameters of Rome's fall and the putative twelfth-century cultural renaissance. However, by 2003, when McNamara rewrote that paper, she found that "even as we try to fit time into categories, labeling the minutes, years, decades, and centuries . . . we have been caught ourselves in its relentless current."[20] In her magistral work, *Sisters in Arms* (1996), McNamara presented the history of Christian vowed women as a history of partnership among women in all-female communities and also between women and men who actively developed the spiritualities and institutions of Christianity.[21] In every period—from Gospel days to the turn of the last millennium—McNamara detected historical moments when inspired women and men transcended the limits of gender ideologies to achieve genuine collaboration in the building of religion.

Perhaps, then, by imitating McNamara and constantly questioning our own most basic assumptions about the practice of history, medievalists can finally begin to appreciate the routine convergence of religion and gender in earlier Europe. Dominant Christian discourses both erased and promoted gender differences, sometimes simultaneously—as when bishops and theologians repeatedly prohibited women from ordination and preaching on the grounds that women who strove for spiritual perfection would eventually achieve the same asexual state as good men. At other points in the medieval past, however, commonly held religious principles helped women and men challenge predictable gender roles and ideologies. For instance, literacy and the ability to write were not among traditional expectations for either women or men in early medieval Europe, yet life in a monastery led a fortunate few from both sexes to careers as scribes, artists, and authors. In fact, throughout all periods of the Middle Ages, only certain kinds of men and women could choose single-sex communal life and celibacy over traditional families.

Likewise, gender ideologies hindered the religious profession of both men and women. Christians who wished to divorce and yet remain orthodox faced difficult and even tragic choices because canon law, based on the epistles of Paul, prohibited the sundering of marriage bonds. But believers also relied on familiar gender roles to shield them as they crossed social and political boundaries—for instance, when women of different faiths shared the secrets of midwifery in fifteenth-century Castile or when fourteenth-century farmwives and noblewomen colluded in hosting and hiding the heretical preachers of Montaillou.[22] Throughout the medieval centuries, discussions of gender led church reformers to question the sexualized hierarchy that privileged virgins. Examples of opinion and practice come from all periods and regions of Europe, from the abbatial dynasties of eighth-century Ireland, to the affair of Heloise and Abelard in eleventh-century France, to Martin Luther's condemnations of a celibate clergy in his printed treatises.

The mutable, organic relation between gender and Christian identities affected every European, even non-Christians. Those men and women who lived in single-sex communities and vowed themselves to lives of social isolation were "religious," but so were Christians who underwent particularly devout periods in their lives. Those who lived consciously and piously, as well as baptized women and men who were not conscientious churchgoers, also professed and practiced religion. Although European intellectuals recognized other human possibilities, most medieval babies after about 600 were quickly gendered and baptized.[23] Only a tiny minority of Europeans was of another, or no apparent, religion. If a baptized infant survived childhood, he or she grew into some kind of Christian—male or female, celibate or sexually active, pious and observant or not, orthodox, recalcitrant, or heretical. Christianity operated in many more mundane arenas than formal rituals, intellectual endeavors, or meditative practices. The rhetoric of medieval documents, however, suggests only a few well-defined ways of publicly professing the faith. Theologies, monastic rules, institutional reports, laws, congregational decrees, spiritual literature, hagiography, and other genres of medieval texts contained only a fraction of the possibilities for living as Christians. The practice of cloistered withdrawal, which was the only official religious career available to women throughout most of the Middle Ages, worked for only a fraction of women and men. Monasticism was neither the norm nor the realistic goal of most self-identified Christians. The great majority of men and women professed religion in other ways every day of their lives.

Medieval Christians defined religious thought and vocations both spatially and temporally, as well as through a wide range of behaviors that scholars have only begun to detect. Public processions, legal oaths, seasonal holiday celebrations, and sudden changes in political regime all resonated with Christian meaning. Private deeds sent religious messages, too. For example, a young woman in late medieval Italy or England could identify and be recognized by contemporaries as a religious practitioner by something as simple as her disgust for cosmetics and costume. She might live quietly at home with her parents and siblings, but when she tossed her best shoes out the door to a beggar or gave away the family meal to hungry vagrants, her family might react with dismay. Her utter disdain for men and marriage, her hours of prayer, and her knees bruised from repetitive penance were more obvious cues. Historians can usually spot these religious professionals only when they caught the attention of neighbors, officials, and record-keepers. When the teenaged Catherine of Siena shut herself in her room around 1360, displaying many of those cues mentioned here, her parents badgered and punished her. At the end of the same century, Margery Kempe (ca. 1373–1438) spent years weeping publicly and arguing with her husband and confessors to be released from marriage so that she might live chastely. Catherine and Margery persevered against refusal, and thus earned their way into history—in fact, some might argue that these women aggressively pursued conflicts with authority that ultimately brought them fame. Catherine did not shun a highly public profile when she marched her clerical retinue off to Avignon to resolve the papal schism, or fired letters of advice to the Italian pontiff. Margery would have faded into oblivion if she had not carefully chosen a malleable confessor, demanded examination by the bishop, or promoted her own story of clashes with religious authorities.[24]

Yet many other self-identified religious probably enjoyed the willing collaboration and amiable society of family and neighbors, with the result that they remain unknown to modern historians. Saint Monenna, an early medieval Irish saint, supposedly took a youthful vow of chastity and remained contentedly in her parents' house *seorsum* (apart), ideologically and possibly spatially. Her folks must have been happy with her decision, for no one objected. We know her early history only because she later became a cloistered abbess and eventually a celebrated saint.[25] The larger community always shaped and responded to an individual's particular professions of gender and religion according to specific local circumstances, and then rendered these believers for history.[26] But medieval authors tended to ignore contented and cooperative religious women, noting mostly the stunning achievements and spectacular failures of vowed women—the runaway nuns and heretic wives—whereas they often littered the documents with the mundane lives of vowed and ordained men. Men simply had more formally recognized opportunities for religious careers, which demanded bureaucratic record-keeping.

When modern historians still fail to see religion in the ordinary events of the medieval past or gender in the daily operations of medieval Christianity, it is because—like suffragists looking at nuns—they are blinkered by their own expectations of religion and gender in their own putatively equitable and secularized modernity. The search for medieval women once brought us to nuns; gender history and gender theory now have led us to a new relationship with the religious past. Gender consciousness offers both theoretical and practical models for religiously sensitive scholarship. To be mindful of Christianity's pervasive presence in medieval Europe does not require taking a confessional stance but only vigilance for the religious implications of events and ideas in historical situations. Like tourists in the field at Cell Craobhnat, we need to notice and wonder about the enigmatic fragments of lived religion and gender in medieval context.

Professing Gender, Professing Christianity

The contributors to this volume train the double lenses of gender and religion on the Christian past of Europe. Collectively, the chapters here explain how medieval people professed Christianity, how they professed gender, and how the two professions coincided. The authors argue that medieval Europeans chose how to be women and men or some complex combination of these, just as they chose whether and how to be religious. Every contributor tries to step back from received assumptions about the intersections of religion and gender to consider what, exactly, the terms "woman," "man," and "religious" mean for historians. In addition, just as gender history has come to include the study of all genders, rather than simply focusing on the recovery of aristocratic women's past, so the chapters here strive for a more generous definition of religious history, which has too often been a history of its most visible participants and dominant discourses.[27]

These attempts to connect gender and religion—and to use one to understand the other—take different approaches. Some of the chapters investigate the boundaries of gender expressed in formal religious discourses. Other tackle religion as medieval Christians lived it in purposely gendered ways. Still others examine the relation between the material contexts of religious behavior, especially the behavior of those who acted contrary to the formal guidelines posed by religious institutions and gender ideologies. Together, the following five chapters expand the parameters of religious profession to include almost everything a Christian woman or man might do. The chapters also suggest the gendered implications of every pious thought and ritual gesture of medieval Christians.

The book begins with Dyan Elliott's reexamination of the metaphorical "bride of Christ" as a formulaic description for medieval vowed women. She traces ideologies of female virginity from Tertullian, the early third-century theologian who first articulated the bridal metaphor in writing, to much later discussions of virginal poetics and politics. Tertullian's virginal spouse was not the veiled medieval mystic but a response to problems of angelology. He was seeking to fit virtuous humans into the hierarchy of Creation. Mortals could only attain angelic status through union with the savior, which Tertullian phrased in nuptial language, as the Psalms wed Israel and God the Father. The problem was further complicated, however, by gender; in the minds of later Christian thinkers, male bodies were stronger and more easily controlled, thus men made better mates for Jesus. Elliott finds that in the medieval centuries, the role of Christ's bride could liberate religious women from social constraints imposed by gender, but often could also restrict their ritual activities and authority within the ecclesiastical hierarchy. She draws implicitly on both queer theory and cultural history for her methods, but she also continues a venerable tradition of using medieval history to invoke later political issues—in this case, anxieties about interracial and same-sex unions.

Jacqueline Murray also examines the early Christian basis for later medieval ideas about bodies. Rather than theology, however, she focuses on medical and philosophical discussions of sex and gender. As she points out, medieval theories about how the body worked did not always match contemporary ideas about gendered Christian practice. If doctors believed that body heat and hairiness signified masculine ardor and virility, she asks, what did medieval people think of monks who shaved their heads? What about holy women who punished themselves with steamy baths? Murray finds that conceptual models for sex and gender proposed by other modern scholars are insufficient to explain the complex ways that medieval thinkers treated bodies. In fact, she argues, the patristic Christian theology of "one flesh" for male and female believers allowed medieval thinkers extraordinary fluidity when thinking about the sexes. Murray concludes that particular venues of religious experience—martyrdom, the cloister, seniority—were important sites of gender slippage.

Whereas Murray and Elliott explicate medieval theologies and theories of bodies, Ruth Karras asks how pre-modern Europeans reconciled ideals of Christian celibacy with sexually grounded masculinity. Karras rejects the seeming contradiction, argued by other modern scholars, between celibacy and manliness. She also denies Michel Foucault's familiar argument that pre-modern Europeans had no sexual identities but instead conceived of and committed discrete sexual acts—a man might be accused of committing sodomy, for instance, but no one could conceive of a man as a homosexual or could self-identify as such. Karras finds that medieval clerics generated a well-defined and highly self-complimentary sexual identity. They elaborated a concept of celibate masculinity as part of their ongoing combat against sexual temptation. Thomas Aquinas, the thirteenth-century saint and philosopher, serves as the model for Karras's argument about virile chastity. Aquinas supposedly fought off seductive female demons, chasing them out of his room and then praying tearfully for a chastity belt to protect his virginity in future duels with temptresses. Like Aquinas, monastic writers considered themselves to be warriors for God and celibacy, and used terms of both gender identity and religious vocation to frame resistance to bodily demands.

Jane Tibbetts Schulenburg's chapter addresses the issue of tempted celibate bodies from a differently gendered perspective. She engages the old historiographical chestnut of cloistered women's sexuality: did they flee to the protection of convent walls or bridle at imprisonment? Instead of analyzing medieval men's statements of praise for or suspicions about nuns, Schulenburg looks at the places where women lived, worked, and prayed. She considers who created and shared those spaces, and who controlled passage in and out. Although other historians have lamented women's claustration, Schulenburg finds that the cloister was less well defined and far more permeable than either modern scholars or medieval theologians previously thought. Professional religious women worked to preserve the sanctity of their communities but also opened doors in their walls for neighbors and pilgrims so that secular men and women might share access to the saints in specially designed shrines. They used the purity of claustration as a platform from which to extend saintly grace to other Christians.

In the last chapter Felice Lifshitz brings together the volume's themes. She links theories of virginity—treated by Karras, Murray, and Elliott—with the gendered practice of celibacy—as in Schulenburg's cloister—in a study of the politics of purity. Lifshitz examines the simple word *virgo.* It meant "virgin," of course, to Latin speakers of the Middle Ages, but it meant many other things as well. Beginning in the eighth century, liturgists who listed and categorized the saints divided holy men into groups of apostles, evangelists, martyrs, or confessors, but they listed all saintly women as virgins (*virgines*). Martyred mothers and widows were *virgines,* along with the ex-prostitute Mary Magdalen, and Mary, mother of Jesus. Lifshitz shows how the term *virgo* both reduced female sanctity, consigning women to nonpriestly models of sanctity, and privileged celibate women as models of purity. She then tracks the efforts of monastic reformers such as the tenth-century Englishman, Archbishop Dunstan, to reclaim the status of the *virgo* for men and to use celibate purity as a warrant for political power not only within the church but across the entire kingdom. The religious, gendered, and political value of virginity did not necessarily coincide—except when men such as Dunstan chose that it should. As Lifshitz notes in closing, in the long run women probably lost more by their banishment from the priesthood than men did by their exclusion from the category of heavenly virgins, but neither group was completely satisfied with the gendered nature of these prescribed ecclesiastical functions.

Together the chapters in this book suggest a shift in focus rather than a particular view of the medieval past. The contributors have not treated—nor will historians ever identify—all the ways that women and men professed religion in all parts and periods of medieval Europe. Unlike saints of old, modern scholars cannot glimpse the entire medieval world in a single glance. In the sixth century, Saint Columcille of Iona could confidently instruct his marveling disciples: "There are some, though very few, who are enabled by divine grace to see most clearly and distinctly the whole compass of the world, and to embrace within their own wondrously enlarged mental capacity the utmost limits of the heavens and the earth at the same moment, as if all were illumined by a single ray of the sun." Such global vision was not exclusively masculine. Six hundred years later and half a continent away from Iona, a woman of Assisi also witnessed the complete world in a moment's dream of St. Francis. Saint Clare saw herself nursing at Francis's breast when his nipple came away in her mouth; she spit it into a bowl and peered at it to see reflected there a golden microcosm of Creation.[28] The strange visions shared by this Irish abbot and Italian noblewoman—as different as any two historical characters could be, yet still both medieval and Christian—teach a disconcerting lesson about historical blindness. Modern scholars can see only bits and pieces of this lost world. We have only begun to understand how to look at the rubble.

By a twist of focus and a twitch of perspective, we are widening the frame of our historical scrutiny from an empty arch to a view that, at least, hints at a shape and a plan. I began this chapter with the combined metaphors of historical tourism and photography, and the lost women of Cell Craobhnat. I end with the less enigmatic remains of Cell Eóin (Killone), another medieval Irish convent about seventy-five miles south of Cell Craobhnat, in County Mayo. In a photo taken by the antiquarian T. J. Westropp in 1898 (Figure 2), a young woman poses in the foreground of the considerable remains of a Romanesque church. She is dressed for fieldwork in a plain dark skirt, starched white shirtwaist, tie, and practical straw hat. No doubt she wears sturdy boots. The church, all its gaudy finery long gone, presides like an aristocratic dowager over what remains of the convent and its graveyard, still clearly in

Fig. 2: Cell Eóin (Killone) Convent, 1898 (Photograph by Thomas Johnson Westropp, by permission of Clare County Library).

use behind the lady. The field-worker takes a businesslike stance meant to suggest scale for viewers of the photographic ruins: She is tiny; they are enormous. She might have been Westropp's wife, who performed this service in others of his photos, or perhaps she was a student of medieval history or archaeology.

The lady represents us, of course, poking through what's left of medieval Christians and using rough scrapings and muddy foundations to map a community, a religion, a whole world. When the photographer took his shot, the lady's clothes were unsullied and her hopes of finding a treasure undimmed. She was facing a modern man with a camera, not the mystery of the convent's past. When she turned to scan the ruins, she would have seen the fine east window of the church, an excellent example of Irish Romanesque and a testament to the success of the ancient monastic community. Perhaps while clambering through the vaulted crypt, though, she began to appreciate the difficult task of conjuring from the stones so many centuries of women and men living ordinary Christian lives. Perhaps, too, she traveled to the parish archives or the antiquarian societies of Dublin. There she would have found that Cell Eóin (also known as the Abbey of Saint John, Ecclesia S. Johannis,

Killane, Killiean, and Killean) was founded about 1189 by Donal Mór Ua Briain, one of the most powerful men in Ireland at the time, or possibly by his son Donnchad Cairprech Ua Briain a few years later. Slaine, Donnchad's daughter, was its first abbess. If our nameless young scholar had read the Book of Lecan in the library of the Royal Irish Academy (which, if a patriotic Irish speaker, she might have called Leabhar Lecain) or pondered the genealogical manuscript of Duald MacFirbis, she could have traced the names of women who had knelt and prayed in the church and now rested in the crypt. Throughout the medieval years, the nuns of Cell Eóin were named, noted, and noble, partnered in charters and genealogies with the monks of Clare Abbey until the mid-sixteenth century. Men and women had worked together for three and a half centuries building Christianity in this corner of northern Europe.

The first modern histories of medieval nuns and convents were newly published around 1898 when this photograph was taken. It was still twenty-six years until Eileen Power's *Medieval People* would be published and almost a century until Jo Ann McNamara would produce her thousand-page survey of religious women. But the antiquarian couple—the lone woman and her partner Westropp—were continuing a project already begun, which feminist historians would continue, and that the authors of this volume push forward. The past century of medieval scholarship has proved that the women and men of Cell Eóin and Cell Craobhnat likely spent much of their lives praying in memory of their patrons, neighbors, and kin. We writers of this volume also commemorate those medieval Christians, body and soul—at least long enough to spy on them going about their everyday business of gender and religion.

Chapter 1
Tertullian, the Angelic Life, and the Bride of Christ

Dyan Elliott

A young woman eschews all mortal ties to unite herself irrevocably with a man who has been dead for centuries yet has nevertheless managed to lure countless women into this suspect arrangement: a polygamist on a grand scale. Although it may sound like something right out of Edgar Allan Poe, I am, of course, alluding to the traditional understanding of the consecrated virgin as bride of Christ—a concept so intrinsic to female spirituality and so familiar to medievalists that it is difficult to imagine a time when it was otherwise. But there was such a time: a time when the bride was just a metaphor unattached to any particular human body, before she tumbled from the symbolic order, became entangled in text, and then finally came to rest on the female body of the consecrated virgin. It was a hard landing which, viewed teleologically, might be characterized as a mismatch of the highest order.[1] For although women had already come to be identified with consecrated virginity by the end of the second century, their preference for this vocation was precisely because they rejected the role of bride and may have continued to resist even if the groom had been Christ himself.

In her groundbreaking work *A New Song: Celibate Women in the First Three Christian Centuries*, Jo Ann McNamara contextualizes the struggle of those women within the radical ideology of the early church, which eschewed the institution of marriage both for its reproductive potential and for the gender roles it sustained. The women who spurned marriage were attempting to turn a sharp metaphysical corner, which, if successfully negotiated, would institute a dramatic transformation of gender that would remove them from the threat of marriage forever. The anticipated change was generally described in two ways. First, by embracing chastity, women were understood to achieve gender parity by being spiritually transformed into "men," a clear promotion in a patriarchal world.[2] But the second and more audacious formulation was to associate the transition to chastity with the *vita angelica* of the resurrection alluded to by Christ (Luke 20:34–36). In this future state when "marriage and giving in marriage" would cease altogether, gender would likewise be abolished.[3]

McNamara has identified the fiery Carthaginian theologian Tertullian (ca. 160–after 220), the first great theological voice in the West, as the person who initially invested the consecrated virgin with the persona of the bride of Christ, the ultimate mechanism for bringing the independent virgin firmly under patriarchal control.[4] Such a paternalistic impulse is abundantly supported by Tertullian's prolific outpourings on female dress. This preoccupation adheres to the Pauline tradition, which had already drawn a parallel between female modesty in dress and submission to masculine authority, citing Eve's seduction as a rationale (1 Tim. 9–14). Tertullian's treatise *On the Apparel of Women* cranks this association up a notch with its famous condemnation of women as the "devil's gateway" by virtue of their association with Eve.[5] His later treatise *On the Veiling of Virgins*, moreover, is an extended indictment of virgins who resist the veil, apparel that does double service as a symbol of both gender and submission.[6] Nor is Tertullian's concern with female subjection limited to these treatises; elsewhere he uses female prominence, especially in Gnostic circles, as a measure of heretical debasement.[7]

Yet despite such celebrated rhetorical sallies, Tertullian's initiative in wedding the virgin to her metaphoric destiny is in many ways at odds with his pronounced views on marriage and virginity. His opinion of marriage was despairing, to say the least, while his most cherished hopes for humanity were peculiarly linked with the adulation of consecrated virginity. The extent of Tertullian's matrimonial pessimism might logically argue against any willingness to associate the consecrated virgin with the marital state, even metaphorically. Moreover, it would be irresponsible to allow Tertullian's potentially misogynist words to trump his deeds: Even the most provocative rhetoric aimed at uppity women does not eclipse the fact that he ended his life as a member of the New Prophecy movement or, as the church fathers would have it, the heretical Montanist church. This sect believed in the continued access to divine revelation through prophecy, a gift peculiarly associated with virginity and one in which women assumed leadership roles as select vessels of prophecy.[8] Moreover, modern reassessments suggest that the virgin prophetesses Priscilla and Maximilla not only enjoyed parity with Montanus, but were possibly senior members of the sect who were regarded as his spiritual superiors. It was the innate sexism of the church fathers that was responsible for reflexively linking the sect to a male founder.[9]

This study revisits the early church's attitudes toward marriage, virginity, and the angelic life in order to better understand the role Tertullian played as "father of the bride" and just what exactly he intended when he married the virgin to Christ. It is difficult, admittedly, to separate the bridal persona from the constraining manner in which it would soon be wielded by the church hierarchy. I would contend, however, that when Tertullian first conferred the title *sponsa Christi* on the consecrated virgin, he believed that there was much more at stake than questions of female discipline or even than the preservation of gender hierarchy. The virgin as *sponsa Christi* was the logical terminus to his long deliberative process over humanity's singular position in the created order. At issue was a concern that probably strains the credulity of our own age: the boundaries between the angelic and the human races, a preoccupation that Dale Martin has assessed in terms of pollution taboos.[10] Tertullian lived under a heightened awareness that these boundaries had been breached in antediluvian times by the so-called Watcher Angels—those sons of God who intermarried with the daughters of men (Gen. 6:2). It was an instance of the *vita angelica* gone desperately wrong, as it not only resulted in the destruction of the world but further unleashed a legion of demons upon the earth whose sole purpose was to work to the detriment of humankind. Ultimately, Tertullian would become apprehensive of any efforts to assimilate humankind and angels, theological or eschatological. The sexed body will emerge as the benchmark of difference in his writings and he will be further inspired to project it into the afterlife, sharply curtailing earlier visions of the *vita angelica*. Although a marriage to Christ placed the virgins firmly under the supreme patriarch and by extension his clerical proxies, it was also Tertullian's way of fending off the possibility of much worse unions with celestial predators. The human race would thus be spared any repetition of the horrors of supernatural miscegenation, while its distinct future glory would be enshrined.

From Brides to Grooms in the Early Church

Metaphors describing humanity's union with God in terms of marriage abound in biblical texts: God's union with Israel had traditionally been described in terms of a marriage.[11] Christ employs the image as well, lending an eschatological twist in his parable about the ten virgins and their state of preparedness when the bridegroom appears for the last judgment (Matt. 10:25). Paul's later invocation of the same symbol is bifurcated, representing both Christ's mystical union with the soul and Christ's more corporate union with the church—each of which will become important in the development of church hierarchy. With regard to the soul's marriage, Paul appropriates the role of nervous father of the bride: "For I am jealous over you with godly jealousy: for I have espoused you to one husband, that I may present you as a chaste virgin to

Christ" (2 Cor. 11:2). Paul's patriarchal watch anticipates the rise of a paternalistic clergy from amid a brood of erstwhile egalitarian siblings in Christ. And yet certain hierarchies are still suspended in Paul. In the spirit of Galatians 5:28—which abolished most of society's canonized boundaries, including the division between male and female—the marriage between God and the soul was gender blind. But this androgynous potential is not sustained in the macrocosmic manifestation of this image in Christ's marriage with the church. Paul, and later his disciples, will align Christ's rule of the church with the husband's rule of the wife, thereby superimposing this image on the temporal institution (Eph. 5: 23).[12] This image was aimed at domestic life, where it could not but fail to strengthen traditional gender roles. Likewise, the corporate realization that will ensue, in which the bishop stands *in loco Christi* in his marriage to his see, confirms the hierarchy that is already implicit in normative gender roles and clerical authority alike.[13]

Paul's understanding of the mystical marriage bends gender one way and one way only: There are male brides, but no female grooms. This is the reading that prevailed in what would be eventually recognized as orthodox circles, but it was by no means the only one. For the Gnostic Christians, every one began as a bride, which designated the carnal nature and literal mindedness of the psychic masses, and everyone had an equal chance to become a groom, to join the pneumatic elite. This egalitarian view was supported by an allegorical reading of the same texts that orthodoxy used to the opposite purpose. Where Paul saw the opportunity to subordinate wives, the Gnostics preferred to encourage the due submission of fledgling psychics to their pneumatic superiors, to whom they were urged to join themselves as carnal wives would to their husbands. For his part, the pneumatic groom would purify his psychic wife in preparation for the ultimate ritual of the bridal chamber, in which all differences in gender and status would be obliterated and humanity united with the divine. In Gnostic exegesis, scriptural references to marriage and sexual union do not correspond with their carnal counterpart, which anyone even remotely interested in being saved would have abandoned long ago. The human institution was but a bad copy of the celestial reality. So while the bride's spiritual profile may be extremely bleak in the Gnostic cosmos, as was anything female, in practical terms the same interpretative trajectory placed the woman in all the inferiority of her physicality on an equal footing with the man, which was her manifest destiny anyway once she had joined the pneumatic elite and became a groom.[14]

So among the Gnostics, no one wanted to be a bride unless en route to becoming a groom. The situation was probably not much different in orthodox circles. Apart from the classic soul marriage, which was the spiritual heritage of every believer, it would be indeed surprising if female virgins felt any special affinity for bridal imagery not only because it gestured toward the institution they spurned but also because of the way Paul used this figure to subject carnal wives. The women in question construed virginity as a conduit to "becoming male" or, better still, the realized eschatology of the *vita angelica* where there was no marriage nor giving in marriage.[15]

Marriage Versus Virginity in Tertullian

Although no friend to Gnosticism, Tertullian shared its prejudices and those of his coreligionists, regarding marriage through the same lens of postlapsarian pessimism rampant in orthodox and Gnostic circles alike. Adam and Eve "had committed murder on themselves" hence "falling from immortality."[16] Their crime eventuated in a hereditary ailment whereby, "given over to death on account of [Adam's] sin, the entire human race, tainted in their descent from him, were made a channel for transmitting his condemnation."[17] Marriage was nothing more than a remedy to sin. The gloomy cycle of marriage, birth, and death would relentlessly perpetuate itself until the resurrection, at which point marriage, both designer to the vestibule and purveyor of victims for death's grim chamber, would be destroyed.[18] Although himself a married man, Tertullian had determined never to marry again were he to be at liberty to do so, nor did he believe anyone else should. The orthodox church's refusal to follow him in this resolve eventually prompted his break with Rome in favor of the Montanist sect, which likewise condemned second marriages.

Remarriage was Tertullian's psychic "trigger issue," and he devoted three treatises to the cause. Doubtless reasoning that chastity begins at home, the first treatise was dedicated to what must surely have proven to be his toughest audience—his wife. For not only did Tertullian need to establish his stance as disinterested moralist versus posthumously possessive husband, but, more important, he had to convince his partner of a lifetime that their marriage was a kind of fool's endgame—a pungent truth spiked with the bitterest of tonics. Yet Tertullian unflinchingly administers the full dose at the outset of the work by anticipating the ultimate dissolution of the married state, "No restoration of marriage is promised in the day of resurrection, translated as they will be into the condition and sanctity of angels. . . . There will at that day be no resumption of voluptuous disgrace between us."[19] The hopeful strains of this greater joy do not, however, drown out the somber melody of his prevailing theme: that marriage is not an absolute good in itself, as it is only conceded by "necessity."[20]

In the treatise *To His Wife*, Tertullian argues the case against remarriage passionately, only to back away from the grim logic of its misogamy rather abruptly. For the second and final book capitulates to human frailty by anticipating the possibility of his wife's remarriage and launches an extended petition for marriage within the faith. This spirit of compromise has entirely dissipated by the two subsequent treatises, however. *An Exhortation to Chastity*, written to a friend on the death of his wife, presents the widower's loss as a cause for celebration—a strategy later made famous by Tertullian's spiritual heir Jerome. Here marriage itself is characterized as "not so much a 'good' as a species of inferior evil," while second marriages are dismissed as a "species of fornication."[21] Tertullian's third treatise, *On Monogamy*, interprets Paul's recommendation that "it is good not to touch a woman" with sophistical cunning, "It follows it is evil to have contact with her; for nothing is contrary to good except evil."[22]

Tertullian's contempt for marriage was not merely shaped by the temporary nature of the institution and its affinity with death but also by his apprehension of the transformation that awaited the prospective couple. Marital relations induced a coarsening of not just the body but also the soul, "dulling" the spiritual senses and "avert[ing] the Holy Spirit."[23] Once united in marriage, husband and wife literally became one flesh, their individual integrity forever compromised. Although the institution itself might come to an end, these deleterious effects endured, constituting a kind of negative transcendence every bit as permanent as that final metamorphosis awaiting the resurrected body. This apprehension of the enduring effects of the married state was progressive, both stimulating and justifying Tertullian's aversion to remarriage.[24]

Tertullian's association of marriage with marital relations was, therefore, absolute. He would have been at a loss to comprehend the chastity debates of the fourth century, when orthodoxy's insistence on the perpetual virginity of Mary ultimately triumphed and the didactic value of her unconsummated union with Joseph was upheld.[25] Not only does Tertullian assume as a matter of course that Mary and Joseph proceeded to beget children in the ordinary way after Christ's birth, but he uses Christ's references to his brethren as evidence of his full humanity to counter dualist arguments against Christ's true incarnation.[26]

Although clearly believing that the ground lost through marriage could never be regained, Tertullian still maintained that sexual renunciation was commendable at whatever stage in life it was undertaken. To this end, *An Exhortation to Chastity* distinguishes three types of "virginity": physical virginity from birth; the kind embarked upon at the "second birth," when married couples agree to renounce sex upon baptism; and instances in which a once-married widow or widower refuses remarriage.[27] Yet, the only true escape from the taint of marriage was to circumvent it altogether. Christ is an exemplar in this context, having been born from "[flesh] not even unsealed by marriage" and inhabiting a body consisting of "[flesh] never to be unsealed by marriage."[28] Thus lifelong virginity alone constitutes "the principal sanctity, because it is free from the affinity with fornication."[29] It is "the virginity of happiness"—a blessed condition by which the virgin's "perfect integrity and entire sanctity shall have the nearest vision of the face of God."[30] Sanctity was a key term for Tertullian because it best expressed God's will for humanity.[31] The fact that words *virginity* and *sanctity* are used as synonyms in Tertullian's lexicon perhaps gestures toward a gradual democratization of the virginal vocation as humanity advances toward the eschaton.[32] Yet while the virgin state in every way realizes humanity's full potential, it nevertheless provides an alibi for the very institution it hobbles. Thus to the Gnostic detractors of marriage, Tertullian will affirm, "If there is to be no marriage, there is no sanctity. All proof of abstinence is lost when excess is impossible."[33]

Virgins and Angels: A Walk in the Dark

Tertullian was aware of the challenges besetting a person who strives for chastity. In particular, the person who was at one time sexually active and later embraces chastity requires considerable virtue and moderation, in contrast to the virgin's "total ignorance of that from which you will afterwards wish to be freed."[34] And yet, Tertullian values virginity over the virtuous struggle of the sexually seasoned.[35] This predisposition reflects his commitment to virginity as an anticipation of the future kingdom where ignorance was, indeed, bliss and in which any exercise of the virtues would, therefore, be otiose. His exhortation to his wife sweetens the abolition of marriage with a promise of the "condition and sanctity of angels,"[36] describing those who choose voluntary chastity as "already counted as belonging to the angelic family."[37]

This is a rare moment for Tertullian. Apart from this rather glib promise to his wife that chastity already secures her place in an illustrious angelic lineage, the sanctity Tertullian attributes to virginity is usually rhetorically aloof from the angelic life, which he reserves for the resurrected body. Thus in his treatise on female dress when he asserts that "the same angelic nature is promised to you, women, the selfsame sex is promised to you as to men," he is gesturing toward a future condition that provides temporary shelter from his steady rain of rhetorical vitriol.[38]

The promise of an "angelic nature" is hardly a transparent one, however, even as not all androgynies are equal.[39] When Tertullian assures women that they are to receive "the selfsame sex" as men, the school of androgyny that he seems to be aligning himself with is not unlike the Gnostic predisposition to regard prelapsarian humanity as male. This prejudice was supported by Christ's initial identification of chastity with eunuchs—an identification that was corroborated by the Revelation of Saint John, when the visionary describes the virgins following the lamb as individuals who "have not defiled their clothes with women."[40] But Tertullian ultimately recoiled from this vision of male-inflected androgyny, which threatened to collapse the angelic and human race, instead favoring a resurrected body that was ineradicably sexed. Intrinsic to this position was Tertullian's preoccupation with the antediluvian history of the Watcher Angels, whose intermarriage with the daughters of men was perceived as so heinous that it precipitated God's decision to flood the earth (Gen. 6:8).

This alternative, and perhaps original, story of the fall was mentioned fleetingly by Paul when he was likewise seeking to impose veils on wives, using "because of the angels" (1 Cor. 11:3ff) as possible justification.[41] Paul tended to favor the story of Adam and Eve as the origin of humanity's fall, keeping the fallen angels in reserve as a kind of trump to enforce female submission. It is easy to imagine that Tertullian did likewise, seizing upon the tale as a pretext for subduing uppity women. Nevertheless Tertullian's obsession with this calamity and the significance it assumed in his understanding of salvation history, suggests that the incident resonated far beyond its undeniable utility as a disciplinary strategy. The apocryphal Book of Enoch offered an extended account of the baleful history of the Watcher Angels, and Tertullian brooded over its contents, arguing at length in favor of the authenticity of the work.[42] His work *On Idolatry* attributes practically every evil known to humanity with the intervention of the rebel angels. Moreover, vestiges of this calamity seemed to be present to Tertullian at every turn. When arguing for the durability of the flesh, he points to the recent discovery of some ancient bones still covered with flesh and hair, construing these as the remains of giants—the cursed progeny of these blighted unions.[43]

The Watcher Angels were the motor behind Tertullian's frequent return to the question of female dress and modesty in general, although it was virgins on whom the penumbra of this evil legacy fell. The virgins who refused to wear veils were, to Tertullian's mind, attempting to deny their sexuality and gender—an effort that he compares with attempts to establish "a third generic class, some monstrosity with a head of its own."[44] He answered these claims by arguing that it was virgins and virgins alone that were the special object of angelic lust, thereby proving that virgins were women and that virginity had always been sexualized. Moreover, his efforts to secure a unique destiny for humanity would lead him to maintain that this sexualization was eternal.

Already in his earliest treatment of the subject, Tertullian maintained that the daughters of men, who were not specifically designated as "wives," must, by process of elimination, be virgins. But this rationale was not simply based on biblical nomenclature or lack thereof: Tertullian's own aversion to sexual activity made it impossible for him to conceive that angels could possibly settle for married women who were no longer virgins.[45] In *On the Veiling of Virgins*, Tertullian expresses disgust as the taint of sex is allowed to flow unchecked, "Who can presume that it was bodies already defiled, and relics of human lust, which such angels yearned after, so as not rather to have been inflamed for virgins, whose bloom pleads an excuse for human lust as well?" Nevertheless, he is careful to have it both ways. Even if the women targeted by the angels were already "contaminated" [*contaminatas*], and hence not virgins, the temptation afforded by virgins would be more potent still: "so much more 'on account of the angels' would it have been the duty of virgins to be veiled."[46]

The unholy union between the angels and erstwhile human virgins was responsible for unleashing a series of unhallowed horrors that spawned every conceivable sin known to humankind. Not only were the fallen angels themselves transformed into demons, but their offspring became a "still more wicked demon brood,"[47] bent on securing humanity's damnation. Their exemplary malevolence was sharpened by revenge. The rebel angels "who certainly thought sometimes of the place whence they had fallen and longed for heaven after the heated impulses of lust had quickly passed," wreaked vengeance on their hapless wives by showering them with every imaginable luxury: tinted cloth, jewels and makeup, seeking to entrap them by their own vanity.[48] Privy to the secrets of the earth, the erstwhile angels introduced metallurgy, a craft that brought weapons and war in its wake. Moreover, the former denizens of heaven exercised immense powers over humans, plaguing the body with diseases and assailing the spirit with "violent assaults . . . hurry[ing] the soul into sudden and extraordinary excesses."[49] On a more metaphysical level, the fallen angels prompted humans to turn away from God through the introduction of idolatry and occult arts such as astrology.[50]

Ultimately, humanity degenerated so completely that God was compelled to turn away altogether, signaling his disaffection with the comment, "My Spirit shall not permanently abide in these men eternally, for that they are flesh" (Gen. 6:6). This was a troubling passage for Tertullian, but he was forced to return to it often because it was flagged by his dualist opponents as evidence that the creation of humanity was a calamity and as further proof that the good god had never intended to mix flesh and spirit.[51] While eschewing this interpretation, Tertullian clearly regarded the text as indicative of a portentous shift, which, in a later work, he interprets as marking the beginning of the ongoing disjunction between flesh and spirit alluded to by Paul (Gal. 5:17).[52]

The virgins' role in the angelic fall loomed sufficiently large in Tertullian's psychic landscape that it threatened to overshadow Eve's transgression in Eden. Yet the two stories were in many ways complementary, constituting formidable proof of woman's ineradicable sexuality, evidenced by her unerring capacity to seduce her superiors—be they men or angels. The opening of *On the Apparel of Women* exploits this cumulative case for female perfidy, whether active or passive, by placing the two accounts of the fall side by side. The first chapter upbraids all women as daughters of Eve who, while seeking finery, are in reality deserving of penitential garb,[53] while the second reveals the identity of the evil agents responsible for the dyes and metallurgical skill necessary for the female fashion: "those angels . . . who rushed from heaven on the daughters of men; so that this ignominy also attaches to woman."[54]

Moreover, Tertullian takes pains at a number of junctures to stress the prelapsarian Eve's status as both woman and virgin, "since she has the appellation *woman* before she was *wedded*, and never *virgin* while she *was* a *virgin*."[55] Not only does this emphasis confound arguments in favor of the special androgyny inherent in the virginal state, it further sets the stage for the remedial intervention of that exemplary virgin (and woman) par excellence, Mary. The Virgin Mary is an antidote to the evil instituted by the primordial Virgin Eve: "It was while Eve was yet a virgin, that the ensnaring word had crept into her ear which was to build the edifice of death. Into a virgin's soul, in like manner, must be introduced that Word of God which was to raise the fabric of life; so that what had been reduced to ruin by this sex, might by the selfsame sex be recovered to salvation. As Eve believed the serpent, so Mary believed the angel."[56]

But while the history of the virginal daughters of men compounds the guilt of Eve, it is a tacit inference achieved by an adroit juxtaposition of references rather than by overt articulation. An invisible barrier seems to be erected between this instance of supernatural miscegenation and the incarnation, even as the daughters of men are excluded from the antiphonal rapport between Eve and Mary. Tertullian has good reasons for textual restraint. Schooled by the Book of Enoch, Tertullian interprets the antediluvian denizens of heaven as being members of the angelic host. Yet so disturbing an appellation as "sons of God" would caution against any close juxtaposition of the Old Testament text with the incarnation of Christ, the true "son of God." If placed alongside Gabriel's annunciation to the Virgin Mary, the angelic dalliance with the daughters of men reads too much like a misbegotten incarnation. Although the incarnation of Christ represents a fresh start for humanity, even as Mary provides the antidote to Eve, there was no remedy for the ongoing destruction wrought by the demonic progeny of the fallen "sons of God," who would continue to plague humankind until the end of time.

Equal of Angels Versus Becoming Angels

Tertullian's reading of the Watcher Angels was a dark tribute to the liminal capacity of virginity. By elevating human nature, virginity created a zone in which angels and humans were permitted to mingle—a propinquity that Tertullian clearly deemed deleterious to both. Although virginity could not raise women to angelic heights, the virgins themselves clearly had the capacity to draw angels down to subhuman depths. And the falling angels would, in turn, do all in their power to drag humanity along with them. It was through the indiscretion of virgins that the sacrosanct boundaries between the human and the angelic races had once been breached. To prevent any recurrence of this abomination, Tertullian attempted to squelch the androgynous pretensions of virgins by asserting their ineradicable womanhood, a cause that was symbolically advanced by the imposition of the veil.

But the hubris of orthodox virgins was not the only thing that threatened the integrity of the human race. Heretical virgins were also contriving to merge the two races through the dissemination of false doctrine. A Gnostic virgin named Philumene taught that Christ was an angel and that his body was not formed from flesh but extracted from the stars, and this doctrine attracted a following.[57] The biblical support for this conviction came from Paul, who had juxtaposed "the first man is of the earth, earthy; the second man is the Lord from heaven."[58] Tertullian recognized that an angelic Christ not only denigrated the human body and, by extension, its creator, but effectively eliminated any salubrious distance between humans and angels. His horror was duly expressed by disparaging Philumene with the racial impurity he so dreaded, characterizing her as "an angel of deceit, 'transformed into an angel of light' (2 Cor. 11:14)."[59] His rebuttal was to develop a theological anthropology that would eventually enshrine the human body in all its particulars by immortalizing it, differentiating humans from angels once and for all.

Tertullian's treatise *On the Flesh of Christ* vigorously rejects an angelic Christ, arguing that Christ was fully human and, hence, possessed of the same flesh as humanity. While granting that there were incidents in the Old Testament where angels appeared as humans, even to the point of assuming human flesh, "it is plain that the angels bore a flesh which was not naturally their own; their nature being of a spiritual substance, although in some sense peculiar to themselves, corporeal; and yet they could be transfigured into human shape." Angels may be able to cast themselves into human form. But no angel, whether encased in borrowed flesh or not, was born to die, as was Christ, and it was only the death of a human Christ which could redeem humankind.[60]

Tertullian was nevertheless aware that his argument for the flesh shared the same vulnerability as the flesh itself: that dualist expressions of incredulity over an incarnate Christ were formulated "lest the Lord should be regarded as inferior to the angels who are not formed of earthly flesh."[61] Initially, Tertullian attempted to quell this objection by insisting on the extraordinary purity of Christ's flesh.[62] But ultimately, this problem was tackled more effectively, albeit more obliquely, through his description of humanity as a coherent and inextricable coalition of flesh and spirit. Not only did such a formulation make it impossible to separate the soul from what the Gnostics considered to be its carnal husk, but it had important implications for gender as well. In line with Stoical thought, Tertullian adhered to the concept of the corporeal soul, one possessed of its own special kind of body. Both types of bodies, carnal and spiritual, were interdependent, having been created by the same act of insemination in which gender was also integral.[63] "The soul, being sown in the womb at the same time as the body, receives likewise along with it its sex; and this indeed so simultaneously, that neither of the two substances can be alone regarded as the cause of the sex. . . . The insemination of the two substances are inseparable in point of time, and their effusion is also one and the same, in consequence of which a community of gender is secured to them."[64]

The profound unity of humanity in its different dimensions is developed in the treatise *On the Resurrection of the Flesh*, a prolonged meditation on the role of the human body. Humankind, the pinnacle of the created world, was created body and soul in the image of God: "And so intimate is the union, that it may be deemed to be uncertain whether the flesh bears about the soul, or the soul the flesh."[65] In opposition to the Gnostic tendency to regard the body as a transitory prison of the soul, Tertullian advances the eternal codependence of body and soul, arguing that "the flesh is the very condition on which salvation hinges." Virginity and all other modes of sexual restraint are thus "but fragrant offerings to God paid out of the good services of the flesh."[66] Body and soul constituted an integral unit. The inner body of the soul was naked without the protective covering of the external body of flesh.[67] Death would transform the outer body "even as corruption must put on incorruption." But even after mortality is "swallowed up," the outer body remains.[68]

Tertullian's perception of humanity as a seamless and integral union of spirit and flesh would naturally augment his awareness of the deleterious impact of sexual relations and heighten his appreciation for virginity. When this pro-virginal stance is considered independently of his vision of humanity, this emphasis seems unreasoned, even fetishistic. Hence, Tertullian has frequently been identified as the turning point after which anatomical virginity begins to eclipse the perception of virginity as a state of mind.[69] Indeed, his tendency to rank the virgin's effortless attainment above the widow's virtuous perseverance only compounds this impression.

Tertullian's ineradicable view of marriage as carnal conditioned his own idiosyncratic evocation of the mystical marriage—a masterful recasting of Gnostic nuptial imagery, one that turned the mystery of the bridal chamber on its head by making the human body the *ne plus ultra* of consummation. The body's fragile coalition of flesh and spirit is consummated and sanctified by the incarnation: "Both natures has He [Christ] already united in His own self: He has fitted them together as bride and bridegroom in the reciprocal bond of wedded life. Now, if any should insist on making the soul the bride, then the flesh will follow the soul as her dowry. The soul shall never be an outcast, to be had home by the bridegroom bare and naked. . . . But suppose the flesh to be the bride, then in Christ she has in the contract of blood received His spirit as her spouse."[70]

Thus in his zeal to discern between the angelic and human race, Tertullian found himself defending the body in all its particulars, and projecting it into the afterlife. Humanity's retention of both sexes was, perhaps, his coup de grâce. For although angelic androgyny could, arguably, accommodate one sex, it could not accommodate two—especially not the female sex. Tertullian nevertheless had to acknowledge that he was up against an inexplicable mystery regarding what possible purpose any body, let alone a gendered body, would serve when death, and hence marriage and procreation, had ceased to exist. And this is where virginity, a condition valued by Catholics and Gnostics alike, came to his aid. Although virginity did not solve the conundrum of the body's continued existence, it nevertheless re-posed the question in striking terms by offering a compelling *figura* for how incomprehensible anomalies are nevertheless consistent with God's plan for humanity. Virginity was a condition in the body but not of the body. To many early Christians, the virgin's sexual abstinence might have anticipated a blissful abolition of gender. But for Tertullian, to whom gender had become inextricably linked to body and soul, the virgin's sexed body was now possessed of a different potential altogether: her untapped fecundity became the most compelling exemplum for the impenetrable mystery of the body's endurance. The treatise *On the Resurrection of the Flesh* raises, but does not answer, the question of "what purpose can be served by loins, conscious of seminal secretions, and all other organs of generation in the two sexes, and the laboratories of embryos, and the fountains of the breast, when concubinage, and pregnancy, and infant nurture shall cease."[71] The answer will be revealed when we reach the future kingdom. Until that time, we must be content to contemplate a parallel set of anomalies that are accommodated within the mundane order of things, prefiguring things to be. "Even in the present life there may be cessations of their office for our stomachs and our generative organs. For forty days Moses and Elias fasted, and lived upon God alone. . . . See here faint outlines of our future strength! We even, as we may be able, excuse our mouths from food, and withdraw our sexes from union. How many voluntary eunuchs are there. How many virgins espoused to Christ! How many, both men and women, whom nature has made sterile, with a structure which cannot procreate!"[72]

The sexed body of the consecrated virgin is but an exemplum framed within a series of seeming anachronisms that prefigure humanity's ultimate destiny. The designation of "bride of Christ" distinguishes her from her male counterpart, the voluntary eunuch. Their bodies, sexually inactive but gendered, are projected into the afterlife, scuttling all hopes for an androgynous *vita angelica*. Thus Tertullian succeeded in bringing what he perceived as hubristic claims for virginity down to earth in order to secure humanity's due place in heaven.

Separate from but Equal to Angels: The *Vita Angelica* and Its Afterlife

Equality with angels did not mean assimilation. What Tertullian sought to establish for the human race was its separate but equal status, both in this world and the next. Angels had often appeared on earth, dwelt among humans, even eaten and drunk with them, without abandoning their spiritual natures. In a similar manner, "We shall not therefore cease to continue in the flesh, because we cease to be importuned by the usual wants of the flesh; just as the angels ceased not therefore to remain in their spiritual substance, because of the suspension of their spiritual incidents. . . . When [Christ] ascribed an angelic likeness to the flesh, He took not from it its proper substance."[73] In Tertullian's later works, humanity's much-awaited angelic life simply becomes a shorthand for eternity and the transformation that the body must undergo when the flesh "is remade and 'angelified' [*angelificatam*] in the kingdom of God."[74] Humans will become " 'equal unto the angels,' (5 John 6:39) inasmuch as they are not to marry, because they are not to die, but are destined to pass into the angelic state by putting on the raiment of incorruption, although with a change in the substance which is restored to life."[75]

So humanity was securely separated from angels by its body of flesh, but nevertheless maintained equality. But Tertullian's claim of a "separate but equal" status for humanity requires close scrutiny. When both heaven and earth abound with hierarchies, the plausibility of the construction is naturally called into question. One might seek an analogy in contemporary politics over the issue of same-sex marriage. The conservative impulse is to withhold the institution of marriage from gays and lesbians, proffering the less volatile alternative of "civil union." This is essentially the solution recently arrived at by New Jersey's Supreme Court when it accorded gay couples parallel rights to those enjoyed by heterosexuals, all the while withholding the designation of matrimony. Canadian Prime Minister Paul Martin had resisted this compromise the previous year, supporting the designation of "gay marriage" with the clearheaded statement that "'separate but equal' is not equal."[76] The marker of difference that would, in the eyes of some, ostensibly bar gays and lesbians from "true" matrimony was the sexed body: that the bodies in question were of one sex rather than two. The same might be said for Tertullian's view of humanity's separate but equal status with the angelic host. Only in this instance, it is the presence of two distinct sexes, as opposed to one, that operates as a chief marker of difference between the two races.

The reinvestment in the sexed body had ramifications that exceeded the constraints of gender, enabling men to be the ultimate beneficiaries of the *vita angelica*. If the Gnostics had won, the body might have been deemed less consequential, and women may have continued to advance toward the male-inflected androgyny associated with the angelic life. Instead, the full weight of gender and the body reasserted itself, rendering women more fully human than ever before and nullifying their attempts to colonize the angelic life. But the logic of male-inflected androgyny— implicit in the fact that the rebel angels of Genesis 6 were, after all, "sons" of God—charted a different course. Men became progressively "angelified," a process that would take its toll on the angels themselves. The angelic corps, already contaminated by their tarnished bonds with the disgraced daughters of men, would suffer further depredations at the hands of earthly brothers-in-law. Disturbed by the far-reaching implications of the incident of the Watcher Angels, theologians such as Augustine would assume the exegetical role of Jacob, wrestling angels down from heaven to their own level. Augustine responded to Genesis 6 allegorically, suggesting that the sons of God were simply men who had lapsed into concupiscence.[77] This line of reasoning becomes canonized in the *Glossa ordinaria*, which interprets the sons of God as the "religious sons of Seth" (*filii seth religiosi*), and the daughters of men as the lineage of Cain (*de stirpe cayn*).[78] Although according to this interpretative strategy, the pleasures of a quasi-angelic status were fleeting, men are still the only group that benefits from this reading. "The sons of God" are permanently demoted into men, while the daughters of men devolve into the wicked brood, sprung from a murderous lineage. But whether the symbolic alchemy at work here is best understood as transforming men into angels or angels into men, there is no doubt that the tendency to perceive angelic androgyny in terms of masculinity was reified even as men gained spiritual prestige by appropriating the charisma of chastity. Felice Lifshitz's chapter suggests that the church began to place an increasingly high premium on male chastity over the course of the early Middle Ages. Finally, the Gregorian reform ensured that it was the celibate clergy who had become the true heirs to the angelic life. And, as Ruth Karras argues, theirs was a stalwart and virile chastity. Hence, in the thirteenth century, William of Auvergne can remark with some complacency that an angel in female form is invariably a demon because the good angels are males.[79] In contrast, the virginity of Christ's brides became progressively embodied, even as their freedoms were increasingly curtailed to correspond with the restricted lifestyle of the secular matron.[80]

Hesitations en Route to the Altar

Tertullian's emphasis on intact virginity and the omnipresence of gender clearly set the stage for the virgin's identification with the bride of Christ. But it is not clear how exactly he arrived at this expedient. McNamara depicts Tertullian as searching in frustration for just such a vehicle, initially confounded by the difficult fact that the virgins were theoretically subject to no one. According to McNamara's account, Tertullian found his answer in the New Testament concept of the eschatological family. "Christians habitually called God their father. . . . It was not, therefore, a giant step for Tertullian to add conjugal imagery to the scheme."[81] Certainly, this string of associations would have helped justify his ultimate decision to change autonomous virgins into dependent brides. But, as we have seen, Tertullian had already availed himself of the nuptial imagery omnipresent in Gnostic exegesis, inverting it so that the human body becomes both bride and dowry for the celestial bridegroom. What could be more natural than to offer a personification of this contract with real women?

As practical as such a solution might seem, however, Tertullian nevertheless hesitates, introducing the motif with uncharacteristic reticence. A measure of his trepidation is reflected in his efforts to try versions of the bridal motif out on other categories of Christians before finally affixing it to virgins. An early attempt at binding individual women to Christ occurs in *On the Apparel of Women* (ca. 198–202), where Tertullian's audience consisted of matrons. His apprehension of marriage, however, is still such that Christ is introduced as an adulterous lover, not as a husband. "Bow your heads to your husbands—and that will be ornament enough for you. Keep your hands busy with spinning and stay at home—and you will be more pleasing than if you were adorned in gold. Dress yourselves in the silk of probity, the fine linen of holiness, and the purple of chastity. Decked out in this manner, you will have God Himself for your lover."[82] By the time Tertullian wrote *To His Wife* (ca. 200), his most fulsome treatment of the nuptial theme, the amorous Christ had been replaced by his father, whose conventionally honorable intentions were resolved into marriage. Widows who forego opportunities to remarry are characterized as "prefer[ring] to be wedded to God. To God their beauty, to God their youth (is dedicated). With Him they live; with Him they converse; Him they 'handle' by day and night; to the Lord they assign their prayers as dowries; from Him, as oft they desire it, they receive His approbation as dotal gifts."[83] In an *Exhortation to Chastity* (204–212), the Father continues to inhabit the role of bridegroom. Yet Tertullian is emboldened to extend the metaphor in two ways, addressing not only those who had perhaps not yet experienced marriage but also members of both sexes. Hence, he commends both men and women in ecclesiastical orders who have preferred to be "wedded to God."[84]

When it comes to consecrated virgins, Tertullian's application of the image is much more halting. And this should come as no surprise: an irreducible contempt for marriage, an ongoing association of virginity and sanctity, and perhaps even a vestigial sentimentality for the very claims for androgyny that he so disparaged, must necessarily have given him pause. It was much simpler to attach women to a celestial bridegroom if they had already had experience with an earthly prototype because the later union would be deemed a promotion. And among these individuals, the title is assigned as if it were an honor. But when it came to virgins, the title "bride" is invoked in a disciplinary fashion that they would doubtless have found offensive. In an early work *On Prayer* (ca. 198–200), Tertullian's tone is defensive and his initial efforts to associate the virgin with the matron fumbling and unlovely, with no heavenly bridegroom in sight: "No one is a 'virgin' from the time when she is capable of marriage; seeing that, in her, age has by that time been wedded to its own husband, that is, to time."[85] Later, when the bridegroom finally shows up, the contract is undercut by the intonation that he is uniting himself to a kind of pseudobride: "You do well in falsely assuming the married character . . . nay you do not *falsely* for you *are* wedded to Christ."[86] Even in the more mature treatment in *On the Veiling of Virgins* (written before 207) Tertullian exhorts his audience: "Recognize the *woman*, ay, recognize the *wedded woman*, by the testimonies both of body and of spirit, which she experiences both in conscience and in flesh. There are the earlier tablets of *natural* espousals and nuptials."[87] In his eventual segue into mystical marriage, Tertullian's tone is awkward and apologetic: "Wear the full garb of woman, to preserve your standing of virgin. Belie somewhat of your inward consciousness, in order to exhibit the truth to God alone. And yet you do not belie yourself in appearing as a bride. For wedded you are to Christ."[88]

In both *On Prayer* and *On the Veiling of Virgins*, the virgin's marriage to her sexed body significantly takes precedence, both sequentially and symbolically, over marriage with Christ. It is only when Tertullian has successfully articulated a nuptial theology that unites body and soul—a union consummated by the incarnation—that the virgin's marriage has the potential to emerge as a true occasion for celebration. Thus in *On the Resurrection of the Flesh* (210–212), Tertullian at last exclaims joyfully over the number of "virgins espoused to Christ"—reveling in the sexed body, inactive but still fecund. Although existing in the temporal order, virginity augured the future bliss of the resurrected body. It was both warrant against the past, negating the sordid bond that had existed between the sons of God and the daughters of men, and the precious dowry of the present that ratified the virgin's union with the only true son of God.[89]

And thus at a time when divorce was rife and the doctrine of indissolubility of marriage but a glint in the clerical eye, the virgin's marriage to Christ was the wave of the future: an institution that was indissoluble, irrevocable, and destined to withstand millennia.

Chapter 2
One Flesh, Two Sexes, Three Genders?

JACQUELINE MURRAY

Until quite recently, the belief that human beings are divided into two distinct sexes has been accepted by society in general and by scholars of past and present more particularly. The two sexes, male and female, have been defined by their biological differences. Physical characteristics, such as musculature and genitalia, distinguish male and female across species. Thus, sex is primarily related to physical characteristics and the role of each in the process of reproduction. Gender refers to the social roles that society assigns to men and women as being appropriate to each sex. Thus, the facts that men emit semen and women can carry a fetus in their uterus are aspects of their sex. The meanings inherent in the notion of a man as provider and protector of the family or a woman as housekeeper and caregiver to children are gender roles ascribed by society to male and female human beings. Finally, society identifies qualities or attributes that imbue men and women and characterize them as masculine or feminine. So, for example, a deep voice might be the result of having a male body, but assertive speech can be viewed as masculine. Similarly, a woman's voice may be soft because of her different physical nature, but speaking in a deferential manner is associated with femininity. A woman who speaks assertively could be considered to be exhibiting masculine qualities. Historically, sex and gender were considered to align with each other so that male people would adopt the social roles of men and behave in masculine ways while female people would adopt the social roles of women and behave in feminine ways. More recently, however, this view of harmonious binaries of sex and gender has been criticized as too simplistic and too rigid to describe human complexity.

The term "third gender" has begun to appear with increasing frequency in medieval studies, to distinguish and make sense of various types of people who, by their behavior, activities, or mode of life, appear to have deviated from the common gender roles ascribed to men and women. It has been applied in a variety of contexts and has been used variously to describe different groups of people. For example, in her excellent study of women, particularly dowagers, in thirteenth-century England, Linda Mitchell has excavated the lives of a number of women who have been neglected or marginalized by earlier historians. Mitchell demonstrates that there were indeed women who were powerful, influential, and important actors in the political and economic spheres. These women, who transcended the contemporary gender system, can by no means be considered to have been subordinate, despite prevailing gender ideology. Consequently, Mitchell argues that, in light of their movement beyond the norms and expectations set for women, they might better be considered as *viragos*, as essentially a third gender.[1]

The medieval clergy has also been identified as a group that functioned as a distinct third gender. In his study of clerical masculinity from the Gregorian Reforms to the Reformation, R. N. Swanson has argued that the clergy were trying to establish two genders for the male sex: masculinity for laymen and emasculinity for celibate clergy.[2] This explicit decoupling of biological sex and socially constructed gender is an important innovation and allows for a more nuanced assessment of how these phenomena were understood in medieval society.

This notion of a separate, clerical third gender is further explored by Patricia Cullum. In her study of the English clergy toward the end of the Middle Ages, she argues that clerical identity, unlike the identity of the laity, whether men or women, was not grown into from infancy.[3] In the early medieval period, the practice of oblation made possible a longer period of inculcation and socialization, stretching from childhood to adulthood. But, how did the fully grown men who entered the clergy in the later Middle Ages acquire their clerical gender identity, in particular, those men in minor orders who were not vowed to celibacy? It would have been particularly challenging for adult men, socialized in the same way as laymen, to accommodate and internalize a different gender identity once they decided to enter the clergy.

Another group frequently identified as a third gender, or sometimes as a third sex, are eunuchs, particularly those in the Byzantine east. Some evidence exists to support a separate category of sex and/or gender for men deprived of their testicles. For example, in the fourth century, Basil of Caesarea (born ca. 329, bishop of Caesarea 370, d. 379) criticized eunuchs as unwomanly, unmanly, and effeminate, while Claudius Mamertinus (flourished mid-late fourth century) said they were "exiles from the human race, belonging to neither one sex nor the other." Severus Alexander (b. 208, emperor 222, d. 235) was even more explicit, observing that eunuchs "are the third sex of the human race."[4] One question that arises from the discussion of eunuchs, however, is the role of the body in establishing considerations of sex and gender. In this case, the absence of testicles is the defining feature, but the critics seem unclear about the exact implications this had for the sex or gender identity of eunuchs.

The study of the social construction of sex and gender in the Middle Ages has been one of Jo Ann McNamara's enduring contributions to medieval scholarship. She has directed the historian's gaze to the study of masculinity as a social construction, and in the process she has also challenged the notion of gender binaries: that the natures of men and women were perceived to be direct opposites. Rather, McNamara has demonstrated how gender was on a spectrum, and a person's place on this spectrum was influenced not only by sex but also by class, mode of life, and personal characteristics. Thus, she has observed that "unmanly servility pressed impotent men down toward the female, inferior end of the scale."[5] McNamara has revealed the inadequacy of a two-gender mode of analysis in studies of how women were pushed out of public roles. Just as Adam did not have a gender until Eve was created, so a womanless space allowed for public men to become the face of ungendered institutions: "their gender masked by their grand titles, their masculinity subsumed by the anthropomorphized institutions they represented."[6] McNamara has also suggested that, in the Merovingian world, monks and nuns were recognized to be outside the prevailing gender system. These chaste people withdrew socially from a society that was preoccupied by sex and violence, with the result that contemporaries such as Gregory of Tours (b. 538, d. 594, bishop 573) perceived them to comprise a third gender, that of the chaste who were not involved in the affairs of the world.[7] Moreover, McNamara has described the syneisactic religious communities of men and women as comprising "the porous center of the sexual continuum established by Aristotelian biology."[8]

This overview has identified five groups that have been characterized as a third gender in recent scholarship. One must ask how it is that so many different people—men and women, sexually active, genitally deprived, formally chaste, lay or religious—could all constitute a third gender? Certainly, medievalists will have an understandable sympathy with the attempt to break out of the tyranny of binaries, the dyads of men/women, male/female, and masculine/feminine, given the tyrannical binaries that dominate the study of the Middle Ages: lord/serf, orthodox/heretic, and secular/ecclesiastical. The attractiveness of a third or more categories by which to understand and describe people in the past is immediately apparent.[9] Nevertheless, we need also to ask how many third genders there can be for the term to continue to be useful or meaningful to explain aspects of medieval society and beliefs.

Two different works, neither with much to say about the Middle Ages, provide a provocative impetus for a discussion of medieval contexts for a third gender. The first is Thomas Laqueur's *Making Sex: Body and Gender from the Greeks to Freud*.[10] Laqueur argues that, from the Greeks, through the Middle Ages and to the end of the early modern period, science and medicine viewed the male and female bodies as homologous. The ovaries were viewed as internalized testicles and the uterus and vagina to be an inverted penis. Male and female developed according to whether there was sufficient heat to externalize the genitals; if not, they remained inside the body. Medievalists have rightly objected that there is a profound weakness inherent in Laqueur's study, which leaps from antiquity to the early modern period, without any explicit discussion of the Middle Ages.[11] More significantly however, Joan Cadden's research has demonstrated that in the Middle Ages multiple understandings of the differences between male and female genitals coexisted. The view of women as inverted men was not widely held, although generally there was a perception that women's genitals were internalized, lesser, smaller, and weaker than those of men. Moreover, there was also recognition that the balance of the humors and the relative qualities of wet and dry and heat and cold were all central to sex difference.[12] Nevertheless, despite these critiques and the limited applicability of the one-sex model in medieval society, Laqueur's work is important for drawing attention to the porous and malleable ideas about sex difference during the Middle Ages. As he succinctly challenges us, "Two sexes are not the necessary, natural consequence of corporeal difference. Nor, for that matter, is one sex."[13]

The second work that is useful for an analysis of the concept of a third gender is the essay collection *Third Sex, Third Gender: Beyond Sexual Dimorphism in Culture and History*.[14] The historians and anthropologists whose work is included in this collection are all concerned with the same issue: "Are two sexes or genders in the nature of things, whether biologically or socially determined?"[15] In the introduction, Gilbert Herdt argues that, since at least the nineteenth century, the dominant ideology has seen sexual nature as bifurcated along the lines of sex, male and female; and gender, men and women.[16] These dyads, he argues, create an inevitable oppositionality between male and female. A third category between these dyadic points, however, would upset this balance and result in a new dynamic. Herdt quotes the sociologist Georg Simmel (1858–1918): "The dyad represents both the first social synthesis and unification, and the first separation and antithesis. The appearance of a third party indicates a transition, conciliation, and abandonment of absolute contrast."[17] Thus, the idea of a third gender is ideologically invested and is intended to disrupt social relations as much as it is meant to describe an existing situation. Arguably, this overtly ideological perspective is useful for scholars, given that it counterbalances the equally ideological blinders of scholarship that emerged under the influence of nineteenth-century sexology, scholarship that posited innate sex differences for all forms of life, not just human beings.[18] Importantly, Herdt challenges the unexamined assumption that gender identity, which is learned in a dimorphic, two-sex system of male and female, necessarily leads to all human beings as either male or female, men or women, masculine or feminine. The congruence of biological sex and social gender is assumed to be in harmony, in part because sex and gender are linked to reproduction.[19] Thus, the concern about a third sex or a third gender is that it admits of nonreproductive sex acts and adds yet another layer of controversy and complication to our understanding of sex and gender difference. Can dyadic sex and gender systems be challenged without reference to choice of sexual object? A wish to avoid confronting issues of sexual orientation and nonreproductive sexuality have resulted in a marginalization of the study of both third-sex and third-gender possibilities, according to Herdt.[20] Can there, then, be a third gender in a two-sex world? Can there be a third sex to destabilize the embodied binaries of sex difference?

So, with Laqueur's reminder about the fluidity and contingency of sex, and Herdt's challenge to the dyadic nature of sex/gender ideology, it is possible to apply the notions of third sex and third gender to the medieval world, and ask how specifically Christian ideas about creation and sex and gender fit with these two concepts, one inherited from the medical discourses of pre-Christian antiquity, the other imposed onto the past by the postmodern, and possibly post-Christian, theorist.

Medicine: One Sex, Two Genders?

Medieval ideas about sex and gender difference were an amalgam of various ideas inherited from antiquity.[21] The notion of sex difference between female and male, distinguished by internal or external genitalia, was also refined by the individual balance of humors, and the relative degrees of heat and cold and wetness and dryness that gave each person a unique complexion and temperament. As a result, the difference between male and female was qualitative as much as rigidly dimorphic. This could have postulated some semblance of gender equality or equivalence between men and women, but it did not do so in part because of the centrality of Aristotelian ideas that considered the differences between male and female to be as much moral as biological. As a result, male and female were considered to be binary and hierarchical: the weak and passive female compared to the strong and active male.

For Aristotle, the female was a defective or incomplete male. As a result, there was a natural and inevitable relationship of inferiority and superiority between male and female (sex) and men and women (gender). These distinctions of sex and gender, however, were not static; they were placed on a continuum and human beings could be found at different points along it. Generally women were found on one end, men on the other, and "unmen," such as slaves, would be located somewhere in the middle. It was the characteristics at either end of the continuum that established and reinforced the ethical and moral qualities that contrasted men and women as a series of binaries: intellect/body, form/matter, active/passive, rational/irrational, reason/emotion, self-control/lust, judgment/mercy, order/disorder, and, most important, perfection/imperfection.[22]

This system of binary differences was influenced by each individual's unique bodily state or complexion, which was determined by the individual's balance of humors—blood, phlegm, black bile, and yellow bile—and relative degree of heat/cold and wetness/dryness. These together placed a person at some point on a continuum, stretching between the perfectly male and perfectly female. This biological continuum, too, was value laden. Men were considered to be fully human and perfect and without mystery, whereas women were the marked category that needed investigation and explanation. Women were by nature colder than men and their internal genitals were smaller, underdeveloped, and inferior to those of men. Women were also wet and porous, whereas men were hot and contained. Women were able to balance their humors naturally and regularly through menstruation, which helped to dry out their excessive wetness. Men expelled their excess heat through sweating, which accounted for the fact men had more pronounced veins than did women.[23] Other differences in complexion or temperament were demonstrated by the physical attributes of men and women's bodies. For example, men's beards were contrasted with women's smooth skin. Women's innate coldness made them unable to form the vapors needed to open the pores and then solidify into hair upon contact with outside air.[24] This explained why women had so much less body hair than men. In animals, which neither menstruated nor sweated, these excess humors were excreted and formed claws, horns, and fur.[25]

This spectrum of sex difference, however, had its challenges and dangers. For example, its midpoint did not represent perfection, a perfect balance of male and female but rather was the location of the monstrous hermaphrodite.[26] And if a man expelled too many humors, for example, by engaging in excessive intercourse, he risked becoming cold and wet and weak, even to the point of death. This biologically based sex continuum melded easily with the ancient hierarchical moral evaluation of men and women posited by Aristotle. They melded together and merged into a single continuum on which sex differences and gender differences were reinforced and arranged hierarchically, with women placed firmly in the subordinate position—physically, mentally, and morally well below their male superiors.[27] The important question for medievalists is how these ancient philosophical, biological, and medical ideas, rooted in a pre-Christian world, meshed with Christian theology,[28] which had a fundamentally different conceptualization of human beings.

Christianity: One Flesh, Two Sexes?

The Christian conception of sex difference found in scripture is as complicated and contradictory as were the ideas of the ancients. The contradictions began with the two stories of creation found in Genesis. The first version is brief and, perhaps for this reason, less dominant in the discourse of creation. The creation of humanity is summarized in one brief sentence: "God created man in his own image, male and female he created them" (Gen. 1:27–28). This is followed by a second, alternative, and more familiar account of how God created Adam from the dust of the earth and Eve, subsequently, from Adam's rib (Gen. 2:21–22). These two versions of creation present a conundrum for the Christian understanding of sex and gender. Genesis 1 presents the cocreation of male and female versions of humans, perhaps better understood as flesh than as human beings, because it then permits the notion of one essence, one flesh, capable of manifesting two sexes.

Creation in Genesis 2 presents man and woman as separate entities, although Adam himself recognizes their unity when he refers to Eve as "bone of my bones, and flesh of my flesh" (Gen. 2:22). Subsequently marriage is characterized as "the two become one flesh" (Gen. 2:24). This, then, carries some limited sense of the inherent sameness of man and woman that is so unambiguous in the Genesis 1 creation story. In the Middle Ages, however, Genesis 2 was conventionally interpreted in a neatly hierarchical way that reinforced a view of woman's secondary place in creation, and thus both her subordination and dependence. This view dominated in Christian theology, although occasionally an understanding reminiscent of the Genesis 1 version reinserted itself. For example, the Apostle Paul affirmed that "there is neither Jew nor Greek, slave nor free, male nor female, for you are all one Christ Jesus" (Gal. 3:28). This assertion challenged the very foundations of the ancient hierarchical understanding of sex and gender by denying the distinctions between men and women and those in-between "not-men" such as slaves.

Nevertheless, the notion of male and female as one flesh in God's image was unstable and easily overlooked or interpreted away in a society ordered along the hierarchical binaries of both sex and gender difference. For example, in the late sixth century, Gregory of Tours records that at the Council of Mâcon there was an argument about whether woman was in fact included in the term "man." The council concluded that in Genesis 1 God had used the word "man" to refer to both Adam and Eve; in Gregory's words, "yet of both he used the word man."[29] This did not mean that the question about women's essential humanity was settled once and for all. For example, in the twelfth century a similar debate took place about whether women were created in the likeness of God. The general conclusion was that men and women were both fully in the spiritual likeness of God, but this was not reflected in their biological differences, which ultimately kept women removed from "fully human status."[30] So the enduring importance of the sexed body and sexual difference in a hierarchical ordering of genders is highlighted.

Following on the sex and gender binaries of ancient philosophical and medical ideas, Christian theologians incorporated their hierarchical sex/gender continuum into the Christian world view. For example, Isidore of Seville (ca. 560–636) reconciled the Christian and ancient continuum. In the *Etymologies*, a foundational text for subsequent medieval thought, Isidore states that man was created from clay and changed into flesh, but from the moment of her creation woman always was flesh. As a result, women's bodies are airy, with thin skin and a thin skull. If women were to feel the same heat as men, they would be sterile, just like the earth is sterile from too much sun.[31] Thus, the qualitative difference between female cold and male heat layered onto the Christian creation story.

It is particularly significant that these various complementary and contradictory understandings of sex and gender support the argument that religious people, saints, and celibate monks and nuns may have formed a third gender. The possibility of slippage, or movement along the continuum can be found quite early in Christian contexts. For example, the early martyr, Perpetua (d. 203), described how she saw herself preparing to go into the arena: "My clothes were stripped off, and suddenly I was a man." Attendants rubbed her with oil and she then engaged in hand-to-hand combat with an Egyptian gladiator. These activities are described in vividly masculine terms: "We drew close to each other and began to let our fists fly." The vision continues, describing in detail Perpetua's very physical fight against the gladiator.[32]

Much later, Hucbald of Saint Amand (b. 840, d. 930 or 932), writing around 907, used a similar metaphor of masculine sports to describe Rictrude's (ca. 614–688) struggles: "Stripped of every worldly care as in the customary nudity of the palastra, she entered the monastic gymnasium where she would run, competing in the arena of this present life, struggling in contention against the Devil. She was anointed with the oil of celestial grace lest the wicked adversary get a hold to restrain her."[33] The language of the arena and gymnasium was useful to describe the struggles of monastic life and was applied to women as well as to men. In his *vita* of Monegund (d. 570), Gregory of Tours observes that, "as examples, He provides not only men but members of the inferior sex who are not sluggish in fighting the good fight but full of manly vigor."[34] Similarly, a seventh-century life of Rusticula (ca. 556–632) notes, "While she was on earth she could always struggle manfully against the Devil who attacked her incessantly."[35] Even as late as the twelfth century, the English mystic Christina of Markyate was sometimes characterized "as more like a man than a woman" and as having "more masculine qualities" because of her superior ability to resist sexual desire.[36]

It was Perpetua alone, however, who appears to have envisioned herself and described her experience explicitly in the language of transsexuality. "I was a man," she says. Rachel Moriarty, among others, has argued that an alternative and equally correct translation of the Latin *masculus* could be *male*.[37] In that case, Perpetua would have been more conventionally appropriating masculine gender qualities rather than transitioning into a biological man. Even if this were the case, however, Perpetua saw herself moving along a sex/gender continuum, away from the weaker female point toward the stronger male end.[38] This movement also pertained to male martyrs, who could be described with the most intimately female imagery, that of childbirth. The account of the martyrdom of a doctor named Alexander states, "It was clear to those standing around the platform that he was, as it were, suffering the pain of giving birth."[39] So it was possible to have slippage, whether it was sex or gender, biological or moral, in both directions.

The notion that men and women were not so much equal as capable of becoming more similar as they moved along the continuum was most frequently used to suggest that women should, and would as they became more spiritual, move toward the masculine end. One of the earliest examples is found in the work of Clement of Alexandria (d. ca. 215) who observed, "Is not woman translated into man, when she is become . . . unfeminine, and manly, and perfect."[40] In a similar vein, Jerome (ca. 340–420) famously urged his female followers to shed their womanliness and strive for virility: "As long as woman is for birth and children, she is different from man as body is from soul. But when she wishes to serve Christ more than the world, she will cease to be a woman and will be called a man."[41] Ambrose of Milan (ca. 340–397) was even more explicit when he wrote, "She who does not believe is a woman and should be designated by the name of her bodily sex, whereas she who believes progresses to complete manhood."[42] This kind of advice was provided by male writers to religious women throughout the Middle Ages. Women would become more virile, more manly, and, by implication, more perfect, if only they would repress their female qualities and deny and overcome their female bodies.[43] So, for example, in the twelfth century, Osbert of Clare (fl. 1136) wrote to Ida of Barking: "Do not let lascivious mirth reduce you to your sex. Conquer the woman; conquer the flesh; conquer desire." He further urged Ida "to become a splendid and radiant *virgo*, or rather a virile and incorrupt *virago*."[44] Thus it was that also in the twelfth century, Peter the Venerable (b. ca. 1092–1156) could find no higher praise for the incomparable Heloise than to tell her, "You have overcome all women and risen above almost all men," a compliment that extolled Heloise's virtue while still reinforcing female inferiority.[45]

If a woman did indeed deny her female body, she could demonstrate incredible strength. James of Vitry described the fortitude of Mary of Oignies (1167–1213), a woman widely admired for her rejection of her own flesh, a rejection that extended to self-mutilation. According to James, Mary was able to suffer trials so severe that "even strong men could barely have endured a third part of her toil."[46] Thus, denial and castigation of the female body led to masculine strength and endurance. It allowed women to move along the continuum and harden their bodies, as much as their souls, so that they were no longer soft, feminine, and weak.

When the sex/gender continuum is examined, it is clear that men needed to move along it as much as women.[47] For example, a man who was too hot would be as much a slave to his flesh as a woman was to hers. In the twelfth century, Hildegard of Bingen (1098–1179) summarized a number of ways that a priest could control his burning lust: "Let him subdue his body with abstinence and fasting and chastise himself with cold and scourging."[48] This was established advice that many believed holy men took at face value. For example, a number of male saints and holy men, including Hildegard's contemporaries Bernard of Clairvaux (1090–1153) and Ælred of Rievaulx (1109–1167), were reported to have jumped into freezing water to cool their burning flesh and extinguish the fires of lust.[49] Others suggested sitting on cold stones would also cool the sexual organs when necessary, surely a remedy that was easily accessible in the stone buildings of northern Europe.[50]

While women had a natural means of expelling excess humors through regular menstruation, men needed to find alternate ways to purge their bodies. Gregory the Great (b. ca. 540, bishop of Rome 590, d. 604) alluded to this in his description of Benedict famously taming his lust by jumping into nettles: "His torn and bleeding skin served to drain the poison of temptation from his body."[51] Much later into the Middle Ages, Arnold of Villanova (ca. 1238–c. 1310) reported that the doctor in a monastery bled monks who experienced seminal emissions because they were too hot.[52] Theologians were well aware that it was easier for some men to tame the flesh than others. Hence, in the thirteenth century, Robert Grosseteste (ca. 1175–1253) admitted that he did not experience movements of the flesh—spontaneous erections and seminal emissions—because, by nature, he was colder than other men.[53] This means that Robert believed himself to be further toward the female end of the continuum and, having a cooler temperament, he was less subject to the insistent movements and desires that characterized the male body.

The very hairiness of the male body was the result of virile heat, which could also be a sign of spiritual pollution. Hildegard of Bingen observed, "Some are hairy of body and seem dirty in the soul, because they are pervaded with unclean human pollution."[54] Thus, a man with a hairless face was assumed to have a cooler temperament because he lacked the prominent body and facial hair that signaled masculinity. He would also, then, have appeared to be less prone to the "fires of lust" than were hairy men.[55] This movement along the sex continuum was symbolized by the tonsure men received upon entering monastic life. For example, in his description of the shearing of Rictrude's son, Maurontus, Hucbald reflected tenth-century ideas about tonsure: "Blessing him according to the ecclesiastical custom, he cut the hair of his head in clerical tonsure and made the sign of the cross on his brow, showing that what was done on the outside was to serve as a sign of what was inscribed within. Clearly the denuded top of his head signified that all the secrets of his heart were bare and open to God. . . . Verily frequent shearing of hair signifies the frequent shearing of superfluous evil thoughts."[56] While the tonsure might remind a monk to banish evil thoughts, being clean shaven and tonsured was also an outward symbol of a man's abandonment of his sex and his gender.[57] It is not without significance that lay brothers could wear beards to distinguish themselves from monks[58] who had, presumably, moved further along the sex/gender continuum. Significantly, as a reversal of the symbolic meaning of tonsure, Gregory of Tours recorded that Bishop Ursicinus of Cahors (d. ca. 585) was punished by not being allowed to shave or cut his hair for three years.[59] The tonsured and clean-shaven monk deliberately signaled his chastity and confirmed publicly that he had rejected and tamed the masculine heat associated with a beard, hair, and, by extension, semen and sexual virility.[60]

Just as hair and a beard was the result of masculine heat and was linked to virility and the production of semen, so, too, natural baldness was a manifestation of a cold temperament. A cold man, who could not produce the heat to externalize the vapors to create a beard or hair, was also less virile and more likely to be impotent.[61] Doctors would diagnose impotence by looking for cold testicles, a lack of hair, tight veins, or cold flesh.[62] This cultural understanding of the relationship between hair and virility was ancient, as the example of Delilah cutting Samson's hair so clearly articulated (Judg. 16:17–19). For the Franks, baldness was associated with slavery and those weak, unmanly creatures found at the center of the sex/gender continuum, so far away from their virile and decidedly hot, long-haired kings.[63]

The tonsure and smooth skin served as external signs of internal chastity. They were a reflection of the cooling of a monk's body. They were also reminiscent of the state of purity, especially the sexual and bodily purity, that characterized prepubertal children. When the twelfth-century English monk Ælred of Rievaulx died, his body was laid out, naked, to be prepared for burial. Walter Daniel, Ælred's friend and hagiographer, described its state: "His flesh was clearer than glass, whiter than snow, as though his members were those of a boy five years old, without a trace of stain, but altogether sweet, and composed and pleasant. . . . pure and immaculate in the radiance of his flesh as a child."[64] Walter also noted that Ælred had not lost any hair and was not bald. This would suggest that, despite his smooth skin and famed continence, Ælred continued to have masculine heat. Indeed, even in his old age, he continued to need the icy vat of water that was installed in his monastic cell to quench his passions through immersion. Walter was able to convey something of the complexity of Ælred's continence by describing him having both the smooth skin of the pure and the hair of the virile.

There are also examples of women who underwent physiological changes as they approached greater holiness, revealing they were moving closer to the masculine side of the continuum. In the sixth century, Venantius Fortunatus (530–609) reported that Radegund (ca. 520–586) employed a number of methods to raise her bodily heat. She had a brass plate in the shape of a cross, which she heated and pressed against her body so that her flesh roasted. "Thus, with her spirit flaming, she caused her very limbs to burn."[65] On another occasion, she filled a water basin with burning coals and threw herself into it, "To cool her fervent soul, she thought to burn her body." Catherine of Siena (1347–1380) used much the same strategy. Her confessor, Raymond of Capua (1330–1399), reported that Catherine's mother would take her to the baths, hoping that the sensual pleasure of bathing would discourage the young saint's austerity. But Catherine, "pretending to be in search of better waters, . . . went off to the channels that carry the sulphurous streams along and received the boiling water on her tender flesh, afflicting her body more than she had ever done, even by beating it with an iron chain."[66] Thus, while men such as Ælred tamed their flesh through immersion in icy waters, Radegund and Catherine used excessive heat to mortify their flesh.

Each sex, then, found that the appropriate way to tame their body was through an excess of the characteristic that was by nature weaker. So, warm men turned to cold and cool women turned to heat.

Other holy women were reported to have had more heat naturally than the norm for the female body, for example the thirteenth-century holy women of Liège. According to James of Vitry, Mary of Oignies "did not fear the external cold at all because she was burning internally. . . . And once, in a wondrous manner when the winter was even more bitter than usual and the icy waters froze over from the cold, her outer body became hot while she was praying in conformity to the way she was glowing in the spirit."[67] Similarly, Thomas of Cantimpré (1201–1272) recorded that another of the early beguines, Lutgard of Aywières (1182–1246), was particularly prone to sweating, a standard means to balance men's humors. He wrote, "It happened one night around the time of Matins that an intense and natural sweat overcame her." Apparently Lutgard "presumed that sweat was helpful for her body"; however, she heard a voice tell her to get up and do penance for sinners "and [do] not indulge yourself in this sweating."[68] Moreover, when she was only twenty-eight years old, Lutgard suffered from a miraculous hemorrhage that resulted in the cessation of her menses. The holy woman was no longer subject to the ultimate characteristic of femaleness, which was understood to be both a miracle and a sign of her holiness. The text clarifies this, stating that Lutgard experienced "the cessation of the nuisance with which God has tamed pride in the sex of Eve."[69] Other saints used more earthly means to tame their bodies and fasted to the point that they stopped menstruating because they no longer needed to purge their humors. It is possible that even Margery Kempe's (ca. 1373–ca. 1438) irritatingly copious tears might have been understood to be a means to purge her female wetness.[70]

Holy women's bodies could reveal other physiological characteristics that indicated they had moved toward the masculine end of the sex/gender continuum. For example, the case of a young widow named Galla appears in the *Dialogues* of Gregory the Great.[71] Galla was a noblewoman who was married at "a very young age" and widowed within a year. Age and status dictated she should remarry; however, Galla preferred to remain a chaste widow. According to Gregory, Galla had "a very passionate nature" and the doctors informed her that if she did not remarry, "she would grow a beard even though she was a woman." This is exactly what happened, although the story concludes with the observation that "the saintly woman was not disturbed by this external disfigurement." In Galla's case, the practice of chastity raised her bodily heat, which must already have been high given her passionate nature. As her body became warmer with continued chastity, she moved away from the female end of the continuum, and began to produce the vapors that opened the pores and allowed whiskers to appear. It is significant that the physicians had warned her in advance that this would occur because they well knew the physiological changes that would result from the renunciation of sexual activity.

The numerous other stories of bearded saints, known variously across Europe by names such as Wilgefortis, Uncumber, or Liberada, suggest that the movement to holiness was not perceived only as a transition of gender but also could involve biological sex characteristics. These bearded women were all reported to have rejected suitors or husbands and, by extension, the sexual aspects of marriage, along with the appropriate gender behavior.[72] This was signified by the miraculous growth of a beard and moustache, which served to disguise the woman's identity as well as reveal the increased heat that accompanied chastity as she moved along the sex continuum. Moreover, tradition held that Wilgefortis was one of a group of septuplets, and had three brothers and three sisters. The three brothers had rested on the hotter right side of the womb, the sisters on the colder left side. Wilgefortis had been in the center of the womb, exposed to a balance of heat and cold, which resulted in her having male attributes, such as the beard, and masculine qualities, such as distaste for marriage.[73]

While certainly legendary, nevertheless, the stories of bearded women saints suggest that the relationship between hair and female holiness was recognized. For example, among the early Christian martyrs, Blandina stands out for being a small and frail slave, hardly one expected to do well in the coliseum. However, as she was hanging in a cross-shape in front of the wild animals, her companions saw her change and appear as the decidedly masculine Christ.[74] Raymond of Capua had a similar experience, while talking to Catherine of Siena. He wrote, "Her face turned into the face of a strange man. . . . It was an oval, middle-aged face with a short beard the colour of corn, and it looked so majestic that it seemed to be that of the Lord."[75] Raymond himself understood the bearded man to be Jesus, but perhaps, too, it was also a means by which Catherine's virile holiness was confirmed in a profound, embodied way. At the time, Raymond had been experiencing doubts concerning Catherine's authenticity. Such a vision substantiated her holiness through an ancient and honorable motif, dating back to the early virgin-martyrs.

There was a caveat to this movement along the sex/gender continuum, however. Just as the ancients had placed slaves and "unmen" at the middle of their gender continuum and hermaphrodites at the middle of their sex continuum, so, too, Christian writers were uncertain about the quality and nature of the midpoint between masculine and feminine, hot and cold. For example, Hildegard of Bingen discussed the moral qualities of middleness. "You are not entirely given over to works of cold evil, and you are not entirely burning for good deeds, but you waver toward each in the instability of your mind, like a lukewarm wind."[76] Hildegard chastised those who considered neither the punishment for their evil deeds nor the potential rewards for their good actions. Such people are "like a lukewarm wind, which gives neither moisture nor heat to the fruits" and they behave with "lukewarm negligence."[77] Even the Aristotelian Albert the Great (b. 1193/1206, d. 1280), who was not inclined to see sex as porous and incremental, admitted to the role of the humors and heat and cold in determining sex difference. He observed, "Sometimes even the complexion of the heart is so intermediate that it is scarcely possible to discern which of the sexes should prevail."[78] Moreover, the indeterminate, lukewarm center of the spectrum was populated not only by biologically anomalous hermaphrodites but by others, as well, who disrupted sex and gender norms; transvestites, eunuchs, and homosexuals were also to be found there, the morally suspect being linked to the biologically ambiguous.[79] This reveals so clearly how medieval people believed that biology and morality, sex and gender intersected and reinforced each other.

Setting aside examples of physical changes, it is also possible to find evidence that medieval people believed, and even promoted, the idea that monks and nuns were more similar to each other than they were different. For example, through "her sober and beneficent demeanor," Bertilla, abbess of Chelles (d. ca. 700), "attracted many women and even men whose hearts were faithful."[80] More compelling is an example provided by Jonas of Bobbio (b. ca. 600, d. after 659). He described how Burgundofara (603–645), the abbess of the mixed community of Faremoutiers, raised the young Ercantrude, who had entered the convent while she was still "an infant": "Our mother [Burgundofara] nurtured her [Ercantrude] so carefully within the convent walls that she could not distinguish between our sexual natures: for she counted male and female the same; female and male just alike."[81] Thus, Jonas portrayed the situation at Faremoutiers as one in which the blurring of sex and gender distinctions was complete and traditional differences were rendered irrelevant. The holy person was a type of its own, a person in whom sex and gender binaries were erased, with the result they could live together as one.

Medieval Synthesis: One Flesh, Two Sexes, Three Genders?

The question remains, however, whether all of this, taken together, substantiates the identification of chastity as a third gender. The introduction to Herdt's *Third Sex, Third Gender* is of particular use to establish an analytical framework. Herdt notes that dyads set up situations of inevitable oppositionality.[82] The very fact that medieval people saw sex and gender as mutable and recognized that every individual could possess greater or lesser amounts of maleness and femaleness demonstrates a worldview that allowed for the accommodation of multiple identities underneath a dominant discourse of binaries. Indeed, the absence of a medieval notion of absolute sex/gender alterity created a conceptual space in which a third gender could exist. Herdt also argues that the intentional actor needs a separate social space in which to search for a new sex/gender identity.[83] The medieval monastery, the hermitage, beguinage, or anchorhold all could have provided exactly such a space in which a third gender—the chaste—were able to develop a separate and unique identity. As Abelard wrote in a letter to Heloise, concerning a request he write a monastic rule specifically for women, "As in name and profession of continence you are at one with us, so nearly all our institutions are suitable for you."[84] Finally, according to Herdt, alternative genders cannot be separated from sexes or sexualities but must be integrated.[85] This then, leads back to the recognition that, in medieval society, chastity was a distinct sexual orientation.[86] Given how closely chastity was linked to the sexed body and to changes to that body, for both men and women, there would appear to have been an integrated understanding of sex, gender, and sexuality. Thus, in the Middle Ages, the conceptual framework necessary for the development of a third gender was indeed available.

If the medieval worldview, with its fluid sex and gender systems, provided space for a third gender to develop, it is necessary to ask what this might have meant in a society that depended formally on a hierarchical sex/gender continuum rooted in the values and beliefs inherited from antiquity. Holy women and men who moved closer together, were also moving away from the extremes of sexed temperament and were becoming more similar in body and in soul. As Dyan Elliott notes in her chapter in this book, women "construed virginity as a conduit to 'becoming male' or, better still, the realized eschatology of the *vita angelica* where there was no marriage nor giving in marriage" (see p. 20). In other words, being freed from sexual activity not only freed women from the constraints of their female bodies but also from their gendered subordination.

If, then, chastity was indeed a third gender, where did it fit in the hierarchical evaluation of sex and gender? Given that the movement along the continuum was in both directions, it was not just the more obvious situation of women becoming more masculine. Men also needed to become cooler, less virile, and more feminine in both bodily temperament and gendered social and moral qualities, for example, by developing the virtues of mercy, meekness, and obedience, and by rejecting the external signs of virile masculinity such as waging war or engaging in sexual intercourse. As Gregory of Tours reported a description of heaven from a vision of Bishop Salvius of Albi (d. 584), it was filled "with a throng of people, neither men nor women . . . not angels but holy saints."[87] In other words, the dichotomies of sex and gender would be swept away in the resurrected bodies of the holy.

At this point, the Christian notion of one flesh is again helpful. A medieval person could not and would not want to be located at the lukewarm center of the sex/gender continuum with the unhappy hermaphrodites, the inferior slaves and "unmen" of antiquity, or the transgressive homosexuals and transvestites. Perhaps, for Christians, the solution to the problem of sex and gender slippage was found in the one flesh of creation, first discussed in Genesis 1. Even in the postlapsarian world of the Middle Ages, some notions of the commonality of male and female flesh endured. For example, a life of Glodesind (ca. 600), written in the ninth century, begins with the invocation: "Oh God, you Who created all things from nothing by the power of your virtue, have made woman's help indispensable to man, for you have decreed that all virile flesh begin in feminine bodies."[88] Significantly, this assertion, appearing in the context of a work celebrating the life of a holy woman, reverses the usual relationship of male and female in the notion of one flesh. Instead of highlighting Adam's first place in the order of creation, and Eve's subsequent creation from his rib, this statement places women first and men second by virtue of their dependence on women for conception, gestation, and birth. How this might have been understood by the medieval reader is interesting to contemplate. The passage stressed not only the notion of cocreation and the union of the flesh, but it may also have enhanced women's place in the order of creation by foregrounding men's dependency on women's wombs.

Even without this kind of reversal of the order of creation, however, it was possible for male and female characteristics to be more closely aligned through the belief in one flesh. For example, Hildegard of Bingen asserted, "Eve was formed from a rib by Adam's engrafted heat and vigor."[89] She continues, "As she is from the man, the man is also from her, lest they dissent from each other in the unity of making their children; for they should work as one in one work."[90] Thus, one flesh enhanced the cooperative and interdependent nature of the relationship between men and women in procreation. But chastity took men and women beyond the tyranny of the body and beyond the tyranny of social expectations. Chastity took human beings back to the prelapsarian one flesh that was created in God's image. This flesh had united male and female before the intrusion of gender into the Garden of Eden and before gender was put in a hierarchical relationship with the Fall and the advent of original sin. As Paul summarized this notion, "Just as woman is for man, so man is for woman but all are from God" (1 Cor. 11:12). Rather than a binary of male and female, one flesh created a triad between men, women, and God.

Given the inextricable relationship between sex and gender, which cannot be decoupled completely from each other, it is perhaps possible to find a third sex or third gender in medieval society. Chastity required biological sex and social gender to be transformed in both men and women. In the process, men and women were reconciled and became more like one another. They could truly imagine themselves as the one flesh of creation, in relationship with each other, without dominance and subordination, or other oppositionalities. Adding the lens of the biological sex to the discussion of chastity as a third gender reinforces the significance of chastity in bridging the gulf that separated medieval men and women, a point made so importantly by Jo Ann McNamara.

Chapter 3

Thomas Aquinas's Chastity Belt
Clerical Masculinity in Medieval Europe

Ruth Mazo Karras

The relatively new scholarly field of masculinity studies has established that masculinity, like femininity, is a construct that varies across cultures and over time. Scholars do not agree, however, about how we decide what constitutes masculinity at a given time. Is it a norm defined by what men actually do, or an ideal? This fundamental interpretative question is particularly relevant to the study of the clergy in the Middle Ages. Clearly the ideal for the clergy (enforced more stringently after the reform movement of the eleventh century) was chastity. Active engagement in sexual and reproductive activity, however, is an important component of masculinity in many, if not all, cultures and medieval western Europe was no exception. Were the clergy, then, being more masculine if they violated the celibate ideal and behaved like the lay majority? As Lisa Bitel suggests in her introduction to this book, was their gender ideology hindering their religious profession, or their religious profession their gender ideology?

Medieval European Christian culture is unusual (though not unique) in the larger scope of world history, in that the members of its cultural elite were under an obligation of chastity. In my 2003 book on medieval masculinities, I touched on the clergy only briefly, in part because it seemed too big a subject to be just one chapter and in part because the book focused on the fourteenth and fifteenth centuries and it is the period before that which is most interesting for the development of an ideology of clerical masculinity. The topic remains too big for one chapter, and this essay attempts only to outline the issues.

A number of scholars who have recently written about the clergy and masculinity have suggested that the medieval clergy were not, in fact, masculine—that by virtue of their renunciation of sexual activity they became "emasculine" or a "third gender."[1] Of course, not all members of the clergy lived up to their vows of chastity (for monks) or requirement of celibacy (for the secular clergy). Records of episcopal visitations and church court prosecutions, as well as anticlerical satires especially from the later Middle Ages, make this abundantly clear.[2] Scholars have found in this sexual—particularly heterosexual—activity by the clergy an attempt to reclaim the masculinity denied to them by their vows or (in the case of the secular clergy) to remain within the masculine culture in which they were raised.[3] I suggest, however, that the clergy, both regular and secular, who did remain celibate and chaste did not thereby abdicate their masculinity. To argue that any person who does not live up to the culture's dominant ideals for his or her gender—as do some of the scholars Jacqueline Murray cites in her essay in this volume—would mean that any woman who exercised any sort of leadership or any man who allowed himself to be led was something other than a woman or a man. I would apply Ockham's Razor here and suggest that genders should not be multiplied beyond necessity. There was considerable play within the medieval gender system, but, as Murray notes, it was "underneath a dominant discourse of binaries" (see p. 49).

Rather than speak of third (or fourth or fifth) genders, it is more useful to speak of multiple variations on the basic two. This approach allows us to observe the tensions inherent in "masculine" and "feminine" gender identities. Dyan Elliott traces the process by which these identities came during the patristic period to be understood as embodied, and they continued to be so during the Middle Ages.[4] It was thus difficult for medieval people, while remaining in their bodies, to transcend them completely. Instead, they lived with contradiction and multiplicity. The fluidity that Murray sees along a spectrum from male to female might instead be seen as fluidity of meaning within the binary categories of masculine and feminine (although I recognize that people could move from one to the other, just as Murray recognizes the existence of the binaries). My earlier work argued that there were distinct models of masculinity in different segments of society during the Middle Ages. The same is true of the clergy. The clerical ideal was a model of masculinity distinct from those models found among the laity, even if many clerics behaved according to the latter. It is not enough to say, "Many clergy behaved like lay men, therefore they accepted the lay model of masculinity and those who did not adhere to it were not masculine." There was more than one lay model and not all emphasized sexual activity. I will argue that there was also a clerical model that in fact emphasized the lack of sexual activity.

Masculinity and Struggle

The association of masculinity with sexual activity and indeed heterosexual aggressiveness is far from alien to the medieval world. We could adduce a number of instances from medieval literature in which men who do not have lovers are taunted as not real men.[5] However, this was far from the only standard of masculinity in the medieval European world. Masculinity also involved fighting; the knight was a powerful medieval ideal of manhood, even if in actual practice the status was only relevant to a small segment of society.[6] Military metaphors were often used for Christianity; all Christians were to some extent *milites Christi*, soldiers or knights of Christ. The phrase could be used particularly of monks, who led a life as regimented as a soldier's and who could be seen as battling continuously for the faith.

Even though military metaphors could be used to describe monks, however, the church and monasteries in particular were dedicated to the cause of peace, and it was hard to make the case that the clergy (regular or secular) were like other men in regard to either sexual activity or aggression. The church responded to this problem with a deliberate, ongoing, and rather successful effort among the clergy to create an ideology in which the standard of masculinity was not sexual activity or aggression but rather strength of will, as evidenced among other things in the avoidance of sexual activity. Participation in sexual activity thus became a sign of weakness, following in the Pauline tradition in which it is better to marry than to burn, but better still to remain a virgin. Indeed, a number of scholars, including Jacqueline Murray and Maureen Miller, have suggested that the church (especially after the reform movement and the "monasticization of the clergy") presented a model of masculinity in which the struggle against temptation, particularly sexual temptation, was depicted as a manly battle.[7] When monks led a life as regimented as a soldier's and battled continuously for the faith through strength of will rather than the use of weapons, were they buying into a secular model of what a man should be or were they transforming it by making chastity, rather than wealth or power, the object of constant struggle?

Indeed, the idea of masculinity achieved through chastity depends on conceiving of chastity as struggle. I have argued elsewhere that chastity could be considered a sexual orientation in the Middle Ages.[8] Although some people were abstinent because of the circumstances in which they found themselves, chastity was more than abstinence. In terms of the acts/identities paradigm popularized by twentieth-century devotees of Michel Foucault, abstinence was an act (or more precisely the absence of an act), whereas chastity was an identity.[9] Sexually active versus chaste was at least as fundamental a difference within society as gay versus straight is today. Both men and women felt themselves drawn to chastity at a very young age, before they would have begun sexual activity anyway. Chastity came as a vocation from God, but it was similar to what people today would describe as an inner compulsion or an orientation.

We might wonder whether men who had to struggle constantly against sexual temptation should really be understood as having this orientation to chastity. Are they not, in fact, closeted heterosexuals, simply repressing their desires? Are they akin to victims of the twentieth-century medicalization of homosexuality, who felt same-sex desires but were persuaded to understand them as a mental illness that needed to be controlled? I would argue, no. An integral part of the orientation to chastity itself was the struggle. If someone were simply without sexual desire, there would be no virtue in not indulging the desire (although, as John Arnold points out, the lack of desire could be a gift from God as a result of a successful struggle).[10] This struggle was not just a way of persuading oneself or others that the chaste could still display the strength and authority that the secular world connected with masculinity; it was integral to many medieval Christians' understanding of their relation to God. It differed from secular expressions of strength and authority in that it could not be carried on independently but required, by its very nature, divine assistance.

This valuation of chastity as more masculine than sexual activity was not, of course, universally adopted in medieval society; just as what is normal in one social class or subculture in the modern era may be deemed effeminate by another, so too within medieval culture the clerical view of things encountered substantial resistance. Yet it cannot be seen simply as a self-serving action by a group of men who are simply protesting too much. It represents a fundamentally different, and enduring, understanding of what it means to be a man—and what it means to be a woman.

This masculine chastity could be exhibited not only by men but also by women. Consider an example from *The Life of Christina of Markyate*, written by an anonymous monk of St. Albans in England in the twelfth century. Christina, a young noblewoman, had made a vow of virginity, but her family in collusion with church authorities forced her into a marriage. She fled and lived in a series of precarious situations before finally taking a formal vow and settling down as an anchoress near St. Albans, where she became a spiritual adviser to its abbot. For a portion of her life she lived with a cleric, unnamed by her biographer, to whom she had been referred by a sympathetic archbishop. The devil attacked the two of them with sexual temptation. He, "out of his senses with passion, came before her without any clothes on and behaved in so scandalous a manner that I cannot make it known, lest I pollute the wax by writing it, or the air by saying it." She was more able to control herself: "And though she herself was struggling with this wretched passion, she wisely pretended that she was untouched by it. Whence he sometimes said that she was more like a man than a woman, though she, with her more masculine qualities [*virtute virili*], might more justifiably have called him a woman."[11] In medieval terms, uncontrollable lust was connected with women, not with men; in a reversal of what we have come to know as the Victorian model, it was men who were expected to exercise self-control and regulate the passions of their partners. Here both of them felt the same passion, but Christina was able to conquer it, and that ability was presented as masculine (even when found in a woman).

Yet, tellingly—and this would be true of a man as well—she did not conquer it through her own virtue. Rather, the help of God was an integral part. Christina both behaved "manfully" in "violently resist[ing] the desires of her flesh" with "long fastings, little food . . . a measure of water to drink, nights spent without sleep, harsh scourgings," but, most important, "she called upon God without ceasing not to allow her, who had taken a vow of virginity and refused the marriage bed, to perish for ever." God accordingly reduced the level of Christina's temptation when the cleric was with her. "For in his absence she used to be so inwardly inflamed that she thought the clothes which clung to her body might be set on fire. Had this occurred whilst she was in his presence, the maiden might well have been unable to control herself." Finally, "the Son of the Virgin looked kindly down upon the low estate of His handmaid and granted her the consolation of an unheard-of grace," appearing to her as a small child and extinguishing forever the fire of lust within her.[12] Only God's grace could accomplish this.

This model of masculinity, rooted in strength and struggle that are to no avail without the help of God, can be traced back to the Desert Fathers tradition, dating to the fourth and fifth centuries. For the writers of this textual tradition, chastity always required a battle. Indeed, the very first desert monk, St. Anthony, who served as a model for so many others, was described as fighting off the temptations of demons *viriliter* (manfully).[13] Some texts denied that it was possible to be without desire, even for the most chaste of men living among chaste men. Abbot Cyrus of Alexandria is reported to have said, "If you do not have thoughts of fornication, you have no hope; for if you do not have the thoughts, you have the deeds."[14] The stories of the Desert Fathers make the point that no one is ever totally safe from temptation. When a "certain old man" told a young brother that the latter was vile and unworthy for admitting into his mind the harassment of the demon of fornication, Abbot Apollo prayed that the old man would feel the same temptation: "Lord, who sends useful temptation, turn the battle that brother suffers against this old man." He told the man that he had not felt temptation before because "you were either unknown or held in contempt by the devil until now, because of which you have not deserved, like men of virtue, to struggle against the devil." However, "No one can bear the ambushes of the enemy, nor extinguish or rein in the fire swelling up in nature, unless the grace of God protects human weakness."[15] The images of aggression—*pugna, luctamenta, insidiae*—stress the masculine nature of the struggle, but it cannot be won by man's strength alone.

Cenobitic monasticism picked up on this idea of struggle. The early fifth-century Rule of Saint Benedict requires chastity but does not go into great detail about the means of maintaining it; John Cassian's *Institutes*, which helped spread the practices of eastern monasticism in the West, have more to say about threats to chastity (such as inappropriate relations between monks, and nocturnal emissions), and provide guidance in the struggle. This struggle is a "brutal war" that can be won only by a combination of fasting, manual labor, and prayer, and even then only through the special gift of God. The status of those "who do not feel the stings of the flesh as an attack of shameful desire" is very difficult to achieve; but "we do not doubt that there are many who are continent and extinguish and restrain the attacks of the flesh, which they sustain either rarely or daily . . . they can never be safe and unscathed. For it is necessary that whoever is in a struggle, no matter how often he defeats or overcomes the enemy, himself will sometimes be thrown into disarray."[16] Victory in the struggle is only possible with God's intervention.

Gregory the Great's late sixth-century life of Benedict continues in the tradition of the desert ascetics when he describes how Benedict, assailed by lust and tempted to leave his monastic vocation, controlled the desires of his flesh by rolling around in nettles. "By the wounds of the skin, he removed the wound of the mind. . . . Thus he defeated sin, because he transformed the burning. . . . From that time on . . . the temptation of pleasure was completely tamed in him."[17] Saint Benedict proved a model for the writing of later lives of other monastic saints, who are reported to have fought similar battles. All these stories make the point that the chaste monks are like other men in having these desires; they are not emasculine. The difference is that they are driven to struggle to control the desires. Theirs is a heroic chastity. As Conrad Leyser points out, it was not just a matter of avoiding sin; it could bring political benefits, "the respect and obedience of [one's] fellows."[18]

A chastity that did not involve struggle and God's intervention was not heroic. Eunuchs did not fight the masculine fight of virtue. In the Eastern church eunuchs did serve as priests, monks, even bishops (although some monasteries refused to admit them because they might become temptations to other monks).[19] But churchmen writing about them did not give them credit for great ascetic virtue because once they were castrated chastity did not require an effort of will. In the early Middle Ages, Eastern Christian writers had tended to regard eunuchs as dangerous (because they were sexually tempting to men) and not especially virtuous. They could not struggle against temptation or achieve the triumph of *apatheia* (sexual disinterest) because it was already physically determined.[20] Those who achieved *apatheia* through divine grace, or metaphorical castration, were not emasculated. If they were considered no longer quite men, it was only because they were considered no longer quite human: They ceased to be embodied at all because the flesh mattered not at all to them.

Monasticism and Desire

Western monasticism in the early Middle Ages, although certainly aware of the Desert Fathers tradition and heavily influenced by Cassian, put less emphasis on the struggle. Albrecht Diem argues that the monastic ideal as found in Merovingian church councils and hagiography is a complete chastity created by the absence of desire, rather than by a constant struggle.[21] The idea of struggle did not disappear entirely. Monks read and copied the Desert Fathers' texts and learned from them. The Merovingian saint Vulmar, founder of several monastic houses in the north of France, was called "the knight of God, manfully fighting in the battle against the vices."[22] The Flemish Saint Bavo (589–654) was described by his (eleventh-century) biographer as a knight of Christ, combating temptation *viriliter*, with the "shield of truth."[23] Diem argues, however, that early medieval monasticism was focused much more on the creation of sacred space than on desert father-style asceticism. The fact that monasteries remained involved in politics, rather than being truly withdrawn from the world, may be a contributing factor. In addition, so many monks in this period were child oblates that their attitude toward worldly temptation (and the need to use the metaphors of worldly activity to combat it) would have been different from those of men who chose the monastic life as mature adults.

Across the channel, Aldhelm's (ca. 639–ca. 709) seventh-century works on virginity associate both male and female saints with "physical strength, aggressive warrior action, and weapon-bearing" in the spiritual battle.[24] Aldhelm apart, however, stories of men afflicted by sexual temptation are much more common than stories of women. Indeed, before the twelfth century, concern about the sexuality of monastic women seems to have focused mainly on their role as occasions of sin for men rather than on their own struggles. They are exhorted to resist, not temptation, but rape; for them, too, divine intervention is often necessary to win the battle.[25]

The notion of chastity as struggle reemerged into prominence in the twelfth century. Scholars who have written about clerical masculinity, indeed, disagree about what kind of changes the twelfth century brought. Jacqueline Murray sees a monasticization of the secular clergy as the model of strength and aggression through renunciation was applied to them, too; R. N. Swanson suggests that the model of aggression fell by the wayside and the clergy became emasculine as they ceased to be sexually active (at least in theory).[26] Both Murray and Swanson assume that the use of military metaphors drawn from secular masculinity was a way of claiming that the cleric could nevertheless live up to a secular model of manhood; men might not be sexually active, but they could still be warriors. However, I suggest that these clerics were not so much trying to live up to a secular model as they were transcending it. It is by no means an insignificant detail that the enemy against whom their aggression was directed was their own desires. And, while they transcended the secular model, they did not transcend masculinity; the idea of aggression, far from falling away, was retained and redefined.

To some extent, the concern with chastity for the secular clergy echoed the renewed interest in chastity—and other moral virtues—which characterized the new monastic orders, beginning with Cluny in the tenth century and continuing through the twelfth century. Odo of Cluny, for instance, wrote a great deal about chastity, not only for monks but also for laypeople. The lay saint whose biography he wrote, Gerald of Aurillac (855–909), was part of a "heavenly army" who fought "*viriliter*" against the vices (described as presenting themselves in a military wedge formation), although the devil "raised up the tempest of war against him" to "capture the citadel of his heart." As with clerics, Gerald's chastity required assistance from God; tempted by the daughter of one of his serfs, he sent word that he was coming to her one night, but he prayed ("though but weakly") to God not to allow him to give in to the temptation. God made the girl appear deformed to him.[27] Yet, as Janet Nelson points out, for Gerald, who lived in a chaste marriage, the secular necessity of marriage posed as large a problem as did sexual temptation; the issue Odo of Cluny faces is whether it is even possible for a layman, whose position requires him to marry, to be holy.[28]

The movement for the reform of the secular clergy may have been influenced in part by the writings of monastic authors like Odo, but the issues were different. Rather than just the personal avoidance of vice, it was the purity of the church—and its independence from dynastic politics—that was at stake in the enforcement of celibacy on the secular clergy. As part of a wider move toward separating the church from the world (but at the same time giving it dominance over the world, particularly over temporal rulers), the popes attempted to set higher standards of moral behavior for priests, including the insistence that they not marry and that if they did so the marriage was not valid.[29] A whole new literature developed about the harms of marriage and the importance of chastity to salvation.[30]

The insistence on clerical celibacy in the West in the wake of the church reform movement of the later eleventh century served to draw a sharp line between clergy and laity, a line that was defined in terms of sexual activity.[31] Much as the church encouraged chastity for the unmarried laity (and even in some cases for the married laity, although chaste marriage was not universally approved), it was a calling only for a few, mainly the regular and secular clergy.[32] The chastity of those few was necessary to maintain their special, sacred status, underscored by a new focus on the Eucharist and the miracle of transubstantiation, which only a priest could perform. By presenting sexual activity as polluting and by requiring purity for the performance of the sacraments, the church could maintain its own representatives on a higher moral plane. This allowed it to justify clerical privileges such as freedom from taxation and from royal justice. The line between clergy and laity thus had immense practical as well as symbolic importance, as Jo Ann McNamara so cogently points out.[33] What is worth noting in this process is the absence of any discourse that implies that the clergy thereby became unmasculine, or even transcended masculinity in a positive sense. Felice Lifshitz points out in this volume, for an earlier period, that virginity conveyed extra authority to a man; this was true a fortiori in the twelfth century. A man might lose secular authority because of not procreating, but he gained another sort of masculine authority.

Murray presents the story of Hugh, a Carthusian who became bishop of Lincoln, as a vivid example of a "new, virile, monastic masculinity" which "reaffirmed to celibate men that they were not a third gender nor were they effeminate or emasculinized."[34] Hugh's biographer, Adam of Eynsham, reports Hugh's description of the events shortly after he joined the Carthusians: "The tempter direct[ed] all the ancient weapons of his infernal armoury against a new recruit to this holy warfare, and in particular, as if from a very powerful crossbow, he shot bolts which, he hoped, I could not resist, since they were part of myself. I mean that he aroused my carnal lusts." Hugh went on to describe how he called on God for help, which was granted.[35] Here too the military metaphor comes through strongly, along with the idea that the struggle can only be won with God's help.

Yet there is a danger in taking stories like that of Hugh of Lincoln as part of an attempt to make a (newly) celibate clergy feel masculine or of the monasticization of the secular clergy. Hugh, of course, was not a secular priest but a monk, and monks had always been required to be celibate. Aristocratic families were eager to place their younger sons in prestigious houses (the sons of the highest nobility as abbots), and a young man raised in a martial environment would have appreciated the idea of the monastic life as a constant battle. Such men, by contrast, were hardly likely to become parish clergy. The stories of men such as Hugh of Lincoln likely circulated mainly within their own orders.[36]

The arguments presented in favor of clerical celibacy seem not to have focused on heroic chastity but rather on the sinfulness of clerical marriage; indeed, the laity were encouraged to put pressure on their priests not to marry or to dismiss their wives. It is not clear exactly what means were used to communicate these ideas to the parish clergy and to the laity. Books of exempla and saints' lives for preachers to use in preparing sermons do not survive from the twelfth century as they do from a later period, nor do sermons to the laity. This is not likely to have been simply an accident of documentary preservation. Before the Fourth Lateran Council (1215) emphasized preaching to the laity, and the Franciscan and especially the Dominican orders began their ministries to provide it, the dissemination of edifying tales like this was much more haphazard. Thus, while the church may have hoped that the secular clergy would become more like monks, the use of monks alone as examples of heroism may not have been the best way to achieve this. The extent to which secular clergy were actively encouraged to live up to these models, or simply criticized for not living up to them, is not clear.

Regardless of the extent to which it extended beyond the monastery to the secular clergy, the Desert Fathers' theme of the combination of struggle and grace had clearly reemerged by the central Middle Ages. In the thirteenth century, the Cistercian author Caesarius of Heisterbach (1170–1240) tells the story of a monk who could not control his lustful feelings. He dreamt that a man with a long knife cut off the dreamer's genitals and fed them to a dog. "Awakening from the horrors of this vision he thought that he had been made a eunuch. This indeed was true, even if not as the vision showed, with a material knife, but by spiritual grace."[37] After this dream, he was no longer troubled by lust, although his testicles physically remained. The castration by the grace of God is metaphorical rather than literal, the testicles remaining to allow him to maintain his bodily manhood. His chastity, then, which came as a gift from God, could be understood as virtuous and manly.

Temptations of the Flesh

Caesarius, in a story about a female recluse, also repeats the point found in the Desert Fathers that temptation is unavoidable. Beset by temptation of the flesh, she prays for its removal. Her prayer is granted, but the carnal temptation is replaced by a temptation to blasphemy. Praying once again for deliverance, she is told by an angel, "Do you claim that you can live without temptation. It is necessary that you have one of these, choose which you will." She chooses the temptation of the flesh.[38] The story makes the point that the struggle is important in the quest for purity: "Temptation is the guardian of humility and the means of practicing virtue." In this particular story, however, the temptation is that of a woman, and the struggle is not described in military terms.

Although some medieval texts questioned the possibility or advisability of the absence of temptation, others presented the removal of temptation as a goal, even if one attainable only by the most virtuous. The absence of desire as a gift from God comes through clearly in the life of Thomas Aquinas. Born in 1227 into a noble family related to many of the royal dynasties of Europe, he had an early vocation to the church, and his family planned to make him abbot of Monte Cassino, a very influential position. However, he chose instead to join the relatively new Dominican order, much to the family's consternation. His family imprisoned him in one of their castles and sent an attractive young woman in seductive clothing to his room to tempt him. (The family apparently thought fornication would be an obstacle to his becoming a Dominican but not a Benedictine.) He chased the young woman out of the room with a burning brand plucked from the fire. On this much, several of his biographers agree. One, William of Tocco, adds the following story:

Then, prostrate on the ground, he tearfully prayed to God, begging for a belt of perpetual virginity, which would allow him to keep himself uncorrupted in the battle. When, thus tearfully praying, he fell asleep, behold two angels of Heaven appeared to him, told him that God had heard him, and that he would achieve victory in his very difficult battle, and bound tight his loins, saying, "Behold, on behalf of God, we gird you with a belt of chastity, as you asked . . . that which may not be had by the merit of human virtue, divine generosity grants you as a gift." . . . And until his death he never felt his virginity violated, which in so grave a battle he preserved unconquered.[39]

I have translated *cingulum* here as belt; other scholars have used the term "girdle," in part, I think, because they do not like the combination "belt of chastity," which sounds too much like the mythical means by which Crusaders kept their wives from straying while they were away. The technical translation for the *cingulum* that is part of an ecclesiastical garment is a cincture. But a *cingulum* also means a sword-belt and, given the references here to the *pugna*, or battle, this connotation is certainly present. Indeed, the term could also, by extension, refer to a military office (*cingere* also meant "to knight") or to "the condition of a warrior, a knight, as contradistinguished from that of an ecclesiastic."[40] The point here, however, is that even so holy a man as Thomas Aquinas was held by his biographers to have felt that his chastity was so frail that it could not be defended without divine assistance. God helps him fight his battle.

Fighting a battle is surely a manly, even knightly, thing to do; that metaphor by no means disappeared after the twelfth century. However, William is not here trying to prove that Thomas was a man by knightly standards, he is using the metaphor to make the point that it is manly to struggle against one's own desires and call on God's help to do so.

The phrases "belt of perpetual virginity" and "belt of chastity" seem here to be used interchangeably. It is useful, however, to distinguish between the two terms, virginity and chastity. Virginity clearly has different meanings for men than for women in the Middle Ages. For women it often meant the physical state of being inviolate, unpenetrated; but there was also substantial discussion of the spiritual component so that someone who was raped, for example, or consented to marriage out of duty, could still be a virgin in the soul, whereas someone who was virgin in body but corrupt in soul was not a true virgin. Jocelyn Wogan-Browne speaks of "honorary virginities."[41] For men virginity was much less a physical state. Arnold suggests that virginity corresponds to that state of sexual anesthesia where the man does not feel erotic desire, whereas chastity is the state of constant struggle.[42] However, as Thomas's example indicates, medieval authors did not make this particular terminological distinction. Thomas does receive the gift of sexual anesthesia that Arnold calls virginity but only because he has struggled so manfully to preserve what William of Tocco calls virginity.

Thomas Aquinas's story provides an example of how churchmen concerned with their own chastity cast women not only as inadvertent triggers for men's lust but as actively sinful themselves. Holy women had not only to shut themselves away from men to remove the occasion of sin but also to monitor their own feelings. Even so, however, women or demons in the shape of women tempted men much more than men or demons in the shape of men tempted women; Christina of Markyate is a rare exception, though not unique. The belief in women's greater natural lustfulness made it dangerous to accord holy women any sexual feelings at all because, if it was difficult for men to control those feelings, it would be all the more so for women. It was more difficult for women to remain chaste than for men, so women had to be more strictly controlled; however, when they did remain chaste, it was more praiseworthy than for men, because they had overcome greater obstacles. As Peter Abelard wrote, "Because the female sex is the weaker . . . their virtue is more pleasing to both God and man."[43] Yet when they did resist, it was considered a masculine thing to do.

Women's heroic chastity often involved maintaining virginity in the face not of temptation but of coercion. In either case, defense of chastity, even if it was not a physical defense, was described as manly. As we have seen, Christina of Markyate behaved "manfully" when she "violently resisted the desires of her flesh, lest her own members should become the agents [*arma*] of wickedness against her."[44] Because Angela of Foligno (1248–1309) "manfully" (*viriliter*) pursued poverty, suffering, contempt of the world, and true obedience, "no vice, no temptation could enter into her."[45] Christina of Stommeln (1242–1312), too, defeated the devil, though not specifically sexual temptation, "viriliter."[46]

Self-Control and Divine Assistance

The ideal of masculinity (whether displayed by men or women) as struggle for self-control plays out not only in the lives of saints but also in the advice and teachings of churchmen on a question of great concern throughout the Middle Ages, namely the moral status of involuntary seminal emission, particularly nocturnal.[47] Medical writers stressed that this emission was part of a natural process by which the body purged itself of superfluities, and was both healthy and beyond the individual's control. Moral theologians generally accepted this position and held that such emissions were not sinful if the man did not encourage them by thinking lascivious thoughts or delight after the fact in the dreams that produced them. According to the fifteenth-century theologian Jean Gerson, citing both medical and theological authorities, a priest who had had a nocturnal emission was not therefore prohibited from celebrating Mass as was a priest who had a waking ejaculation.[48] Yet theologians also generally agreed that it was better not to have such emissions, the existence of which represented, in Dyan Elliott's words, "a sensitive gauge for clocking the relative success or failure of disciplinary efforts to gain mastery over the body."[49] A man who was victorious in those efforts would not be troubled by nocturnal emissions. But that victory, which brought with it the cessation of the need to struggle, was won with God's assistance.

As mentioned earlier, some scholars argue that it was the clergy who did not practice chastity who maintained a masculine identity. However, those clerics who did give in to the temptations of the flesh, who followed a lay rather than clerical model of masculinity, could be cast in an effeminate position, both by clerical writers like the anonymous monastic author of the *Life of Christina* and also by authors of secular texts like the twelfth- and thirteenth-century French fabliaux, which make lascivious clerics as well as lascivious women figures of fun. Indeed, in medieval texts the man who spends too much time with women, even for heterosexual purposes, could sometimes be constructed as effeminate for this reason (although I take issue with scholars who have referred to a "feminization of knighthood" with the development of so-called courtly ideals).[50] More masculine was the man who spent his time with other men, often for military purposes, and used women occasionally and instrumentally. The male world of the celibate clergy, then, could be likened to that of the military in that both considered women a dangerous distraction.

This discussion begs the question, of course, of the relation of attitudes found in texts to attitudes among medieval people themselves. If the church, or some within it, promoted the image of the struggle for self-control and chastity as masculine and indulgence in sex with women as (at least implicitly) effeminate, were they shaping societal attitudes or were they protesting too much and thereby indicating to us that matters actually stood somewhat differently than they would have liked? The answer is undoubtedly both. Saints' lives, in particular, were written for exemplary or didactic purposes; but saints were saints precisely because their behavior differed from that of ordinary people. The fact that the struggle for chastity was constructed as masculine in the lives of both male and female saints is perhaps an indication that the case needed to be made, but it is also an indication that this alternative model of masculinity did exist, and was espoused by those who were in a position to disseminate their views. The term *viriliter* was used to describe the struggle against heresy, against enemies of the faith, against wrong teaching, as well as against temptation.

Although medieval clerics in theory renounced the sexual aspects of manhood, they did not reject the patriarchal privilege that went along with it. The conscious adoption of "Father" as a title of authority (with the pope, of course, as the holiest father of them all) removed it from the realm of procreation and gave the clergy the privileges of those who had the right to make decisions for their families and the responsibility to care for them. The use of the term was taken seriously enough that a priest who had sexual relations with a woman who was his spiritual daughter in the sense that he was her confessor was considered to have committed incest.[51] Caroline Walker Bynum pointed out that Cistercian writers especially spoke of Jesus as a mother and of Cistercian abbots as mothers as well (in the sense of nurturing rather than birthing).[52] This is indeed an important image. But it is important precisely because it goes so strikingly against the current of Christian discourse which makes the priest a father.

The fact that abbots could be called mother as well as father, however, indicates another feature of clerical, in particular monastic, masculinity: its appropriation of the positive aspects of femininity. When Christina resisted temptation, she was acting manfully; when an abbot is tender to his monks, he is acting maternally. But all clerics, indeed all believers, were in a position that could be considered feminine in relation to God. Humans were suppliant, dependent, passive in relation to a powerful, dominant, and active God, without whom the struggle could never be won.

In medieval understandings of human love, suppliant did not always go with passive. The literary tradition that has come to be termed "courtly love" places the man as seeker, the woman as grantor; but the man is active, seeking her out, and if she follows the so-called "rules of love" she is obliged to give her love or withhold it based on the man's worth, rather than on her own choices. The dominance accorded to her was largely fictive. One party was the lover, one the beloved. The lover seeks, the beloved receptively awaits him (or her, but usually him). This may be largely a literary conceit, but it is so pervasive in so many literary forms that it would have shaped the way many people thought about their interpersonal relations.

In reference to God, however, the gendered dichotomy of lover and beloved was manipulated in significant ways. The soul could be said to seek God as a lover seeks his beloved, but God had to be the active party, not simply waiting for a lover to come knocking. For the most part the soul, or the church, played the part of the beloved or bride to God's lover or groom.[53] This is in accordance with the grammatical gender of the word for soul, *anima*, but it is not simply an accidental function of it. God was always the authority figure in the relationship. This reflected the role of God in the struggle: it was the battle against temptation that masculinized the monk or cleric, but that battle could not be won without God's assistance. If we say that the clergy were placed in a feminized position because they were powerless before God, however, we distort the meanings of gender terminology beyond any usefulness: if to be powerless before God is to be feminine, then no believer could ever be masculine or understand anyone else to be masculine. That is demonstrably not the case in the Middle Ages or any other period.

Even though they depended on God for their final victory and were passive and weak in relation to his creative strength, monks still fought the battle against sexual sin and were held up as models to those who were not monks. As the fourteenth-century English text *Ancrene Wisse* puts it, "St. Benedict, St. Anthony, and the others, well you know how they were tempted, and through the temptations tested as true champions. And they deserved a champion's crown."[54] To be chaste was to identify oneself as someone devoted enough to spiritual matters that one could transcend the flesh. This is an even more profound aspect of personal identity than simply a question of whether someone was ritually pure or not. The men who adopted an orientation toward chastity displayed their manhood.

I do not suggest—far from it—that all the clergy accepted this model of heroic chastity. I do suggest, however, that we cannot label those who behaved as secular men masculine and those who did not nonmasculine. There was a distinct model, even if current among only a small elite within medieval culture (and not even universally accepted among them). Rather than argue that the clergy during the Middle Ages were not masculine or were masculine only to the extent that they imitated secular behavior that was forbidden to them, it makes more sense to see an alternative model of masculinity as having existed from the early years of Christian monasticism.

Competing Models

Those who renounced secular masculinity renounced both sexual and military activity; but the military resurfaced metaphorically to explain the erasure of the sexual. Caesarius of Heisterbach tells a story in which a knight leaves his marriage to join the Cistercian order. His wife, who joined a women's house, soon thought better of the arrangement and attempted to seduce her husband in order to get him to return to her. However, "Christ . . . delivered His soldier from the illicit embraces of his legitimate wife."[55] The knight becomes a soldier of Christ not because he joins a military order or because he fights against the infidel, but because he fights against his own temptation. Christians could be soldiers without fighting; they could be sexual beings without committing sexual sin. A saint like Aquinas might to some extent, and with divine intervention, transcend manhood, moving beyond masculine desires but only through the use of a manly military metaphor.

This did not mean that monks or secular clergy were buying into the secular aristocratic model of masculinity that required military prowess. Everyone understood quite clearly that the military metaphors were metaphors; to their writers, what they represented was more powerful than the physical warfare to which it was compared. Language familiar from a different model of masculinity was used to express something quite different. Aristocratic men who prided themselves on their progeny, legitimate and illegitimate, might not accept this clerical model as real manhood, but conflicting models of masculinity at differing social classes have coexisted in many societies, and medieval Europe is no exception. Religion profoundly affected medieval men's experience of their gender, as did gender their experience of religion.

Chapter 4

Women's Monasteries and Sacred Space

The Promotion of Saints' Cults and Miracles

JANE TIBBETTS SCHULENBURG

Among the ninth-century posthumous miracle cures attributed to the Merovingian Saint Glodesind, abbess of the monastery of Subterius in Metz (ca. 600), is that of a certain woman named Imma. She had been ill for a long time and finally decided to set out for the saint's tomb and ask for her assistance. According to the *vita*, "As soon as she entered the monastery walls, she began giving thanks to almighty God for there she deserved to feel a little strength. . . . As soon as she went through the gates of the monastery, she felt the sickness recede from her. The nearer she came to the church where the virgin's body lay buried, the more steadily did the infirmity recede, and she got better and better. As she passed through the church, she gave great thanks to God praying for her sins as she approached the altar and tomb of the holy virgin. Soon after, praying intently by the virgin's tomb in the same church, she was restored to her original health and so received a complete cure by the prayers of the blessed Glodesind."[1]

This narrative provides a wonderful glimpse of a female pilgrim, seeking out the nearby tomb of a female saint, housed in a women's monastery. Primed with the expectant hope of receiving a healing miracle, it underscores the belief in the gradations or zones of sacred space, divine *potentia*, and the special efficacy of the saint's tomb as the primary site for the production of miracles.[2]

For much of the medieval period, monasteries played a major role in the development and promotion of the cult of saints and pilgrimage centers. Male and female religious composed *vitae*, collected miracle stories, and advertised the miraculous deeds of their holy dead, especially those of healing. The recorders of miracles were especially careful to provide information on the sacred spaces in which the saint was accustomed or "seen" to perform his or her miracles. Although they noted their saints' unlimited powers and ability to perform "long-distance" miracles, they stressed the importance for petitioners of proximity to or direct contact with the tombs and shrines of their patron saints. Special churches, chapels, and crypts were built to properly house and display their precious relics and accommodate the crowds of miracle seekers. They strategically arranged and decorated the sacred spaces of their pilgrimage sites to encourage a heightened expectation of miracles. It appears that for some communities their power, their prestige, and even their very survival depended on their ability to procure holy relics and then to "package" or promote them in such a way as to attract crowds of pilgrims along with their gifts and donations.[3]

In general, male monasteries controlled the greatest number and most prestigious pilgrimage sites of the period; they also produced and maintained collections of postmortem miracles. Although women were attracted to and participated in many of these male monastic cult sites, for the most part, miracles there privileged male petitioners—with a few exceptions.[4] Moreover, a number of these major pilgrimage centers, at one time or another, actively discouraged visits by female pilgrims; they strictly forbade women's entry into their churches and access to their patron saints' shrines. And, as I have argued elsewhere, these prevalent attitudes and proscriptive spatial policies help to explain, in part, the disparity in numbers of male and female recipients of miracles at some of these major sites.[5]

Although there has been much interest in the male monasteries and the establishment of major saints' cults and pilgrimage centers, the involvement and success of women's monasteries in this culture of pilgrimage has not received the kind of attention from scholars that it deserves. This study provides a preliminary look at the development of a few of the early cult centers established in women's houses in France, England, and Germany from the sixth through the mid-eleventh centuries. It explores some issues of spatial arrangement as related to access, lay traffic, hospitality, and the special difficulties and challenges, as well as economic benefits, brought about by the pilgrimage trade.

Female Communities and the Cult of Relics

Chronicles, saints' lives, miracle collections, and other sources of the period recognized the primary role of queens, noblewomen, abbesses, and nuns as collectors of relics for their own private use and for the prestige and welfare of their monastic foundations. Thus in endowing their monasteries, the generous benefactors frequently provided the new communities of female religious with extensive landed properties as well as important relics of saints. The holy dead would then serve as patrons, protectors, sources of power and privilege, as well as important income producers for the new foundations. For some of the recently Christianized areas, with few relics of their own, political connections and wide networks of friends and relatives were called upon to help these women acquire relics from Rome and the Holy Land.

For this early period, Saint Radegund (d. ca. 587) is perhaps the best-known example of a passionate collector of relics. According to Baudonivia's *vita*, "While she was still at the villa of Saix . . . she determined, with great devotion, to collect relics of all the saints. At her request, a venerable priest named Magnus brought her relics of Lord Andrew and many others which she placed above the altar."[6] She sent her priest Reoval to Jerusalem where he was successful in acquiring the little finger of St. Mammas.[7] Commenting on Radegund's voracious desire for relics, Baudonivia notes, "Had it been possible, she would have petitioned the Lord Himself in the seat of His Majesty to dwell here in sight of all."[8] Failing that, she did acquire from the emperor her most treasured relic: a piece of wood from the True Cross along with many relics of saints from the East.[9] As these most holy relics were ceremoniously translated to her monastery, Baudonivia notes that Radegund "had felt in her soul that they [her disciples] might have all too little after her passing. Thus, though she would always be able to help them when she was in glory with the King of Heaven, this best provider, this good shepherdess, would not leave her sheep in disarray. She bequeathed a heavenly gift, the ransom of the world from Christ's relics, which she had searched out from faraway places for the honor of the place and the salvation of the people of the monastery."[10]

Although not in the same league as Radegund, many other royal and noble women, noble men, abbesses, and others assumed important roles in the acquisition of relics for Merovingian and early Carolingian women's houses. The following is only a sampling of this religious activity. The *vita* (life) of Saint Gertrude of Nivelles (626–659), for example, notes that "with God's inspiration she deservedly obtained through her envoys, men of good reputation, relics of the saints and holy books from Rome, and from the regions across the sea [Britain or Ireland].[11] About thirty years after Saint Gertrude's death, her sister Begga came to Nivelles. She planned to establish a monastery of her own and was given by the community of Nivelles a contingent of nuns, sacred books, and an indispensable collection of relics, including a fragment of St. Gertrude's holy bed.[12] The Anglo-Saxon Saint Mildred, abbess of Minster-in-Thanet (ca. 660–ca. 725), while studying at the monastery of Chelles, was said to have obtained many relics, including a nail of the cross of Christ. When she returned to Britain, she brought these relics with her and they became part of the collection of her monastery of Minster-in-Thanet.[13] At the end of the eighth or in the early ninth century, Chelles acquired an important collection of relics, probably through Abbess Gisela, the sister of Charlemagne. The collection contained 139 relics, each identified or authenticated with a small band of parchment with the name of the saint and place of origin.[14] According to tradition, Rothilde or Rotrude, daughter of Charlemagne and abbess of Faremoutiers, received from her father a reliquary of gilded silver, which held a large piece of the True Cross.[15]

Such relic-acquisition activities continued into the late Carolingian period and beyond. Around 874, Empress Richilde (wife of Charles the Bald) was able to obtain the "greater" part of the relics of Saint Scholastica from the bishop of Le Mans for the new church and monastery of Juvigny les Dames, which she founded and built on lands inherited from her parents. It appears from a description of the relic collection preserved at Juvigny that their number increased greatly after 874.[16] Saint Richarde, wife of Charles III, "the Fat" (d. ca. 893–894), founded on her own lands and endowed with property and relics brought back from a pilgrimage, a monastery at Andlau. Among her treasured relics was the precious body of Saint Lazarus, said to have been brought back from the dead by Christ.[17] The monastery of Herford was known as "Holy Herford" because of its rich collection of bones and other holy relics. One of Herford's early abbesses, Hadewy, was sent as a gift from her brother, Kobbo, the miracle-working body of Saint Pusinna, translated around 860 (under protest) from Corbie to Herford.[18] Saint Oda, the mother of Saint Hathumoda (ninth century), along with her husband, Liudolf, brought back from Rome the relics of Pope Anastasius and Pope Innocent for their new monastic foundation at Gandersheim, and the nobleman Gero brought back from Rome the arm of Saint Cyriacus for his new convent at Gernrode.[19] In 961, Saint Mathilda, the widow of Henry I, acquired part of the relics of Saint Servais from Maastricht for her new foundation of Quedlinburg.[20] Finally, Saint Wulfthryth, abbess of Wilton (d. ca. 1000), used a Wilton priest and former canon of Trier to negotiate the purchase (for two thousand *solidi* or gold pieces) of one of the nails of the passion from the monastery of Saint Paulinus at Trier. Wulfthryth was also able, through somewhat duplicitous dealings, to extricate (for the identical exorbitant sum of money) the relics of Saint Iwi from a group of foreign clerks who had unfortunately accepted hospitality at her monastery. As noted by Susan Ridyard, although these large figures might be exaggerated, the key to Wulfthryth's relic-collecting success was the wealth that she had at her disposal.[21]

One of the most detailed examples of the importance of relics for the survival of a women's community concerns the monastery of Jouarre. Abbess Ermentrude (first half of the ninth century) had a great passion for relics and seized every possible opportunity to acquire them. In 836,

during the translation of Saint Vitus's relics, Ermentrude received a finger of the saint and the linen that had been used to wrap his body.[22] Her
major coup, however, was her success in procuring for her monastery
the body of Saint Potentianus in 847. Overcome by insurmountable
problems associated with the great poverty of her monastery, Ermentrude in desperation begged her relative, Ganelon, bishop of Sens, to
allow her to furtively carry off Potentianus's relics to her monastery.
From then on, according to the sources, the monastery no longer experienced poverty, want, or grave problems. Jouarre's fame spread near
and far as immense crowds of the sick and infirm streamed there. As a
pilgrimage center, it became celebrated for the expulsion of demons
and for a variety of cures.[23] Nine women and seven men were cured at
Potentianus's tomb at Jouarre.[24] Moreover, a catalogue of Ermentrude's
relic collection notes that she commissioned three reliquaries (a large
decorated cross which held 140 relics; a small cross with about 30 relics;
and another reliquary, which contained an additional 50 relics) and
owned, among other things, two pieces of the True Cross and relics of
Queen/Saint Balthilda, founder of Chelles.[25]

Along with the successful acquisition of relics through donation or
"negotiation"—sometimes bordering on theft, as noted earlier—we also
find a few cases of abbesses and nuns involved in rather blatant relic
theft. In 930, for example, the nuns of the monastery of Maubeuge stole
the body of Saint Gislenus, abbot of Hainault, from the neighboring
abbey of Mons. However, under threat of excommunication by Bishop
Stephen of Cambrai, the nuns were forced to return the body to its
rightful owner.[26] Another case of a thwarted attempt concerns Weren-
trude, abbess of Hohenbourg, who sent a priest to cut off the hand of
her recently deceased friend, Saint Attala, abbess of Saint Etienne of
Strasbourg, and to bring the relic back to Hohenbourg. The priest was
caught in the act and this blatant theft was foiled.[27]

Much evidence is then available that points to the active involvement
of women's communities in the procurement of relics and the culture of
saints. And it is through the promotion and advertisement of miracles of
their in-house patron saints and their other special relics, along with the
successful management of the cult site, that some of these convents
would become recognized and flourish as busy pilgrimage centers.

Women's Houses and the Development of
Merovingian Pilgrimage Centers

In light of various gender-based policies of the period, it would appear to
be extremely difficult, if not impossible, for female religious to encourage
a flourishing pilgrimage business within their monastic churches yet still

remain holy and avoid accusations of moral impropriety. They needed to protect themselves and their cloisters from the secular world with all of its temptations and potential for contamination.[28] Thus we find in the church councils and monastic *regulae* of this early period an emphasis on the different protective spatial requirements for nuns and monks. The policies of passive enclosure, for example, found in Caesarius of Arles' *Rule for Nuns* warned, "Above all, in order to guard your reputation, let no man enter the cloistered part of the monastery [*secreta parte in monasterio*] and the oratories except bishops, the provisor and priest, the deacon and the subdeacon and one or two lectors whose age and life commends them, and who are needed to offer Mass sometimes."[29]

The application of these policies of strict enclosure can perhaps be best seen in the famous and extremely moving descriptions of the funeral procession of Saint Radegund. According to Baudonivia's *vita*, "Since it was ordained that no living person should issue out of the gates of the monastery, the whole flock stood on the walls while they bore the holy body with psalms beneath the walls. They lamented so loudly that their grief drowned out the psalms. . . . Suffering the loss of her most bitterly, they cried out from above that the bier on which the blessed woman was carried might pause under the tower. And as the holy body rested there, the Lord, to reveal his faithful servant in the midst of the people, gave sight to a blind person." Or, as Gregory of Tours described the event, "As we passed by beneath the wall, a crowd of virgins began to cry and weep from the windows of the towers and from the tops of the fortifications of the wall, with the result that in the midst of the sobbing and the rejoicing of the psalms no one could keep themselves from weeping."[30]

A similar scene occurred in 632 with the death of Rusticula, abbess of Saint Jean of Arles (Caesarius's convent). According to the *vita* of Saint Rusticula, her holy body was carried "outside of the monastery" by the bishop, the clergy, and the faithful. The nuns, however, were not permitted to leave the cloister and participate in the funeral. The saint was then buried in a place of honor in the church of Saint Mary. This church of Saint Mary was then the convent's funerary church and was located at a distance from the monastery, perhaps outside the city walls. It was here that Saint Caesarius of Arles had buried his sister Saint Caesaria, first abbess of the convent, and where he also chose to have his own tomb.[31]

How then could these early women's communities promote the cults of their patron saints, attract pilgrims of both genders, and allow them access to their cult sites and hospices, while at the same time carry on the duties of their profession and maintain the reputation of their convents? One solution was the tradition of multiple churches in Merovingian women's houses.[32] Most of the early women's monasteries had at least two and often three or more churches. The monastery of Jouarre, for example, had three churches; Blagny, three churches; Nivelles and Soissons, four churches; Montivilliers, at least four; Pavilly, perhaps five; Laon, six churches; and Begga's monastery in Andenne is noted as having seven churches.[33] One of these churches would be built as the convent's primary church, another as the priests' church, while another—often located outside the city walls—would serve as a funerary church. At Saint Croix of Poitiers, the burial church of Saint Mary was certainly outside the walls and was served by a community of monks; however, scholars continue to debate the intramural or extramural location of the funerary church of Saint Jean of Arles. Thus the nuns of Saint Croix (and perhaps of the Arles community), having adopted the rule of Caesarius, were theoretically not permitted to leave their cloisters and visit the tombs of their patron saint; nevertheless, according to her *vita,* Abbess Rusticula of Saint Jean, at the time of the plague, went to the tomb of Saint Caesarius to pray for her nuns.[34] Clearly, there was some flexibility in practice.

With the multiplicity of churches it was also possible for monasteries to have their patron saint's tomb in one place and their other important secondary relics in another church. For example, Saint Gertrude's holy bed (which was decorated "with gold and precious jewels and most beautiful hangings") was specifically not displayed in the convent's funerary church of Saint Peter, where Saints Itta and Gertrude were buried, but rather in Saint Paul's church.[35] Radegund's relic of the Holy Cross, along with the other relics from the East, was placed in a silver reliquary in the main church of her monastery at Poitiers. It was here, on Good Friday, while the nuns were spending the night in vigils in the private space of their choir, that they were said to experience a divine light before the altar, which was seen as a miracle of the cross.[36] However, as Barbara Rosenwein noted, Baudonivia claimed that "anyone who comes in faith, whatever the infirmity that binds them, goes away healed by the virtue of the Holy Cross."[37] The tradition of multiple churches seems to have provided unlimited access, for the laity, to miracle-working saints' tombs, as William Klingshirn has discerned in regard to the nunnery at Arles.[38] Furthermore, the sacred space of the nuns' primary churches was not reduced to accommodate pilgrims. The female religious could remain undisturbed in their churches and choirs while they also fostered an active pilgrimage center.

For a few of the strictly enclosed communities, such as that of Saint Radegund's monastery and perhaps that of Saint Caesaria of Arles, the multiple-church solution seems to have deprived them of direct access to their patron saints in this lifetime. They had to be satisfied with the saint's secondary relics and other relics found in their private collections. Yet, practice could be flexible. For example, in a number of communities that were not strictly cloistered, accommodations were made to allow the nuns to have access to their funerary churches and their patron saints' tombs. This seems to have been the case at Metz where, according to the *vita*, the burial church of Saint Glodesind and her nuns was built outside the city walls. A special gate was cut through the wall to allow the nuns of the monastery to pass from their monastery and enter the burial church.[39] It therefore appears that these communities shared this space and their holy relics with pilgrims of both genders. Some monastic rules for women allowed pilgrims, laymen and laywomen, within the monastic enclosure and thus provided the latter access to the churches and tombs of the community's saints.[40]

Finally, some recorded miracles clearly assume a degree of access to women's religious houses. In the *vita* of Saint Anstrude, abbess of Laon, for example, a possessed nun was warned three times by the saint to go in all haste to her tomb where she should bite the stone three times after which she would receive a cure.[41] We also find examples of pilgrims practicing incubation in women's churches. They were placed on or near the saint's tomb where they then spent the night sleeping. When they awoke, they found themselves freed of their demons and various illnesses through the intervention of the saint.[42] Others were brought to the important secondary relics of saints, for example, the chair of Saint Anstrude or the bed of Saint Gertrude, and were healed.[43] The miracle cures of Saint Austreberta of Pavilly, following her death (ca. 703), were described as occurring at her tomb and fountain (located under the altar). They list eighteen women (many of whom were nuns), and four male pilgrims.[44] The seventeen miracle cures reported at Saint Anstrude of Laon's tomb and her holy chair, which occurred shortly after her death (ca. 709), all concerned women—mainly nuns of the community.[45] Thus, while we do see a few male petitioners and recipients of miracles in women's houses, they are in a distinct minority. It is possible that these early miracle collections were not written to advertise relics and miracles and to promote pilgrimage business but were composed as proof of the saint's power, mainly as didactic works for the community. Nevertheless, they indicate that the boundaries of Merovingian women's houses were far from impermeable.

Pilgrimage and Women's Cult Centers: The Carolingian Period Through the Mid-Eleventh Century

In the Carolingian period, saints' cults and pilgrimage became increasingly popular among all levels of society. Sources note an attempt on the part of the church to introduce some sort of control and order over this rapidly expanding, competitive religious movement. To curb the abuses in the multiplication of saints' cults, episcopal approval was required for any new cults of saints. Well aware of the authority, power, prestige, and economic advantage associated with saints and pilgrimage centers, bishops attempted to monitor these saints' cults and the whole area of the production of miracles.[46] There also appeared a growing concern by churchmen in regard to the ordering of sacred space and a growing segregation between the laity and clergy inside church spaces. The major altar was moved back to the base of the apse, and laypeople—especially women—were frequently reminded of their need to piously avoid, or to be distanced or removed from, the altar and its surrounding area.[47] Monks and nuns were warned to avoid contact with laymen and laywomen, and especially members of the opposite sex.[48] At least a dozen separate pieces of legislation from about 750 to 850 required strict active and passive cloistering for nuns and canonesses, and provided specifications for creating a physical cloister to ensure enclosure.[49]

Another area of spatial concern for the Carolingian reformers, given the increasing popularity of pilgrimage and cult centers, focused on the need to regulate and control the access of pilgrims to saints' tombs housed in monasteries. The Council of Frankfurt, 794, for example, introduced measures to try to protect monasteries and their saints from continually being disturbed by hoards of invading pilgrims. They stipulated that monastic oratories (with their saints' tombs or shrines) were to be located in the interior of the cloister where offices could be held during the night, a measure that inevitably reduced pilgrim access to cult sites.[50] Another major spatial shift that occurred during the Carolingian period was the placing of the tombs of the holy dead in the choir behind or directly below (in a crypt) the main altar of a monastery's principal church. With these spatial changes, monastic attitudes toward pilgrimage, lay traffic, hospitality, and the disturbances to monastic life were tested, and a variety of new policies and arrangements were introduced.[51]

We are especially well informed in regard to the wide variety of solutions adopted by men's houses. Many men's monastic sites, for example, enlarged their churches; they added external or ring crypts to handle the flow of pilgrims and minimize the noise and distraction of the crowds of miracle seekers.[52] They introduced "bi-polar" arrangements, which separated the relics into two reliquaries that were then placed in different parts of the church.[53] Some male communities refused to encourage cult sites and simply closed their doors altogether to the pilgrimage business, while others allowed access to male pilgrims but prohibited entry to women; still others made provisions to display their relics to the laity only at certain times, or they constructed small chapels outside of their monastery walls to accommodate female pilgrims.[54] But it is possible to know something about the arrangements made at women's communities as well. Compared to men's houses, with their rich collections of miracles, only a few official collections of postmortem miracles are extant for women's monasteries. Nevertheless, by examining the miracle collections of four different women's houses from the ninth through the mid-eleventh centuries, we can follow in some detail the origins, development, spatial arrangements, and involvement of these houses as cult sites and centers of the pilgrimage trade.

THE CULT OF SAINT GLODESIND

The official collection of miracles of Abbess/Saint Glodesind of the monastery of Subterius in Metz dates to about 830 and shortly after 882. Glodesind was the founding abbess and patron saint of this convent in Metz.[55] Because her new community did not have a cemetery of its own, the saint was originally buried in the cemetery associated with the church of Saint Arnulf or the Holy Apostles, which was located some distance from the convent.[56] After twenty-five years, Saint Glodesind was said to have appeared to a nun of Subterius and designated to her the exact spot where a church in honor of Saint Mary was to be built. As this burial church was located outside of the city walls, Saint Glodesind also showed the nun where a gate should be cut through the wall to allow the nuns to visit the church.[57] Glodesind was translated to the church of Saint Mary but, in about 830, "the sepulcher in which the blessed virgin Glodesind lay entombed began to emerge from the earth in an extraordinary manner." A short time later the saint was "provided with a sepulcher in the monastery's older church behind the altar." There, miracles soon occurred "so that the blind could see and the lame walk and the infirm be restored to health most generously."[58] Among the recipients of the posthumous healing miracles reported at Saint Glodesind's tomb, we find about twenty-eight women and ten men cured of blindness, fevers, paralysis, lameness, possession by devils, and the like. We are not well informed as to the status of the pilgrims and their place of origin, but from the available information Glodesind's cult appears to have been mainly local, with pilgrims recruited from the lower classes of society.

One of the miraculous aspects of Saint Glodesind's cult was the oil that flowed from the side of her tomb onto the pavement. This holy liquid was collected by custodians with sponges and then transferred into a glass vessel that was placed above the saint's tomb. According to the miracles, "Then many persons with injuries to head or eyes or other members earned cures in that church from a touch of that liquid unction helped by the intercession of Christ's virgin." A woman (nun?) named Doda is recorded as the custodian of the altar and saint's tomb and as the guardian of the sacred vessel. She no doubt assisted with the miraculous cures involving the use of Saint Glodesind's holy oil. The miracles also report a miracle of punishment directed by Saint Glodesind against Doda when she attempted to remove some of the saint's holy oil from her shrine. In this act, we can see the saint's need to control the location of her primary and secondary relics and herself to determine the beneficiaries of her miracles.[59]

The miracles of Saint Glodesind are reported as occurring at the saint's tomb, behind the altar, in the convent's main church. The redactor of the miracles notes the various spaces associated with the cult: the entrance gates, the walls of the monastery, the threshold of the church, the steps to the altar, the area or pavement before the tomb, the head of the tomb, and so on.[60] The case of Imma, noted at the beginning of this chapter, clearly describes the belief in an increasing density of sacrality as one approached the church, its altar, and finally the holy relics.[61] At this holiest spot, incubation was also practiced. A certain blind woman named Plectrude was said to approach the virgin's tomb and "with innumerable other sick persons she lay there the whole night in vigils and prayer." During matins she opened her eyes and found she was miraculously cured.[62] However, later in the collection, there is mention of a certain crippled man who was brought into the court of the monastery around vespers. He wanted to be allowed "to pass the night lying before the altar of the blessed virgin which the custodian of the altar never allowed." Instead, he spent the night lying on his pallet before the entrance gates of the monastery. In the morning, when he awoke, he discovered that he had been cured.[63] It is impossible to determine whether the contrast with Plectrude reflects a change in policy, or a policy of excluding men from incubation at this site, or even the simple fact that the petitioner arrived after the time that pilgrims were accepted into the church, once the doors had been locked. Whatever the explanation, it is clear that the women's house of Subterius at Metz was a significant center of pilgrimage.

Saint Walpurgis's Shrine at Monheim

The Benedictine house of Monheim was founded in 893 by a relative of the Carolingians, Abbess Liubila, who procured a portion of the relics of Saint Walpurgis (ca. 710–ca. 779) from the bishop of Eichstatt.[64] The house's miracle collection, in four books, dates from 894–899. It describes (among other miracles) forty-six individuals who received healing miracles at Saint Walpurgis's shrine. They include nineteen men, thirteen women, eight boys, and six girls.[65] The petitioners especially suffered from paralysis, lameness, blindness, and other maladies.[66] The cult center attracted a variety of pilgrims who came in tour groups or on their own. The list includes Hildegard, the daughter of the East Frankish King Louis II, the Younger (876–882), who had connections with the abbess of Monheim, and who traveled with Margrave Liutpold (also seeking a cure) plus a number of their servants.[67] Also listed were several noblewomen who traveled with their family members in their own wagons and brought along for comfort special head cushions and pillows.[68] As noted by Bauch, the successful cures that this group of nobles experienced at the Monheim shrine would be important in spreading the propaganda for this new cult site.[69] In addition to the nobility came townsmen and women, a seamstress and a weaver, and servants (including a woman from the royal male monastery of Kempten and a lame man from the Abbey of Fulda). While some of the pilgrims lived in Monheim, close to the church, in general, the pilgrims seem to have been recruited from a rather wide area, mainly in the south of Germany, with the most distant traveling from Fulda, Kempten, Mainz, and Regensburg.[70]

The miracle collection gives a unique snapshot of the day-to-day operations of the monastic cult center. Liubila, with her nuns and servants, personally looked after the pilgrims from their arrival in the north porch (which was used as a type of vestibule or reception area for the crowds) to the time of their departure.[71] Many of the miracles are described as having taken place immediately upon arrival in the church, with the pilgrims thus able to return home fully cured on the same day. We find, for example, in the miracles repetition of the words *statim, mox, subito,* and *paulatim.*[72] The miracles were said to take place at the main altar in the monastery's principal church where the Saint's relic shrine, still on its bier, was located. Pilgrims were cured on the pavement before the main altar, under the reliquary shrine, or near the votive lamp with oil; those men and women who did not experience the anticipated quick recovery at the saint's shrine remained in the convent's hospice, sometimes for several weeks, before they received a cure.[73] The abbess herself looked after a few of the sick pilgrims.[74] Those who were especially disruptive or who overstayed their welcome, such as the woman with the eating disorder, were moved to the nearby parish church to be watched over by a nun (the administrator of the church) and the cloister priest.[75] One of the pilgrims, a woman possessed by the devil, became extremely disruptive with her frightening screams and gnashing teeth, and refused to stay away despite being banned from Monheim. Even she, however, was gradually cured.[76]

Monheim pilgrims are described as participating, along with the nuns and servants, in the various services of the monastery.[77] At the altar, the pilgrims prayed, placed their offerings, and described both their illnesses and their miraculous cures to the nuns. According to the miracles, three nuns were stationed at the altar where they offered the chalice to the pilgrims and handed out blessed bread for their journey home.[78] As noted by Bauch, Diethild, the *procuratrix* (verger) and *custrix* (administrator) of the church, and her assistant, Ruathild, were especially involved with the pilgrims, who confided in them the details of their illnesses and troubles. In this role, they therefore were able to collect and write down important information which they then passed on to the priest Wolfhard, who compiled the official miracles in four books.[79]

THE CULT OF SAINT EDBURGA OF NUNNAMINSTER

The late Anglo-Saxon "List of Saints' Resting-places" (ca. 1013–1031) includes, along with male foundations, a number of women's monastic churches with active tomb or shrine cults: Polesworth, Leominster, Barking, Romsey, Wilton, Shaftesbury, Wimborne, Amesbury, and Nunnaminster.[80] The *vita* and miracles of Saint Edburga, royal patron and patron saint at Nunnaminster, Winchester (b. ca. 921, d. ca. 960), are especially informative. Saint Edburga was the daughter of Edward the Elder and granddaughter of Alfred the Great. Nunnaminster was founded by King Alfred the Great and his consort, Alswitha, while Edburga's father further expanded and completed the buildings of the convent as well as endowed it with generous gifts.[81] Edburga was originally buried outside of the monastic church in an *ignobili sepultura* (unworthy sepulcher), but a miraculous "sign" made the nuns realize that they should provide a more worthy resting place for their saintly sister. She was subsequently translated to a tomb within the church, specifically outside of the choir (*extra chorum*), and it was discovered that her body was undecayed.[82] Saint Edburga, apparently still dissatisfied with her resting place, again began to exert pressure on the nuns to move her to a more appropriate place. Bishop Ethelwold of Winchester, who had witnessed her miracles, with the assistance of Abbess Alfgheua, had her bones translated to a costly silver shrine, which was then placed beside the high altar of the nun's church.[83] Many people who were afflicted and physically languishing came to her tomb and received a cure. Miracles were reported as taking place there every day.[84]

Susan Ridyard has discerned both competition and cooperation between the neighboring cults of Saints Edburga and Swithun in Winchester. It appears that, before Edburga's cult was revitalized or reinvented at the time of the second translation by Bishop Ethelwold, her shrine was eclipsed by Saint Swithun's, and the convent suffered accordingly.[85] Osbert of Clare in his *Vita Edburge* notes, "The fame of God's bishop Swithun drew everybody to the festive celebration of his miracles, and on that account the neglected virgins [of Nunnaminster] were tormented by their decline and desperation. But after the sun of justice shone upon them in the splendour of the glorious virgin's miracles there grew in that church the rites of heaven, and the joy of the saints was multiplied."[86] Osbert then reports the successful partnership of the saints in their performance of miracles: "To those whom the holy bishop Swithun seemed to deny a remedy the blessed virgin Edburga held out her hand in compassion. And those to whom she did not grant freedom from sickness the glorious man of God deemed worthy of intercession."[87]

Osbert's account of Edburga's miracles briefly records five posthumous healing miracles at Nunnaminster: a local Winchester man who was crippled, two poor women who were ill, a churchman of Saint-Quentin who had been staying at the convent and suffered from a mental illness, and a man from Wilton who was "possessed by a devil." A final miracle concerned a man who was freed of his chains by the saint's intercession.[88] As noted by Ridyard, Saint Edburga's cult was essentially local with its miracle seekers drawn from the area around Winchester and from the lower classes of society, although the sources do mention the involvement of "devout queens" in the refurbishment of the shrine.[89]

It is significant that the shrine was not harmed by Bishop Ethelwold's reform of the minsters in Winchester. With the institution of a new Benedictine order, the nuns were seen as requiring greater quiet, solitude, and enclosure to carry out their religious functions. At Nunnaminster, the secular buildings within the complex were cleared away and the monastery was enclosed by high walls to separate it from the distractions of the town. Nevertheless, its main church with the reliquary of Saint Edburga, located at the high altar, remained open to the public.[90] The women of the community encouraged the business of pilgrims, male and female; they also provided hospitality and care of the pilgrims and poor, of both genders, in their hospice.

THE CULT OF SAINT ADELHEID OF VILICH

The miracles of Saint Adelheid of Vilich (ca. 970–1015) also yield fascinating details in regard to the establishment of her eleventh-century cult center.[91] Saint Adelheid's parents, the count and countess of Gueldre, founded Vilich for a community of canonesses with the intention of using the monastery as their family burial site. According to the *vita*, Adelheid unfortunately died while she was in Cologne, with the result that the bishop of Cologne wanted to have her buried in his episcopal city. Thus the community had to prevail upon him to allow them to take her body back to Vilich for burial in her beloved convent. Before her death, Adelheid, out of humility, had specifically requested that she not be buried in a sacred place but rather in the cloister.[92] Less than a month after her burial in this fairly well-trafficked spot, the first miracle occurred. It concerned a blind man who came as part of a crowd of the poor into the cloisters to receive their alms. However, because of the negligence of his guide, he fell and (conveniently) hit his head against the saint's tomb. He arose cured of his blindness.[93]

After the occurrence of several miracles at the tomb, the nun Bertha, author of the collection of miracles, notes, "As the news of this and more signs and divine favors were spread abroad, the number of people gathering from the far corners of the world was as great as those living nearby. Though the cloister was by no means small, the proper quiet for the regular observance of the religious life of the sisters was much disturbed—more than seemed decent."[94] Bertha captures here the frequent complaint of female and male religious in regard to the general disruption caused by pilgrims and their effect on the community. In response to the inadequacy of space and disturbance of monastic life, the saint's body was translated to a more holy place in the convent church.[95] A new church was built around the old one with a ring crypt—which contained Adelheid's tomb—located directly under the altar.[96] This arrangement facilitated the movement of the pilgrims, allowing them to venerate the saint without restraining the space or disturbing the nuns in choir. After the translation, according to the miracles: "As henceforth in more and more places the fame of the signs grew, everyone who was plagued by an illness or another trouble swiftly came to that place, certain that they would be healed, the number of those assembling at her tomb knew no end."[97] Four men, two women, and one boy were cured of blindness, lameness, and diabolic possession at the saint's tomb.[98] We are not informed concerning either the status or places of origin of the pilgrims, with the exception of a nobleman, cared for directly by the abbess. He was freed of his penitential chains at the shrine; then, "after the numbed arms and legs had gradually been revitalized to their former strength through the alleviating treatment of such kindness, the Abbess helped them [the nobleman and his accompanying brother] with clothes and horses and allowed them to return home, joyful in their hearts."[99]

Gifts to the Saints

Authors of miracle collections were not in the least reticent to discuss the expectation of pilgrim donations to the saint and his or her monastery.

The miracle collections thus frequently mention, in a variety of contexts, the importance for petitioners to bring gifts to the saints. They point out, for example, the direct correlation between the miracle seeker's gift and his or her treatment by the saint as well as the guardian of the shrine. According to the *vita* of Saint Glodesind, a certain poor man wanted to make a pilgrimage to Saint Glodesind's tomb; however, "He did not wish to go there empty-handed for he was heedful of the divine precept which we read in the law: 'Thou shalt not appear empty before the Lord.'" Thus through the miraculous intervention of the saint, this poor man caught a large fish which he was then able to "offer the warden of the virgin's monastery so that he would get a better place among those praying there and be more kindly received among them."[100] In the *vita* of Saint Adelheid, one of the miracles notes: "If a peasant brought a gift, not from among his abundant possessions but, of his free will, to show her his pure intentions, then he would win an increase in all that he needed through her faithful intervention."[101] This miracle concerned a poor peasant woman who was approached by Saint Adelheid in a nocturnal dream. The saint then commanded the woman to make a white alb for her. When she objected because she was too poor, the saint told her to petition her neighbors at her command. According to the *vita*, when she did this "she received so much linen that not only did she make the alb but a much needed dress for herself as well. After she had placed the alb at the sepulcher, she received so many gifts that for the rest of her life, at the anniversary of that date, she made a donation of an ox or some such thing."[102]

Donations given to the saint as an expression of gratitude for the miracles of healing were seen as part of the ritual and were expected by the saint and guardians of the shrines. The donations varied greatly from extremely modest tokens of appreciation by the poor to rather substantial gifts by noble and royal families. Baudonivia, for example, notes the grateful nobleman named Leo who was cured of temporary blindness by lying on Radegund's haircloth in the church of Saint Mary. (She also mentions that he had daughters who had taken the veil at Saint Croix.) He then gave the convent the substantial sum of 100 solidi for the construction of a new church.[103] Or, at the end of the eighth century, we learn of the famous visit of Ricburgis to Saint Gertrude's monastery of Nivelles and her miraculous cure. Ricburgis had gained the sympathy of Queen Hildegard and was sent in 782 by the queen to Nivelles for a cure which she received on January 6, 785. In appreciation for the saint's assistance, Ricburgis ceded to the monastery all of the land she possessed at Binfels, that is, twelve manses, a church, and all of the serfs attached to her property.[104]

Some, in gratitude for their miraculous cures, brought a gift to the saint's shrine each year. This was the case, for example, of the man who was freed by Saint Adelheid from possession by the devil: "As long as he lived, annually he brought a gift to her tomb in recompense for his sanity."[105] A rather extensive list of donations was compiled for the shrine of Saint Walpurgis at Monheim. Included among these gifts to the saint are a cross, a great candle, a little sword, a costly copper hair ornament, cushions, a headscarf, gloves, many crutches, a three-legged stool, a silver container holding a bone splinter of a woman healed by the saint (hung as a votive gift on the wall), a fish, a sack with blessed bread, bread, and other items. There are also many passing references to small gifts left at the shrine.[106] Moreover, several of the people who received cures at Monheim gave themselves in life service to the saint and monastery.[107]

Conclusions

A variety of evidence points to an active involvement on the part of women's communities in the medieval culture of relics, pilgrimage, and miracles. As avid collectors of relics, they built impressive collections, which vied with those of contemporary men's houses.[108] The women in these communities were involved in the reinvention or revitalization of their cults through translations and through the commissioning of new churches, tombs, and reliquaries. The spatial challenges of segregation, enclosure of the nuns, and development of cult sites were met in a variety of ways, including adopting multiple churches, constructing ring crypts, or simply allowing pilgrims access to their principal churches. Despite regulations for strict enclosure for women's houses, the walls of women's convents were not as impervious as one might think. Rather it seems that they shared their sacred space and holy relics with miracle seekers of both genders: miracles occurred in public within their churches and within the walls of their cloisters. Moreover, contrary to a number of men's houses of the period, which specifically prohibited female access to their monastic churches and saints' tombs or shrines, I have not found any indication of gender-based exclusionary policies practiced by these women's communities. Sources even note a merging of the "public" and "private" spaces at some of these cult centers; abbesses and nuns, in the Benedictine tradition of hospitality, were directly involved with pilgrims and the poor in their churches and hospices, and a number of male pilgrims are reported as staying overnight before saints' shrines in nuns' churches as well as for extended periods in their hospices. The miracle collections, especially those of the Carolingian period and later, note the nearly equal presence of women and men as beneficiaries of posthumous curative miracles.

In their hyperbole, authors of miracles (whether free-standing collections or appended to *vitae*) stress the impressive thaumaturgical power of their saints, the latters' great fame and popularity, and how a given convent's prosperity and very survival depended on their patron saint's performance of miracles. The four-book miracle collection for the shrine at Monheim, with its great numbers of petitioners and miraculous cures and its wide sphere of influence, is similar to the miracle collections found at men's houses. Nevertheless, the total numbers of specific miracles recorded for some of these women's cult sites seem somewhat less than one might perhaps expect.

Osbert of Clare, in his praise for Saint Edburga, compares her ability to work miracles with that of Saint Swithun. He notes that Swithun "gleamed everywhere with various miracles just like the heavenly sun, and the royal offspring Eadburg gleamed with miracles, surrounded by holy virgins as the moon with stars."[109] However, based on Edburga's five posthumous miracles, her cult appears to have been rather limited, local, and obscure compared to the wide popularity of that of Saint Swithun. For example, Lantfred's record of the translation and miracles of Saint Swithun, written soon after 971, provides information on Saint Swithun's curative miracles for eighteen individual men and eleven individual women, as well as for a group of sixteen blind Londoners of both sexes, additional groups of twenty-five and thirty-six from various regions, and a final enormous crowd of 124 sick people from all over England.[110] Lantfred also records the case of a young blind man who "promised that he would keep vigil by night in the monastery at Shaftesbury [a royal convent of nuns], where the body of the venerable St. Elfgifu lies in repose, who was the mother of Edgar King of the English, and at whose tomb many bodies of sick persons receive medication." Disregarding his wife's suggestions that he go to Winchester, the blind man set off to Shaftesbury where, in addition to his blindness, he became inflicted with a painful swelling tumor over his eye. Following his wife's advice, he then hurried to Saint Swithun's tomb and received a complete cure.[111]

Although there appears to be a great deal of evidence that miracles occurred at women's houses, we have only a few official collections of such miracles. In some cases, residents of the sites simply failed to record the miracles of their patron saints. For instance, Flodoard notes that the numerous miracles that occurred at the tomb of Saint Bertha of Blagny were not preserved in writing "*causa negligentiae*" (due to negligence).[112] Other hagiographers and chroniclers mention miracles at saints' tombs housed within female communities, but they do not elaborate or provide specific details. In some cases, they must have relied on oral traditions preserved and handed down by the nuns of the relevant convents. The failure actually to record the miracles might be related to the basic problem that Elizabeth Van Houts has discussed in regard to women as witnesses, namely, a reluctance to accept the authenticity of their accounts and the authority of their testimonies.[113] Thus, compared to men's houses, few extensive official collections of posthumous miracles associated with female communities exist.

However, the cases we have looked at, especially those of Monheim and Vilich, provide us with important information about cults that were established and run by women, and whose miracles were witnessed and recorded by women. Based on this rather limited sampling of the various sources available to us, women's zeal for the cult of saints and relics appears to have been neither less fervent nor more limited than that of their male contemporaries. These women seem to have played a much larger role and had a greater investment in the culture of pilgrimage, shrine cults, and miracles than has been recognized.

Chapter 5

Priestly Women, Virginal Men

Litanies and Their Discontents

FELICE LIFSHITZ

Gender in the Early Litanies of the Saints: What Is a Virgo?

Not all litanies are litanies of the saints. Liturgists define "litanies"
rather broadly, both as repetitive supplications for divine aid and as the
processions in which those supplications may be enacted.[1] Before the
seventh century (at the earliest), such repetitive supplications were not
addressed to saints but rather to the persons of the Christian Trinity or
to Jesus' mother Mary. The appearance of litanies of saints' names in
Continental Latin churches dates from some time during the eighth
century.[2] Beginning at the very end of that century, compilers of litanies
of saints' names began to organize the saints according to a series of explicitly labeled categories. They divided the male heroes of the Christian past into a number of different types: apostles, evangelists, martyrs,
confessors, and sometimes also hermits or other subcategories. In contrast, all the venerated female heroines of Christian history were ghet-
toized into a single category, placed at the end of the list of holy names,
and designated by a single label: *virgines* (plural; singular: *virgo*).

This ghettoization of female saints was not a feature of liturgical practice, as witnessed by extant manuscripts, before the very end of the
eighth century, when the litany category *virgo* appears to have been in-
vented. I have argued elsewhere that the liturgical *virgo* functioned as an
ideological tool that aided male ecclesiastics of the Carolingian era in
their struggle to bar women both from sacred space and from important
official roles in Latin churches.[3] The structure of litanies was important
in this struggle to "reform" liturgical and other practices, in that it excluded women from key categories of Christian historical agency such as
apostle and martyr, roles that were understood as predecessors of leadership positions in the church. A link between those put to death in the
name of Jesus in the past, and those exercising a sacerdotal ministry in

the present, was established at least as early as the third century, for instance in the writings of Origen of Alexandria.[4] By approximately 600, male ecclesiastics in Gaul had begun regularly to express the view that martyrs were typological antecedents for priests, and that both drew their authority from Jesus Christ, model martyr and model priest.[5]

The male-dominated project to limit the activities of professionally religious women was generally successful, but that success was, for many reasons, incomplete. Resistance to the restrictions on consecrated women's activities was underpinned by a variety of political, social, and economic forces, which cannot be explored here. The focus of this essay concerns how the litany category *virgo* itself helped resist women's erasure from Christian liturgical activity and Christian officialdom. The negative power of the new practice of reciting saints' name litanies, the power to exclude women from sacred space and from official positions, derived principally from the female saints' exclusion from those categories of sanctity gendered as male, categories such as "apostle" and "martyr," and not from inclusion in the category labeled "*virgo*." Ironically, the *virgo* label was a potential source of affirmation for women's liturgical ambitions.

Virgo cannot simply be translated by the English "virgin." The reason that the term could plausibly be used to label all female saints is the same reason that it was incompletely effective as an antiwoman device: because (as I argue here) it created a symbolic association between the sainted *virgines* on the litany list and the paradigmatic *virgo*, Mary mother of Jesus. Largely because of that Marian association but also for other reasons, the label *virgo* was perceived as a desirable moniker not only by women but also by men, a topic to which I turn in the second part of this chapter.

Dyan Elliott's discussion in this volume of Tertullian's contribution to the development of the Christian concept of virginity reveals some of the many potential permutations of the concept. Already in the third century, as McNamara long ago demonstrated, the notion of virginity could subsume all sorts of women, including widows and wives, as long as they lived without sexual expression.[6] As one self-described virginologist puts it, "The idea of virginity in the Middle Ages was not monologic and therefore unproblematic, but heteroglossic, conflicted and conditional."[7] Medical and other relevant literature did not necessarily consider the presence of an "intact" hymen to be the determining characteristic of a (female) virgin. Over time, penetration of the vagina by the penis did come to be defined as "the" sex act; concomitantly, there did develop a physiological definition of the female who had not had "sex" as a female whose vagina had not been penetrated.[8] Given that the creation of the conventional litany category *virgo* long predates the physiological definition of virginity, we should not be surprised to learn that the category always encompassed women who must have undergone the experience of vaginal penetration.

From the beginning of the development of categorized litanies, liturgists included Felicitas and her seven children and Symphorosa and her seven children in the list of *virgines*.[9] Mary Magdalen, who was commonly understood to have been a prostitute by the time her cult began fully to flourish, appeared in litanies of the eleventh century at the head of the list of *virgines*.[10] Late medieval visionary matrons and their biographers claimed that corporeal virginal purity could be, and often was, restored to those who had previously lost it. The preeminent beneficiary of this miraculous beneficence was the Magdalen, but others hoped to share in her good fortune. Margaret of Cortona, for instance, who had been sexually active before her conversion to a life of holiness, was assured by Christ, "Your contrition will restore your virginal purity."[11] It would therefore be possible to argue that sanctity guaranteed and/or restored corporeal virginity, rendering the litany label *virgo* effectively valid for all female saints. But to make that argument would be to put undue weight on a corporeal definition of the term *virgo*. It is possible that the term was considered applicable to holy women of all bodily conditions for entirely other reasons and that the term carried no physiological implication whatsoever. Because the period of the creation of the litany categories long predates the development of the concept of the intact hymen, we would be well advised to avoid any physiological understanding of the liturgical *virgo*.

Eighth-century evidence, more directly relevant to the moment of invention of saints' name litanies, also supports a nonphysiological understanding of the word *virgo*. Helvétius notes the use of *virgo* in biographies of female saints to describe both a widow and a married woman, although she goes on to elide the heroic *virgo* in favor of a focus on the *virago*, that is, the "virile" woman.[12] She argues that a *virgo* would have been considered a "*virago* spirituelle" as a result of her conformity to an ascetic ideal.[13] She writes, "The virility that was expected from them [widows and married women] was the same as that of virgins."[14] Although this represents a step in the right direction in terms of recognizing a conceptual, rather than a corporeal, definition of the *virgo*, Helvétius' approach seems to make all female sanctity dependent on a conformity to a cultural standard (namely, virility) gendered as masculine. Yet the word *virago* only appears once in any of the relevant sources,[15] and it appears not to deserve the conceptual centrality Helvétius assigns to it. In her careful study of saints' biographies and other edifying literature from the Carolingian period, the philologist Katrien Heene has shown that the concept of the *mulier virilis* (the manly woman) is actually quite rare, and is confined in the sources to very specific contexts having to do with extraordinary courage.[16] More important, discussions of virility or exhortations to act *viriliter* (manfully) are far more numerous and significant in texts concerning male saints than female ones. Heene even argues that the entire complex of terms (*virilitas/virilis/viriliter* or virility/virile/manfully) had lost any sex-specific connotations already in biblical usage and had come to connote energy and strength with no resonance of manliness, an even broader conclusion, which does not mesh well with Karras's treatment in this volume of the adverb *viriliter* in high and late medieval sources.

In contrast to the rare word *virago*, or even the virile woman, the word *virgo* is ubiquitous. *Virgo* is the word that matters and not because it stands for or is synonymous with something else. *Virgo* was a term far more commonly associated with female persons than with male ones. If the creators of litany categories had wished to underline the virility of holy women, they would not have chosen a generic label whose connotations were predominately female. *Virgo* is one of the words least capable of conveying the status of honorary maleness, although it can convey an extraordinary range of things. Indeed, Eudes of Châteauroux justified the Magdalen's preeminent position among the *virgines* precisely through her manifold achievements as an apostle, a martyr of compassion, and a preacher of the truth, implying that *virgo* might be understood as the sum of those other, partial, categories.[17] It is above all the multivalence of the concept *virgo*, as understood by Eudes, that I would like to emphasize in this essay. *Virgo* is powerful and complex not because it refers narrowly to a particular bodily characteristic (an intact hymen) and not because it can be a synonym for another equally narrow term (a virile woman, or a person who conforms to an ascetic ideal) but rather because it—like the mysterious Christian Trinity—comprehends within itself multiple personae. *Virgo* did not convey the message that a holy woman was like a man but rather that she was like a very special woman, namely Mary, who was known as a *virgo* but who lived an exemplary life both as a wife and, after the death of her spouse, as a widow.[18]

The saintly women's litany ghetto could have been stamped with any number of homogenizing labels, such as *mulieres sanctae* (holy women), *sanctimoniales* (sisters, nuns), *Deo sacratae* (women consecrated to God), *Deo dedicate* (women dedicated to God), *ancillae Dei* (God's nursemaids), all terms current during the early medieval period to describe pious women or female saints. Instead, the litany category came to be known by the one word, *virgo*, already deeply and inextricably associated with an enormously important and powerful female figure. If there was not intentionality in the choice, then there was nevertheless a raft of consequences to this symbolic association of holy women with the Mother of God.

Most of the oldest extant saints' name litanies (from the eighth and early ninth centuries) come from England and from areas on the continent in which insular individuals were active. In that cultural zone at that time, Mary was possessed of an extraordinary multiplicity of personae. To be a *virgo* is to be like Mary, a figure who simultaneously embodies multiple aspects that we might consider mutually exclusive, most prominently virginity and motherhood. On some level, Mary is "la vièrge qui n'en est pas une,"[19] who could—in and of herself—represent the attributes and characteristics of various litany categories . . . and more![20]

That Mary was a virgin was an important aspect of her persona from at least the fourth century.[21] Equally important and equally well known, was her status as a mother and, from the fifth century, as the Mother of God (*Theotokos*).[22] The physical reality of Mary's corporeal motherhood was underlined by the celebration of the feast of her Purification (after the uncleanness of parturition) on February 2, a feast that was well established by the latter part of the eighth century.[23] Far less well known is her status as a martyr, recognized by numerous Frankish and Anglo-Saxon authors from Paschasius Radbertus to Ælfric, as well as in a multitude of pseudonymous texts that circulated on both sides of the channel during the eighth and ninth centuries. In the view of these authors, Mary had won her martyr's palm by suffering emotionally at the sight of her son's physical suffering.[24] Furthermore, evidence from the visual arts indicates that some Latin Christians around the year 800 pictured Mary as a priestly figure. The most famous example of this sort of imagery is the decorated initial of Mary dressed in priestly vestments and swinging a censer in the Sacramentary of Gellone, which was written and illustrated during the 790s (Figure 3).[25] From another, more public medium comes the Breedon (Leicestershire) stone panel carving of Mary as a fully frontal and solitary figure with a disproportionately large right hand whose fingers are raised in the gesture of blessing, while she holds a book in her left hand. This priestly pose and these iconographic attributes are those of Christ and, on rare occasions, the apostles. Here they are used in a female cult image created, either around 800 or during the 830s, for a Marian church.[26]

Adding to the complexity of Mary's multiple personae is her status—from the fifth century—as a majestic and crown-wearing ruling figure, whether an empress or the queen of the angels (*regina angelorum*).[27] According to the ninth-century Mercian *Old English Martyrology*, this "noble queen of celestial citizens, stands on the right side of the High Father and High King," a position reserved in the Nicene Creed for Jesus, Son of God.[28] Such an exalted vision of Mary as God's right-hand woman is consistent with her imagined position as the Daughter of God (*filia Dei*),

Fig. 3: Bibliothèque Nationale de France, Sacramentary of Gellone (Ms latin 12048), fol. 1v: Mary officiating as priest.

the *redemptrix* (redeemer) who "salutem et feminae gessit et viro" (brought salvation both to woman and to man) and who—at the Last Judgment—would save souls condemned by her son.[29] A few manuscripts attest even to the practice of having spiritual recourse to Mary, without any counterbalancing references to male members of the Christian Trinity. The production of such manuscripts was concentrated in England during the late eighth and early ninth centuries and thus coincides both temporally and geographically with the most voluminous evidence for the new practice of saints' name litanies.[30] It is therefore in part against the background of such prayers that the litany categories were developed. The most radical Marian prayers appear in the Books of Nunnaminster[31] and Cerne,[32] addressing Mary as *pia dominatrix* (compassionate ruler), *cordis mei inluminatrix* (illuminator of my heart), *adiutrix apud Deum Patrem* (helper before God the Father), *salvatrix* (savior), and the like. Mary as *domina* (lady, the feminine form of the standard Latin word for Christ, namely *dominus*) dominates the entire story of the Christmas season in the Old English poem *Advent.*[33]

The polyvalence of Mary herself, the archetypical *virgo*, would have infused the litany category of *virgo* with multiple connotations, indeed multiple personae. The conventional litany categories were able to spread and harden during the ninth century because they were not uniformly oppressive to religious women but rather suspended male and female aspirations in a delicate balance, much in the same way that the Gellone image of Mary the priest may have satisfied the identificatory desires of all concerned. (The Gellone Mary may also offer a concrete example of how some medieval people visualized a member of the "third gender," a concept explored by Jacqueline Murray in this volume). Whereas the exclusion of sainted women from litany categories such as martyr and apostle was detrimental to their positions in the Latin churches, the inclusion of sainted women in the litany category *virgo* was potentially beneficial, even if the extent of the latter benefits was circumscribed by another structural aspect of the litanies, namely a certain distancing of the *virgo* Mary from the sainted *virgines*. Mary, mother of Jesus, did not appear in the litanies among or at the head of the *virgines* but rather at or near the top of the entire list of holy names. Such a position was in keeping with her exalted status, as explored in the previous paragraphs, above all other human beings but also resulted (as I discuss below) from the fact that Christian litanies developed in two distinct stages.

A close look at a few specific early litanies (chosen more or less at random) is necessary to illustrate concretely the various points made thus far in this chapter. I begin with one of the oldest extant examples, an eighth-century litany in a Mercian prayer book, probably written in

Worcester.[34] This list of names groups, but does not explicitly label or graphically segregate, the saints as archangels, New Testament figures, male martyrs, male confessors, and women. Eleven women are listed, among whom are two figures (Perpetua and Felicitas) known to have been mothers.[35] Mary appears as the fifth name, effectively as a New Testament figure, after the archangels and John. Nothing directs a reader or listener to think about the women as *virgines*, and nothing discourages a reader or listener from thinking about them as martyrs or confessors or from thinking about the men as *virgines*.

A later stage of litany development is witnessed by a codex created in Bavaria (perhaps at Mondsee) during the first quarter of the ninth century.[36] The litanist maximized the categorical multiformity of revered males, calling on angels, archangels, patriarchs, prophets, apostles, martyrs, confessors, and monks, all labeled as such. At the end of the list come the *virgines*, represented by thirty-eight women's names. However, the practice of categorical division had not yet fully taken hold so that—despite the categorical labels—a number of names appear in the "wrong" category. For instance, Beatrix appears among the martyrs and a number of male martyrs appear among the confessors. Mary both precedes the entire list (including the angels) and is invoked thrice and in more complex terms than the simple *ora* (pray), which follows all the other names. She is asked "ora pro nobis" ("pray for us"), "intercede pro me peccatore" ("intercede for me, a sinner"), and "adiuva me in die exitus mei" ("help me on the day of my death"). At a separate location in the same manuscript, the scribe/liturgist inserted a second litany, containing no names except Mary, Michael, Gabriel, and Raphael, and otherwise consisting entirely of categorical labels. The labels expand on those of the saints' name litany discussed here by adding, after *virgines*, widows, penitents, and *infantes*. Liturgists were clearly still thinking through alternative structures.

Finally, there is the early ninth-century Freiburg Pontifical, containing the liturgical rites exclusively performed by bishops (pontiffs), to which a number of additions were made toward the end of the same century.[37] These additions include a very "well ordered" saints' name litany (folios 50v–52r), beginning with Mary and the archangels, and moving through the (male) apostles, (male) martyrs, (male) confessors, and monks, and culminating in the (female) virgins. This litany is clearly related to the litany in the Bavarian manuscript described in the previous paragraph, in that there is almost total overlap in the names included on both lists; however, all the "confusions" of saints who had jumped category boundaries are rectified in the Freiburg list. Even more interesting is another set of additions (besides the litany itself) that the late ninth-century liturgist made to the early ninth-century pontifical, namely a series of differentiated intercessory prayer formulae addressed to apostles, martyrs, and confessors (grammatically gendered as masculine) or virgins (grammatically gendered as feminine).[38] This late ninth-century addition was apparently intended to remedy a perceived failing of the pontifical, whose early ninth-century compiler had not distinguished between male and female saints when composing benedictional formulae (folios 12r–17r), although he was clearly aware of gender. The original liturgist had provided rites for the ordination of priests, exorcists, deacons, and the like that are gendered masculine (folios 1r–10r); rites for the consecration of virgins and widows that are gendered feminine (folios 33r–33v); plus a rite for the installation of the head of a religious community in both masculine and feminine forms to serve for abbots and abbesses (folios 30v–32r).

Despite these changes in saints' name litanies, Mary always stood at the head of the lists, indicative of her special position. The structure that separated Mary from other holy women on litany lists resulted in part from the fact that Christians had already developed the practice of calling on Mary in liturgical processions before they began to construct saints' name litanies. When, in the eighth century, liturgists began both compiling lists of saints' names for recitation, and segregating male and female saints, the position of Mary in the opening sections of ritual invocations had been established for centuries, and it would have been insulting to the Mother of God to demote her from her position in the immediate vicinity of the Trinity in order to locate her near other sainted women. It was even more unthinkable to put the *virgines*—together with Mary, the paradigmatic *virgo*—at the top of the list. However, despite the formal separation of the *virgo* Mary from the other *virgines*, which resulted from this historical development, the fact that the same word was used to describe both Mary and the female saints rendered a conceptual association between them inevitable. Furthermore, this association was frequently made explicit, such as in a series of formulae added late in the ninth century to the Freiburg Pontifical. There the bishop was instructed to use one formula for the feast of St. John and for the feasts of all the apostles, another for the feast of the Holy Innocents and for the feasts of all the martyrs, a third for the feast of St. Silvester and for the feasts of all the confessors, and a fourth for the Purification of Mary and for the feasts of all the virgins (folios 48v–50r). Thus, the more female saints were conceptualized as belonging to their own thoroughly feminine category of *virgo*, the more closely tied they were to the *Virgo* Mary, Mother of God; the link was not weakened by the insertion of male names in the litany lists between Mary and the other women.

The Vir as *Virgo*: The Question of Virginal Men

We should not permit ourselves to be duped by the exclusive presence of female saints in the *virgo* category of litanies to such an extent that we ignore the importance, to men, of virginity. Although the word *virgo* was (as I have discussed here at length) not a straightforward synonym for virgin, virginity was definitely one of the component characteristics of the *virgo*. During the entire Carolingian period (750–900), that is, precisely when saints' name litanies and litany categories were being developed, authors of saints' lives and edifying tractates consistently attached great value to both the spiritual and corporeal virginity of men.[39] But the fact that virginity was valued for men did not necessarily make it easy to preserve. As Ruth Karras shows in this volume, the struggle of men to remain virginal and/or chaste could be seen as an extremely masculine endeavor, requiring Herculean willpower and perseverance (along with divine aid, a sine qua non of full success). The valiant struggle of each new generation of men was repeatedly narrated, the successes of male comrades publicized. For instance, William of Tocco told how the loins of Thomas Aquinas were miraculously girded by angels with a "belt of chastity," to such happy effect that "until his death he never felt his virginity violated, which in so grave a battle he preserved unconquered."[40]

Clearly men needed emotional and social supports for their virginal vocations. The relatively new field of masculinity studies has sensitized us to the need to think about the emotional and psychological struggles of men. As Jo Ann McNamara writes, "The masculine gender is fragile and tentative, with weaker biological underpinnings than the feminine."[41] Holy women were excluded from "official" categories such as apostle and martyr, but holy men also faced gender discrimination, through exclusion from the category *virgo*, with the result that the ability to identify themselves with the Virgin Mary, at least in a liturgical context, as support for their purity or for any other project, was theoretically denied to them. The creation of the litany category *virgo* and the exclusion of male saints from that category appeared to send—in a liturgical context—the message that the status of virgin was not particularly relevant to men.

Adding consideration of men to the themes discussed thus far deepens our understanding of the power of the image of the sacerdotal Mary in the Sacramentary of Gellone. This sacerdotal Mary could dissolve tensions for two groups whose personal identities were frustrated by the conventional litany categories just then coming into use: women with liturgical ambitions and men committed to sexual continence. A woman is shown as a priest, and a priest is shown as the Virgin. Identities kept separate by liturgical classifications are conflated in the image's letter I, simultaneously the (Roman) numeral for "one." Truly Mary is "la vièrge qui n'en est pas une," both in the image and in the Gellone Sacramentary's own litany, where she heads a list of otherwise entirely male names.[42] It is fitting that this synthesizing image of Mary as priest was created to grace the opening folio of a manuscript produced within the confines of an unidentified heterosocial environment in which male and female scribes and illuminators (among them the male David and the female Madalberta) collaborated.[43]

The fact that some men would have seen inclusion under *virgines* as beneficial and as a support for their own attempts to maintain a chaste body is most easily demonstrated by reference to Aldhelm of Malmesbury (c. 639–c. 709), who—in a social context (Anglo-Saxon England), which provided no previous tradition of male virginity—wrote a treatise celebrating male and female virgins.[44] The phenomenal popularity of Aldhelm's *De virginitate* (On Virginity) has frequently been seen as a result of its author's unusual prose style.[45] I argue, instead, that the popularity of the treatise derived primarily from its ability to provide inspirational models for male virgins.

Among Aldhelm's paragons of virginity were numerous male saints who would soon appear in saints' name litanies as prophets, patriarchs, evangelists, apostles, martyrs, and confessors but who are treated by Aldhelm as virgins. What is more, these men are not simply said to be virgins; their virginity is represented as the source of their powers and their dramatic defense of their bodily virginity is itself narratized as they resist or outwit attempts to force or trick or tempt them into capitulation. Furthermore, Aldhelm's inspirational models of male virgins were not limited to stories of individual men but also included couples, enabling the author to provide a range of models and experiences for a variety of men. The male half of one virgin couple, Chrysanthus, maintains his bodily purity despite being locked in a cellar by his father along with a copious supply of wine and a bevy of beautiful women engaged in erotic play; having bested this challenge, he is free to engage in a chaste marriage with Daria, a marriage devoted to study, teaching, and missionary activity, and ultimately crowned by martyrdom.[46]

Mary, Mother of Jesus, appears in Aldhelm's *De virginitate* at the end of the long list of male heroes who occupy the opening sections of the work. She does not appear alone but in the company of St. Cecilia and (in the background) both women's chaste husbands.[47] Mary, paired with Cecilia, forms the bridge between the male and female exemplars. Through his placement of Mary, Aldhelm provides models for chaste men married to virginal women and removes the eponymous virgin (Mary) from the exclusive preserve of female saints. It is not hard to understand why Aldhelm would have wanted to safeguard some of the exemplary power of Mary for male virgins at a time when the Virgin Mary could symbolize so much. He was himself a devotee of Mary and built a church in her honor (dedicated to Saint Mary the Perpetual Virgin) at Malmesbury.[48] Aldhelm conceived of Mary in the sorts of plenitudinous terms we have seen to be typical of Anglo-Saxon England in and around his lifetime. Mary was, for Aldhelm, "the daughter-in-law of the father, the mother and sister and likewise the spouse of the son . . . the mother-in-law of holy souls, the queen of the citizens of heaven."[49]

Aldhelm was probably both a first-generation Anglo-Saxon Christian and a first-generation Anglo-Saxon Christian cleric, conversion of the ruling elites of the various regions of England having only begun at the very end of the sixth century.[50] Aldhelm lived in a world in which rival religions, none of which valorized virginity to any degree, were vigorous. In his own lifetime and immediately after, the models of male virginity contained in the *De virginitate* must have been especially needed. Yet scholarly traditions of commentary on Aldhelm's ideology of militant virginity have focused on how his writings would have been helpful to female readers,[51] although nothing in the treatise makes it obviously of particular interest to a female audience, unless we assume that anything concerned with virginity is ipso facto essentially a women's text. Aldhelm does not even begin to discuss virginal women ("secundi sexus personae," or persons of the second sex) until page 577 (out of 761 total pages in Gwara's edition).

Formally speaking, Aldhelm did write for, or at least to, women. The *De virginitate* is a treatise in the form of a letter, dedicated to abbess Hildelith of Barking and a number of other named women who have long been identified as prominent nuns of the Barking community but who were more likely other Wessex or Hwiccan abbesses, rendering the treatise something of a circular letter to the double monastic communities of the area, which included both male and female religious, under the leadership of a woman.[52] Such houses were, in Aldhelm's lifetime, the customary form of monastic organization both in England and in the Neustrian portions of Frankish Gaul.[53] Monks as well as nuns would have to be reached, if one respected proper channels, through their abbesses, and there is every reason to believe that Aldhelm did intend his treatise to come to the attention of the men in the double houses. However, Aldhelm's authorial intentions are to some extent beside the point. Whether he wrote for men, for women, or for both, he was read—as far as it is possible to determine—only by men.[54] Indeed, the evidence of men's reception tells of more than mere interest: it reveals a deep embrace of the text by men over the course of many centuries. For women, inspirational texts to help with their maintenance of virginity and chastity were relatively easy to come by and would even have included the saints' name litanies. For men, that was less the case, and therefore Aldhelm's text became a men's book, with a passionate niche audience, filling what would otherwise have been a major gap.

All of the extant manuscript evidence points to men as copyists, readers, and commentators of Aldhelm's *De virginitate*. The main manuscript, the basis of both modern critical editions, was produced by and for the cathedral clergy of Würzburg under Bishop Gozbald between 842 and 855 (just as the Carolingian church reform movement was going into high gear) and was simultaneously annotated with over a hundred Latin and Old High German glosses in many hands.[55] Twelve of the remaining manuscripts were produced (between the eighth and the eleventh centuries) and glossed (by multiple hands, in both Latin and Old English, between the tenth and the twelfth centuries) at men's monastic communities in Canterbury (Saint Augustine's or Christ Church), Glastonbury, Worcester, Exeter, and/or Abingdon.[56] Like the Würzburg cathedral chapter, all of those English men's communities were actively embracing chastity because of either a monastic or an ecclesiastical reform movement at the very moment when their members engaged with Aldhelm's treatise. The treatise constituted such gripping reading that Aldhelm's recent editor has referred to "the mania for Aldhelm which was sweeping England" during the 960s and 970s, that is, during the height of the Benedictine monastic reform movement.[57] The final two manuscripts, from the twelfth century, were also read and glossed in men's monastic communities.[58]

The possibility that virginal men may have been especially interested in Aldhelm's glorification of virginal men has been raised before, only to be dismissed.[59] A massive amount of circumstantial evidence connects passionately committed virginal men (indeed, leaders in men's virginity movements) with Aldhelm's text, but no explicit statement from any of them asserts that their interest in it derived from their desire for self-affirming models of male purity. However, through their glosses on the text, these men have left us oblique indicators of their concern for virginal male predecessors. The bulk of the glosses were part of a standard set that always accompanied the main text, probably from as early as the eighth century.[60] New glosses were consistently added and some were then transferred from one manuscript to another, but the core corpus remained consistent over centuries. For the most part, therefore, they do not provide evidence of individual responses to the text, but rather constitute a semipermanent interpretive framework for the text. While this may diminish the importance of the glosses as evidence of individual responses to Aldhelm, it increases their importance as evidence of his general reception. Out of some 20,000 potential lemmata (headwords) in *De virginitate*, around 5,500 are glossed in Old English and

Latin and another 8,500 are glossed only in Latin—a staggering number of glosses![61]

It is unimaginable that the men who pored over Aldhelm's text and its elaborate gloss apparatus neither noticed nor absorbed the content of the treatise. It is true that the glosses include no overt discussion of virginity at all, let alone male virginity in particular. Nevertheless, the sheer number of glosses tells us something about the intensity of male readers' engagement with the treatise, and the distribution of the glosses tells us even more. Indeed, the distribution of the glosses makes clear that some sections of the treatise were more interesting to its male readers than were others, despite the fact that the language of the treatise is equally challenging throughout. The amount of glossing for different sections can be gauged easily from the proportions of text to gloss in Gwara's edition, namely how many lines of Latin text can fit on the right-hand page of the edition to accommodate the (bilingual) glosses printed on the left-hand page. The proportion of text to gloss varies considerably over the course of the work. The most telling point is that the amount of glossing drops precipitously, by something on the order of half, when the subject of the treatise shifts from male to female virgins.[62]

One man who intensely engaged with Aldhelm's *De virginitate* was Dunstan, the "pioneer" and "guiding hand" of the [Benedictine] revival in tenth-century England.[63] The hallmark of this Benedictine revival was the strict practice of chastity, enforced through the threat of significant financial penalties for breach of chastity.[64] We possess Dunstan's personal copy of Aldhelm's treatise, which he "attentively studied" and glossed extensively in his own hand (to such an extent it has been called a "comprehensive revision"), and which he used to teach as abbot of Glastonbury (940–956), as bishop of Worcester (from 958), and as archbishop of Canterbury (from 960 until his death in 988).[65] Having been tonsured at Glastonbury at the age of fourteen, Dunstan moved in the highest political circles (including the royal court) from his teenage years, and was alienated from the movers and shakers of England only during one year-long exile on the continent.[66] Adherents of the reform movement powered by Dunstan themselves monopolized (and in some cases founded) the most influential monasteries and bishoprics in England, played key roles at the royal court and in the witan (where they helped to shape the law of the land), and worked to convert Scandinavia to Christianity. At Glastonbury, Winchester, and Abingdon, they assumed the function of producing royal charters.[67] They dominated the English church until the Conquest, and not just the church, for "monastic bishops and abbots . . . came to hold large estates in peripheral areas, and exercised much local government, including judicial and military elements."[68] They "were great political figures who should not be disobeyed in any of the things they prescribed for the good of the Christian people."[69] And they were Aldhelm's main readers.

Scholars have recently become attuned to the extent to which an emphasis on virginal purity has been used by men as a tactic in their struggle for public authority.[70] This has enabled specialists to recognize how high the stakes could be for men who, like Dunstan, committed themselves to the appearance and the reality of chastity. Virginity did matter for men, and a man who successfully achieved recognition for his virginal status could parlay that into major earthly rewards (superadded, of course, to the celestial ones which perhaps interested him more). As Conrad Leyser has written, ascetic masculinity is not "an introverted discourse of sexual anxiety, but . . . [a feature of] a fiercely competitive culture of public power. . . . The language of bodily purity and pollution represents neither infant trauma nor cultural neurosis, but a set of claims to power."[71] At least in one context, however, that of saints' name litanies, recognition of virginal status was categorically denied to men, as if it were insignificant to them socially, spiritually, and politically. Yet men such as Dunstan built claims on their sexual purity, claims that were bigger than the exclusive right to perform the miracle of the mass (as supported by the litany categorization of their predecessors as apostles and martyrs and confessors). Furthermore, men such as Dunstan claimed public authority based on something other than mere office; he wielded influence in the witan not because he held the office of archbishop of Canterbury, but because he was the reformed, chaste holder of that office. The possibility of being conceptualized, in a liturgical context, as a *virgo* would surely not have hurt Dunstan's career.

Litany categories may seem like, and in many ways are, minor aspects of the entire discourse surrounding both sanctity and virginity. Yet it is their very discursive nature that renders them so potentially important. As Leyser has shown, the appearance of chastity in a male ascetic's persona was a necessary complement to its reality if he wished to achieve public power. Power accrued to virginal men not merely because they were virgins, but also because they knew how to deploy a "language of moral authority" and a "language of spiritual expertise."[72] Their power had a lot to do with their control of a discourse, with what they said about their chastity and how they said it, in addition to their actual ascetic practices. The importance of an upright sexual reputation for male ascetics is amplified by Jane Schulenburg's surprising finding that women's monastic communities appear to have had greater leeway in permitting miracle-hungry laypersons (including men), into their sacred spaces, than did men's monastic communities (p. 84). Whereas monks often felt compelled to forbid all women entrance to their relic-rich enclosures, nuns created cult centers at which one could even find a "merging of the public and private spaces." This differential may reflect a greater willingness among medieval Christians to believe the chastity claims of women than those of men. Considerations of rhetoric and reputation highlight how a discursive element such as the categories of a saints' name litany could be important in a male ascetic's overall strategy of self-presentation.

Leyser studied the language of Cassian of Marseilles, of the Rule of Benedict, of Gregory the Great. So did Aldhelm himself, who devoted a chapter to the writings of Cassian and Gregory (chapter xiii), and one to the life of Benedict (chapter xxx). Men like Dunstan studied both that originally late antique "language of moral authority,"[73] and Aldhelm's language, his way of talking about the heroics of male virginity.[74] The virginal men who maniacally glossed Aldhelm were not academic philologists, vaguely curious about the connotations of words; rather, they were politically active leaders studying the language of ascetic authority in connection with male virgins.[75] There were still many married priests in tenth- and eleventh-century England,[76] but only committed virgins such as Dunstan and Wulfstan achieved power.[77]

In the tenth century, at least some virginal men were keen to (re)assert their status as *virgines*, even as the (by then) increasingly standard gendered litany categories denied their claims to that title. It is presumably not coincidental that the litany in the missal used at Dunstan's Glastonbury itself gave the holy names as a single, uninterrupted list, with no categorical divisions.[78] The litany category *virgo* may have been originally intended by clerical inventors to exclude women from certain social roles, and to support men's exclusive claim to those roles. However, such categorization could not achieve those intended goals, in part because of the multivalence of the word *virgo* itself, which stemmed from the dynamic potency and potent dynamism of the cult of the Virgin Mary, and in part because of the often neglected fact that men too could experience the *virgo* identification label as an object of desire. To be seen as a *virgo* could be a source of power, indeed of a more flexible, plenitudinous power than that which might be derived from the labels "martyr" and "confessor." It is not as clear-cut as it might, at first glance, have appeared to be, which group—priestly women or virginal men— had more reason to be discontented with Christian liturgical categories. On balance, it is probably the case that professionally religious women were more disfavored by their exclusion from the priesthood than were professionally religious men by their sometimes socially unsupported struggle to maintain chastity. Yet, as the intriguing image of the sacerdotal Mary from the Sacramentary of Gellone makes clear, neither side was completely satisfied with the dominant gender roles negotiated by Christian Europeans during the early Middle Ages.

Notes

Introduction. Convent Ruins and Christian Profession

My thanks go to the anonymous readers of this chapter who offered valuable suggestions for its revision and for the shape of the entire volume. I have relied on their reports especially for describing the contents and context of the other chapters published here.

1. Monastic Matrix, http://monasticmatrix.org/monasticon, #556 (accessed March 25, 2007); Dianne Hall, *Women and the Church in Medieval Ireland, c. 1140–1540* (Dublin: Four Courts Press, 2003), 75–80, 207–10; Mervyn Archdall, *Monasticon hibernicum, or, An History of the Abbeys, Priories, and Other Religious Houses in Ireland* (Dublin: G. G. J. and J. Robinson . . . and Luke White, 1786), 799.

2. Mary Bateson, "The Origin and Early History of Double Monasteries," *Transactions of the Royal Historical Society* 13 (1899): 137–98; Lina Eckenstein, *Women Under Monasticism: Chapters on Saint-Lore and Convent Life Between A.D. 500 and A.D. 1500* (Cambridge: Cambridge University Press, 1896); Eileen Power, *Medieval English Nunneries c. 1275 to 1535* (Cambridge: Cambridge University Press, 1922).

3. Ellen Jacobs, "Eileen Power (1889–1940)," in *Medieval Scholarship: Biographical Studies on the Formation of a Discipline*, vol. 1, *History*, ed. Helen Damico and Joseph B. Zavadil (New York: Routledge, 1995), 219–31.

4. Eileen Power, *Medieval People* (London: Methuen, 1924), 81; see also Power, *Medieval Women* (Cambridge: Cambridge University Press, 1975), 89: "Nuns . . . provided a career for girls of gentle birth for whom the only alternative was marriage." See also Margaret L. King, "Book-Lined Cells: Women and Humanism in the Early Italian Renaissance," in *Beyond Their Sex: Learned Women of the European Past*, ed. Patricia H. LaBalme (New York: New York University Press, 1980), esp. 78.

5. H. Grundmann, *Religiöse Bewegungen im Mittelalter* (Berlin: E. Ebering, 1935).

6. David Herlihy and Christiane Klapisch-Zuber, *Les Toscans et leurs familles: Une étude du "catasto" florentin de 1427* (Paris: Fondation nationale des sciences politiques, EESS, 1978); David Herlihy, *Pistoia nel Medioevo e nel Rinascimento, 1200–1430* (Florence: Olschki, 1972); Peter Laslett, *Household and Family in Past Time; Comparative Studies in the Size and Structure of the Domestic Group over the Last Three Centuries in England, France, Serbia, Japan and Colonial North America, with further materials from Western Europe* (Cambridge: Cambridge University Press,

1972); Josiah Cox Russell, *Late Ancient and Medieval Population Control* (Philadelphia: American Philosophical Society, 1985).

7. Suzanne Fonay Wemple, *Women in Frankish Society: Marriage and the Cloister, 500 to 900* (Philadelphia: University of Pennsylvania Press, 1981); Jo Ann McNamara and Suzanne Fonay Wemple, "The Power of Women Through the Family," *Feminist Studies* 1 (1973): 126–41.

8. Janet L. Nelson, "Queens as Jezebels: The Careers of Brunhild and Balthild in Merovingian History," in *Medieval Women: Essays Dedicated and Presented to Professor Rosalind M. T. Hill*, ed. D. Baker, Studies in Church History: Subsidia 1 (Oxford: Blackwell, 1978), 31–77.

9. Joan M. Ferrante, *Woman as Image in Medieval Literature: From the Twelfth Century to Dante* (New York: Columbia University Press, 1975); Karen Cherewatuk and Ulrike Wiethaus, eds., *Dear Sister: Medieval Women and the Epistolary Genre* (Philadelphia: University of Pennsylvania Press, 1993). See also the revision of the medieval canon to include "women's" literature, such as romance, accomplished by Mary Martin McLaughlin and James Bruce Ross, *The Portable Medieval Reader* (New York: Viking, 1949), ed. James Bruce Ross with an introduction by James Bruce Ross and Mary Martin McLaughlin.

10. Bernadette Barrière, "The Cistercian Monastery of Coyroux in the Province of Limousin in the XIIth–XIIIth Centuries," *Gesta* 30 (1992): 76–82.

11. Roberta Gilchrist, *Gender and Material Culture: The Archaeology of Religious Women* (London: Routledge, 1994).

12. David Herlihy, *Opera Muliebria: Women and Work in Medieval Europe* (Philadelphia: University of Pennsylvania Press, 1980); Mary Erler and Maryanne Kowaleski, eds., *Women and Power in the Middle Ages* (Athens: University of Georgia Press, 1988); Martha C. Howell, *Women, Production, and Patriarchy in Late Medieval Cities* (Chicago: University of Chicago Press, 1986); Judith Bennett, "History That Stands Still: Women's Work in the European Past," *Feminist Studies* 14 (1988): 269–83.

13. Alison I. Beach, *Women as Scribes: Book Production and Monastic Reform in Twelfth-Century Bavaria* (Cambridge: Cambridge University Press, 2004); Constance H. Berman, "Cistercian Women and Tithes," *Cîteaux: Commentarii cistercienses* 49 (1998): 95–128; Fiona Griffiths, *The Garden of Delights: Reform and Renaissance for Women in the Twelfth Century* (Philadelphia: University of Pennsylvania Press, 2007); Bruce Venarde, *Women's Monasticism and Medieval Society: Nunneries in France and England, 890–1215* (Ithaca, N.Y.: Cornell University Press, 1997); Jane Tibbetts Schulenburg, "Sexism and the Celestial Gynaeceum—from 500 to 1200," *Journal of Medieval History* 4 (1978): 117–33.

14. Joan Wallach Scott, "Gender: A Useful Category of Analysis," *American Historical Review* 91 (1986): 1053–75; Ruth Mazo Karras, *From Boys to Men: Formations of Masculinity in Late Medieval Europe* (Philadelphia: University of Pennsylvania Press, 2003); Mary C. Erler and Maryanne Kowaleski, eds., *Gendering the Master Narrative: Gender and Power in the Middle Ages* (Ithaca, N.Y.: Cornell University Press, 2003); Leslie Brubaker and Julia M. H. Smith, eds., *Gender in the Early Medieval World: East and West, 300–900* (Cambridge: Cambridge University Press, 2004).

15. Willis Johnson, "The Myth of Jewish Male Menses," *Journal of Medieval History* 24 (1998): 273–95; Kathleen Biddick, *The Shock of Medievalism* (Durham, N.C.: Duke University Press, 1998); Caroline Walker Bynum, *Jesus as Mother: Studies in the Spirituality of the High Middle Ages* (Berkeley: University of California Press, 1984).

16. Jo Ann McNamara, "Women and Power Through the Family Revisited," in *Gendering the Master Narrative: Women and Power in the Middle Ages*, ed. Mary C. Erler and Maryanne Kowaleski (Ithaca, N.Y.: Cornell University Press, 2003), 17–30; Jo Ann McNamara, "The *Herrenfrage*: The Restructuring of the Gender System, 1050–1150," in *Medieval Masculinities: Regarding Men in the Middle Ages*, ed. Clare A. Lees, with the assistance of Thelma Fenster and Jo Ann McNamara (Minneapolis: University of Minnesota Press, 1994), 3–29.

17. For example, Renée Levine Melammed, "Castilian 'Conversas' at Work," in *Women at Work in Spain: From the Middle Ages to Early Modern Times*, ed. Marilyn Stone and Carmen Benito-Vessels (New York: Peter Lang, 1998), 81–100; Renée Levine Melammed, *Heretics or Daughters of Israel? The Crypto-Jewish Women of Castile* (Oxford: Oxford University Press, 1999); David Nirenberg, *Communities of Violence: Persecution of Minorities in the Middle Ages* (Princeton, N.J: Princeton University Press, 1996).

18. Dyan Elliott, *Proving Woman: Female Spirituality and Inquisitional Culture in the Later Middle Ages* (Princeton, N.J.: Princeton University Press, 2004); Dyan Elliott, *Fallen Bodies: Pollution, Sexuality, and Demonology in the Middle Ages* (Philadelphia: University, of Pennsylvania Press, 1999).

19. Bynum, *Jesus as Mother*; Caroline Walker Bynum, *Holy Feast and Holy Fast: The Religious Significance of Food to Medieval Women* (Berkeley: University of California Press, 1987).

20. McNamara, "Women and Power Through the Family Revisited," 19, n. 6, also 17; McNamara and Wemple, "The Power of Women," 126–41; McNamara, "The *Herrenfrage*," 3–30.

21. Jo Ann McNamara, *Sisters in Arms: Catholic Nuns Through Two Millennia* (Cambridge, Mass.: Harvard University Press, 1996).

22. Melammed, *Heretics or Daughters of Israel?*; Emmanuel LeRoy Ladurie, *Montaillou, village occitan de 1294 à 1324* (Paris: Gallimard, 1975); published as *Montaillou: The Promised Land of Error*, trans. Barbara Bray (New York: G. Braziller, 1978).

23. Joan Cadden, *Meanings of Sex Difference in the Middle Ages: Medicine, Science, and Culture* (Cambridge: Cambridge University Press, 1993), esp. 201–18.

24. Barry Windeatt, ed., *The Book of Margery Kempe* (New York: Longman, 2000), 72–76; Raymond of Capua, *Legenda S. Catharinae Senensis, AASS Apr.* III (April 30), 2.4.

25. Ulster Society for Medieval Latin Studies, "The Life of Saint Monenna by Conchubranus," *Seanchas Ardmhacha* 9 (1979): 250–73; 10 (1980–81): 117–40; 11 (1982): 426–54.

26. See, for instance, the expanded definitions of religious women assumed in Mary L. McLaughlin, "Creating and Recreating Communities of Women: The Case of Corpus Domini, Ferrara, 1406–1452," *Signs* 14.2 (1989), 293–320; Sarah Foot, *Veiled Women* (Aldershot: Ashgate, 2000), 2 vols.; Monastic Matrix, http://monasticmatrix.org/monasticon (accessed March 27, 2007).

27. As in Rodney Stark, *The Victory of Reason: How Christianity Led to Freedom, Capitalism, and Western Success* (New York: Random, 2005); Christopher Dawson, *The Making of Europe: An Introduction to the History of European Unity* (London: Sheed & Ward, 1932); Max Weber, *The Protestant Ethic and the Spirit of Capitalism*, trans. Talcott Parsons (New York: Scribner, 1930).

28. A. O. Anderson and M. O. Anderson, eds., *Adomnan's Life of Columba* (Oxford: Clarendon, Press, 1961), 18–19; Regis J. Armstrong, ed. and trans., *Clare of Assisi: Early Documents* (New York: Paulist Press, 1988), 152.

Chapter 1. Tertullian, the Angelic Life, and the Bride of Christ

I would like to thank David Brakke for his comments on this chapter.

1. On constraining aspects of the virginal vocation that emerged very early, see Elizabeth Castelli, "Virginity and Its Meaning for Women's Sexuality in Early Christianity," *Journal of Feminist Studies in Religion* 2 (1986): 61–88. Also see David Brakke's analysis of Athanasius's efforts to control consecrated virgins precisely by developing the implications of the bridal persona in *Athanasius and Asceticism* (Baltimore: Johns Hopkins University Press, 1995), esp. 17–57; Susanna Elm, *Virgins of God: The Making of Asceticism in Late Antiquity* (Oxford: Clarendon Press, 1994), 117–120, 335ff. Also see David Hunter, "The Virgin, the Bride, and the Church: Reading Psalm 45 in Ambrose, Jerome, and Augustine," *Church History* 69. 2 (June 2000): 281–303. This entire issue of *Church History* explicitly addresses the way the metaphor of the bride is wielded in Christian tradition.

2. Jo Ann McNamara, *A New Song: Celibate Women in the First Three Christian Centuries* (Binghamton, N.Y.: Harrington Park Press, 1983), 77–84, 108–9. Also see Ross Kraemer, "The Conversion of Women to Ascetic Forms of Christianity," *Signs* 6 (1980): 298–307.

3. See John Bugge, *Virginitas: An Essay in the History of a Medieval Idea* (The Hague: Martinus Nijhoff, 1975), 330–35. According to Peter Brown, the *vita angelica* had particular currency in Syrian circles (*The Body and Society: Men, Women, and Sexual Renunciation in Early Christianity* [New York: Columbia University Press, 1988], 323–38).

4. McNamara, *New Song*, 121.

5. Tertullian, *On the Apparel of Women* 1.1, *ANF* 4:14. For a more sympathetic reading that attempts to get beyond the "devil's gateway" trope, see F. Forrester Church, "Sex and Salvation in Tertullian," *Harvard Theological Review* 68 (1975): 85–101. McNamara is also aware of this more positive side (*New Song*, 94–95, 110–11).

6. See Wayne Meeks's classic article, "The Image of the Androgyne: Some Uses of a Symbol in Earliest Christianity," *History of Religions* 13 (1974): 165–208.

7. Tertullian, *On Prescription Against Heretics* c. 41, *ANF* 3:263; compare this with his indictment of an anonymous woman's heretical teaching on baptism in *On Baptism* c. 1, *ANF*, 3:669. For his discussion of the virgin Philumene, see p. 39 On the disparate sets of beliefs associated with the term *Gnosticism*, see David Brakke, "Self-Differentiation Among Christian Groups: The Gnostics and Their Opponents," in *Origins to Constantine*, Vol. 1, The Cambridge History of Christianity, ed. Margaret M. Mitchell and Frances Young (Cambridge: Cambridge University Press, 2006), 245–60.

8. Tertullian, *Against Praxeas* c. 1, *ANF*, 3:597.

9. See Christine Trevett, *Montanism: Gender, Authority, and the New Prophecy* (Cambridge: Cambridge University Press, 1996), 159–162.

10. Dale Martin, *The Corinthian Body* (New Haven, Conn.: Yale University Press, 1995).

11. See Perre Adnès, "Le mariage spirituel," in *Dictionnaire de la spiritualité ascetique et mystique: Doctrine et histoire*, Vol. 10, ed. Marcel Viller et al. (Paris: G. Beauchesne, 1937–1995), 388–91.

12. For a review of this set of associations, see Dyan Elliott, "Flesh and Spirit: Women and the Body," introductory chapter to *The Yale Companion to Medieval Religious Women*, ed. Alastair Minnis and Rosalynn Voaden (New Haven, Conn.: Yale University Press, forthcoming).

13. See Jean Gaudemet, "Note sur le symbolisme médiévale: Le mariage de l'evêque," *L'année canonique* 22 (1978): 71–80. For the later period, see Megan McLaughlin, "The Bishop as Bridegroom: Marital Imagery and Clerical Celibacy in the Eleventh and Twelfth Centuries," in *Medieval Purity and Piety: Essays on Medieval Clerical Celibacy and Religious Reform*, ed. Michael Frassetto (New York: Garland, 1998), 210–37.

14. Elaine Pagels, *The Gnostic Paul: Gnostic Exegesis of the Pauline Letters* (Philadelphia: Fortress Press, 1975), 68ff., 115, 124–27; compare this with Brown, *Body and Society*, 103–121. McNamara, *New Song*, 68–70. On the mystery of the bridal chamber, see especially the Valentinian *Gospel of Philip*, in *The Nag Hammadi Library*, ed. James Robinson (San Francisco: Harper and Row, 1977), c. 64–65, 67, 69–72, 75–76, 82, 84–85, 185–86, (pp. 139–43, 145, 149–51, 185–86.) For the antifemale content in Gnosticism, see Jorunn Jacobsen Buckley, *Female Fault and Fulfillment in Gnosticism* (Chapel Hill, N.C.: University of North Carolina Press, 1986).

15. Compare with the rhetoric of the Ps.-Clementine epistles on virginity, which extends this expectation to virgins. See Ep. 1, c. 4, in *Ante-Nicene Christian Library: The Writings of Methodius, etc.*, ed. Alexander Roberts and James Donaldson (Edinburgh: T. and T. Clark, 1869), c. 4, 370–71.

16. Tertullian, *An Answer to the Jews* c. 2, *ANF*, 3:152. Compare with Ton H. C. Van Eijk's discussion of formative ancient and early Christian thinkers on this nexus of ideas in "Marriage and Virginity, Death and Immortality," in *Epektasis: Mélanges patristiques offerts au Cardinal Jean Daniélou*, ed. Jacques Fontaine and Charles Kannengiesser (Paris: Beauchesne, 1972), 209–35.

17. Tertullian, *Soul's Testimony* c. 3, *ANF*, 3:177.

18. Tertullian, *Resurrection of the Flesh* c. 36, *ANF*, 3:571.

19. Tertullian, *To His Wife* 1.1, *ANF*, 4:39.

20. *To His Wife* 1.3, *ANF*, 4:40.

21. Tertullian, *Exhortation to Chastity* c. 3, *ANF*, 4:52; c. 9, 4:55.

22. Tertullian, *On Monogamy* c. 3, *ANF*, 4:60.

23. *Exhortation to Chastity* c. 11, *ANF*, 4:56.

24. *To His Wife* 2.6, *ANF*, 4:48; *On Monogamy* c. 10, *ANF*, 4:67.

25. The closest Tertullian came to endorsing an arrangement was, in fact, an argument against marriage to counter his recently widowed friend's hypothetical use of domestic needs in favor: "Take to yourself from among the widows one fair in faith, dowered with poverty, sealed with age. You will (thus) make a good marriage. A plurality of *such* wives is pleasing to God" (*Exhortation to Chastity* c. 12, *ANF*, 4:56).

26. Matt. 12:18; Luke 8:20, 21; Tertullian, *On the Flesh of Christ* c. 7, *ANF*, 3:527.

27. *Exhortation to Chastity* c. 1, *ANF*, 4:50.

28. *On Modesty* c. 6, *ANF*, 4:79.

29. *Exhortation to Chastity* c. 9, *ANF*, 4:55.

30. *To His Wife* 1.8, *ANF*, 4:43.

31. *Exhortation to Chastity* c. 1, *ANF*, 4:50.

32. This occurs repeatedly in Tertullian, *Against Marcion* 1.29, *ANF*, 3:294; compare with Tertullian, *On the Veiling of Virgins* c. 2, *ANF*, 4:28; c. 3, 4:28.

33. *Against Marcion* 1.29, *ANF*, 3:293–94.

34. *Exhortation to Chastity* c. 1, *ANF*, 4:50; compare with *Veiling of Virgins* where he assigns greater merit to male virgins because their struggle in maintaining chastity is greater (c. 10, *ANF*, 4:33).

35. *To His Wife* 1.8, *ANF*, 4:43.

36. Ibid. 1.1, *ANF*, 4:39.

37. Ibid 1.3, *ANF*, 4:41.

38. *On the Apparel of Women* 1.2, *ANF*, 4:15.

39. See Dale Martin's discussion of the inequality implicit in the concept of androgyny in *Corinthian Body*, 230–32.

40. Rev. 3.4; 14.4; compare with Tertullian's *On the Resurrection of the Flesh* c. 27, *ANF*, 3:564. Certain theologians, such as Gregory of Nyssa, retain the concept of prelapsarian androgyne humanity that became divided into two sexes through sin (Bugge, *Virginitas*, 16–19; N. P. Williams, *The Ideas of the Fall and of Original Sin* [London: Longman's, Green, and Company, 1927], 271–74).

41. See Thomas Schirrmacher, *Paul in Conflict with the Veil* (Nuremberg: Verlag für Theologie und Religionswissenschaft, 2002); also see Lloyd Llewellyn-Jones, *Aphrodite's Tortoise: The Veiled Women of Ancient Greece* (Swansea: Classical Press of Wales, 2002). Martin analyzes the custom of Greco-Roman veiling and its association with the closed womb. Paul seems to have regarded angels as sexed beings, but his fleeting allusion is perhaps intentionally ambiguous. Thus Martin uses Tertullian to articulate what is hidden in the Pauline text (*Corinthian Body*, 233–39, 242–48). On Genesis 6 as the original legend of the fall, see Williams, *Ideas of the Fall*, 20–28.

42. *On the Apparel of Women* 1.2, *ANF*, 4:15. See *The Book of Enoch* c. 6–22, in *Apocrypha and Pseudepigrapha of the Old Testament*, trans. R. H. Charles (Oxford: Clarendon Press, 1913).

43. *On the Resurrection of the Flesh* c. 42, *ANF*, 3:676.

44. *On the Veiling of Virgins* c. 7, *ANF*, 4:31. See Brown, *Body and Society*, 80–82; McNamara, *New Song*, 109–12.

45. Tertullian, *On Prayer* c. 22, *ANF*, 3:687.

46. *On the Veiling of Virgins* c. 7, *ANF*, 4:32.

47. *Apology* c. 22, *ANF*, 3:36.

48. *On the Apparel of Women* 1.2, *ANF*, 4:14–15.

49. Tertullian, *Apology* c. 22, *ANF*, 3: 36.

50. Ibid. c. 4, *ANF*, 3:62–63; c. 9, 3:65.

51. *Resurrection* c. 10, *ANF*, 3:552; *Against Praxeas* c. 16, *ANF*, 3:612.

52. *On Monogamy* c. 1, *ANF*, 4:59.

53. *On the Apparel of Women* c. 1, *ANF*, 117–18.

54. Ibid 1.2, *ANF*, 4:14. In *Against Marcion* Tertullian describes the angels as "entrapped in sin by the daughters of men" c. 18, *ANF*, 3:470.

55. *On the Veiling of Virgins* c. 5, *ANF*, 4:30.

56. *On the Flesh of Christ* c. 17, *ANF*, 3:536; see the discussion of Mary's womanhood in *On the Veiling of Virgins* c. 6, *ANF*, 4:31.

57. *On the Flesh of Christ* c. 6, 3:526.

58. 1 Cor. 15:47; *On the Flesh of Christ* c. 8, *ANF*, 3:529.

59. *On Prescription Against Heretics* c. 7, *ANF*, 3:246; compare with 30, 3:257. Also see *Against Marcion* c. 11, *ANF*, 3:330. According to Tertullian, Apelles, a one-time follower of Marcion, learned this heresy from Philumene and became its main proponent. The two were said to have become lovers.

60. *On the Flesh of Christ* c. 6, *ANF*, 3:527; 526, c. 13, 3:533–34; on angels' assumption of human flesh, also see c. 3, 3:523; *Against Marcion* c. 11, *ANF*, 3:330; c. 9, 3:328–29.

61. *On the Flesh of Christ* c. 15, *ANF*, 3:534.m

62. Ibid c. 16, *ANF*, 3:535.

63. See Tertullian, *Treatise on the Soul* c. 5–9, *ANF*, 3:184–88, c. 27, 3:208; compare with *On the Resurrection of the Flesh* c. 53, *ANF*, 3:587. On the negative

ramifications of Tertullian's emphasis on seminal identity and its role in establishing original sin, see Williams, *Ideas of the Fall*, 233–38.

64. *On the Soul* c. 36, *ANF*, 3:217.

65. *On the Resurrection of the Flesh* c. 7, *ANF*, 3:550; Caroline Walker Bynum, *The Resurrection of the Body in Western Christianity, 200–1336* (New York: Columbia University Press, 1995), 34–43.

66. *On the Resurrection of the Flesh* c. 8, *ANF*, 3:551.

67. *On the Resurrection of the Flesh* c. 43, *ANF*, 3:577; c. 42, 3:576.

68. Ibid., c. 41, *ANF*, 3:575; c. 54–55, 3: 587–89.

69. Claude Rambaux, *Tertullian face aux morales des trois premiers siècles* (Paris: Société d'Edition "Les Belles Lettres," 1979), 213.

70. *On the Resurrection of the Flesh* c. 41, *ANF*, 3:575; c. 54–55, 3: 587–89. A similar logic is present in the Pauline inflected logic of his antidualist treatise *Against Marcion*: Christ's love for his bride, *ecclesia*, is equated with the husband's love for his wife, and hence the flesh, dignifying the created world in general and the body in particular. (5.18, *ANF*, 3:469).

71. *On the Resurrection of the Flesh* c. 60, *ANF*, 3:592.

72. Ibid c. 50, *ANF*, 3:592.

73. Ibid c. 62, *ANF*, 3:593.

74. Ibid c. 26, *ANF*, 3:564; "in regno dei reformatam et angelificatam" (26.7, PL 2:832; translation mine). Compare with *On the Soul*: "We therefore maintain that every soul, whatever be its age on quitting the body, remains unchanged in the same, until the time shall come when the promised perfection shall be realized in a state duly tempered to the measure of the peerless angels" (c. 56, *ANF*, 3:232–33).

75. *On the Resurrection of the Flesh* c. 36, *ANF* 3:571.

76. Address by Prime Minister Paul Martin on Bill C-38 (The Civil Marriage Act), February 16, 2005, Ottawa, Ontario. Martin's position has been reiterated by critics of the New Jersey ruling. See Evan Wolfson's letter to the editor in the *New York Times*, October 27, 2006. I am indebted to Fred Rodenhausen for his perspective on this issue.

77. Augustine, *Quaestionum in Heptateuchum libri VIII*, 1, q. 3, ed. I Fraipont, *CCSL* 33 (Turnhout: Brepols, 1958), 3. See Dyan Elliott, *Fallen Bodies: Pollution, Sexuality, and Demonology in the Middle Ages* (Philadelphia: University of Pennsylvania Press, 1999), 9–10, 52–53.

78. *Biblia Latina cum glossa ordinaria: Facsimile Reprint of the Editio Princeps of Strassburg 1480/81*, with an introduction by Adolph Rusch, Karlfried Froehlich, and Margaret Gibson (Turnhout: Brepols, 1992), *Gen. 6 ad v. filii dei*, 35.

79. See Dyan Elliott, *Proving Woman: Female Spirituality and Inquisitional Culture in the Later Middle Ages* (Princeton, N.J.: Princeton University Press, 2004), 251–52.

80. See R. N. Swanson, "Angels Incarnate: Clergy and Masculinity from Gregorian Reform to Reformation," in *Masculinity in Medieval Europe*, ed. D. M. Hadley (London: Longman, 1999), 160–77.

81. McNamara, *New Song*, 121.

82. *On the Apparel of Women* 2.13, *ANF*, 4:25.

83. *To His Wife* 1.4, *ANF*, 4:41.

84. *Exhortation to Chastity* c. 13, *ANF*, 4:58.

85. *On Prayer* c. 22, *ANF*, 3:688.

86. Ibid. c. 22, *ANF*, 3:689.

87. *On the Veiling of Virgins* c. 12, *ANF*, 4:34–35.

88. Ibid c. 16, *ANF*, 4:37
89. *On the Resurrection of the Flesh* c. 61, *ANF*, 3:593.

Chapter 2. One Flesh, Two Sexes, Three Genders?

I would like to acknowledge and thank the Social Sciences and Humanities Research Council of Canada for their generous support of this research. Earlier versions of this chapter were presented at the Gender and Medieval Studies Conference, University of Leeds, Leeds, UK, January 2005, and at the Fortieth International Medieval Congress, Western Michigan University, Kalamazoo, May 2005.

1. Linda E. Mitchell, *Portraits of Medieval Women: Family, Marriage, and Politics in England, 1225–1350* (New York: Palgrave, 2003), 133-36.

2. R. N. Swanson, "Angels Incarnate: Clergy and Masculinity from Gregorian Reform to Reformation," in *Masculinity in Medieval Europe*, ed. D. M Hadley (London: Longman, 1999), 160–77.

3. P. H. Cullum, "Clergy, Masculinity and Transgression in Late Medieval England," in Hadley, *Masculinity in Medieval Europe*, 178–96.

4. Cited in Shaun Tougher, "Social Transformation, Gender Transformation: The Court Eunuch, 300–900," in *Gender in the Early Medieval World: East and West, 300–900*, ed. Leslie Brubaker and Julia M. H. Smith (Cambridge: Cambridge University Press, 2004), 71. Kathryn M. Ringrose is generally more positive about the role of eunuchs as a third gender, arguing that by the ninth century, they had clear and distinctive roles, dress, and even sexual status. This was not necessarily in the negative sense that appears to have dominated earlier writers such as those consulted by Tougher. Kathryn M. Ringrose, "Living in the Shadows: Eunuchs and Gender in Byzantium," in *Third Sex, Third Gender: Beyond Sexual Dimorphism in Culture and History*, ed. Gilbert Herdt (New York: Zone Books, 1994), 85–109.

5. Jo Ann McNamara, "City Air Makes Men Free and Women Bound," in *Text and Territory: Geographical Imagination in the European Middle Ages*, ed. S. Tomasch and S. Gilles (Philadelphia: University of Pennsylvania Press, 1998), 144.

6. Jo Ann McNamara, "Canossa and the Ungendering of the Public Man," in *Render Unto Caesar: The Religious Sphere in World Politics*, ed. Sabrina Petra Ramet and Donald W. Treadgold (Washington, D.C.: American University Press, 1995), 131–49. This point is also made in "City Air Makes Men Free," which provides an excellent overview of the process in the twelfth and thirteenth centuries.

7. Jo Ann McNamara, "An Unresolved Syllogism," in *Conflicted Identities and Multiple Masculinities: Men in the Medieval West*, ed. Jacqueline Murray (New York: Garland, 1999), 1–24; and Jo Ann McNamara, "Chastity as a Third Gender in the History and Hagiography of Gregory of Tours," in *The World of Gregory of Tours*, ed. Kathleen Mitchell and Ian Wood (Leiden: Brill, 2002), 199–209.

8. McNamara, "City Air Makes Men Free," 144.

9. Nancy Partner has argued persuasively that the binaries of sex and gender and body and society are too limited to assess the diversity and complexity of psychosocial identity in society. It appears that the ubiquity of third genders is an attempt to address delimiting categories. Partner has suggested a third or middle term, such as self or sexuality, to address how people negotiate their individual identities, which still are appearing as part of the main collectivity. "No Sex, No Gender," in *Studying Medieval Women: Sex, Gender, Feminism*, ed. Nancy Partner (Cambridge, Mass.: Medieval Academy of America, 1993), 117–41. In the

present discussion, however, the focus is not internal, on individual self-identity, so much as external, on how society viewed and understood some individuals.

10. Thomas Laqueur, *Making Sex: Body and Gender from the Greeks to Freud* (Cambridge, Mass: Harvard University Press, 1990).

11. See, for example, the early review by Katharine Park and Robert A. Nye, "Destiny Is Anatomy," *New Republic,* February 18, 1991, 3–57. Monica Green provides an overview of Laqueur's thesis and its subsequent critique by medievalists in "Bodies, Gender, Health, Disease: Recent Work on Medieval Women's Medicine," *Studies in Medieval and Renaissance History,* 3rd ser., 2 (2005): 6–9.

12. Joan Cadden, *Meanings of Sex Difference in the Middle Ages: Medicine, Science, and Culture* (Cambridge: Cambridge University Press, 1993), 170–72.

13. Laqueur, *Making Sex* 243.

14. Gilbert Herdt, ed., *Third Sex, Third Gender: Beyond Sexual Dimorphism in Culture and History* (New York: Zone Books, 1994).

15. Herdt, Preface to *Third Sex,* 11.

16. Herdt, "Introduction: Third Sexes and Third Genders," in Herdt, *Third Sex,* 14.

17. Quoted in Herdt, "Introduction," 19.

18. Herdt, "Introduction," 28.

19. Ibid., 3–33.

20. Ibid., 44. Herdt further posits that there is no link between sexual orientation and third sex or third gender, see 50. Significantly, Ruth Karras has identified chastity as a sexual orientation in medieval society because the men and women who transcended sexual desire were perceived to have become a different type of person. Ruth Mazo Karras, *Sexuality in Medieval Europe: Doing Unto Others* (New York: Routledge, 2005), 40, 56.

21. See the important discussion of this ancient inheritance and its deployment in the early Middle Ages in McNamara, "An Unresolved Syllogism." McNamara's work provides the main edifice for this discussion, which adds but a small brick to her structure.

22. See the useful discussion of binaries in Caroline Walker Bynum, "'. . . And Woman His Humanity': Female Imagery in the Religious Writings of the Later Middle Ages," in *Gender and Religion: On the Complexity of Symbols,* ed. C. W. Bynum, S. Harrell, and P. Richman (Boston: Beacon Press, 1986), 257–88.

23. See the discussion of this Salernitan understanding in Danielle Jacquart and Claude Thomasset, *Sexuality and Medicine in the Middle Ages,* trans. Matthew Adamson (Princeton, N.J.: Princeton University Press, 1988), 71.

24. Cadden, *Meanings of Sex Difference,* 171.

25. Discussed in Jacquart and Thomasset, *Sexuality and Medicine,* 73.

26. According to Salernitan tradition, a hermaphrodite was conceived when the conceptus was in the center of the womb: Cadden, *Meanings of Sex Difference,* 198. See also Jacquart and Thomasset, *Sexuality and Medicine,* 141.

27. Jo Ann McNamara, "The *Herrenfrage*: The Restructuring of the Gender System, 1050–1150," in *Medieval Masculinities: Regarding Men in the Middle Ages,* ed. Clare A. Lees (Minneapolis: University of Minnesota, 1994), 2–4.

28. Discussed in Jacquart and Thomasset, *Sexuality and Medicine,* 73.

29. Gregory of Tours, *History of the Franks* trans. Lewis Thorpe (Harmondsworth: Penguin, 1974), 8.20.

30. Discussed in McNamara, "*Herrenfrage,*" 20.

31. Vern L. Bullough, "On Being a Male in the Middle Ages," in *Medieval Masculinities,* 33.

32. H. Musurillo, ed. and trans., *The Acts of the Christian Martyrs* (Oxford: Oxford University Press, 1972), 117. This passage is discussed at length by Joyce Salisbury in *Perpetua's Passion: The Death and Memory of a Young Roman Woman* (New York: Routledge, 1997), 107–12.

33. *Sainted Women of the Dark Ages*, ed. and trans. Jo Ann McNamara and John E. Halborg with E. Gordon Whatley (Durham, N.C.: Duke University Press, 1992), 209.

34. Ibid., 54.

35. Ibid., 133.

36. *The Life of Christina of Markyate, a Twelfth-Century Recluse*, ed. and trans. C. H. Talbot (Oxford: Clarendon Press, 1959), 114–19.

37. Rachel Moriarty, "'Playing the Man': The Courage of Christian Martyrs, Translated and Transposed," in *Gender and Christian Religion*, ed. R. N. Swanson, Studies in Church History 34 (Woodbridge: Boydell, 1998), 9.

38. Caroline Walker Bynum has observed that the vision of becoming male was a motif found in the lives of early Christian women and fell into disuse in the later Middle Ages; see "Female Religious Imagery," 272.

39. *Acts of the Christian Martyrs*, 76–77.

40. Clement of Alexandria, *Stromateis*, 6.12 in *ANF*, 2: 503.

41. Jerome, *Commentary to the Ephesians*, 16.

42. Cited in Cadden, *Meanings of Sex Difference*, 206.

43. See Bynum ("Female Religious Imagery," esp. 268–69) for a nuanced discussion of how male authors exhorted women to be more virile and masculine.

44. Cited in Barbara Newman, *From Virile Woman to WomanChrist: Studies in Medieval Religion and Literature* (Philadelphia: University of Pennsylvania Press, 1995), 23. In commenting on this passage, Newman argues that the notion of a *virago* or *femina virilis* relies on an androcentric notion of the male as normative and femaleness as defect that can be overcome by women denying their sexed bodies.

45. Cited in Cadden, *Meanings of Sex Difference*, 206.

46. Jacques de Vitry, *The Life of Marie D'Oignies*, trans. Margot H. King (Toronto: Peregrina Publishing, 1993), 72.

47. McNamara has suggested that Gregory of Tours was aware that the ascetic movement of early Christianity made women masculine and, to an extent, feminized men. "Chastity as a Third Gender," 200.

48. Hildegard of Bingen, *Scivias*, trans. Columba Hart and Jane Bishop (New York: Paulist Press, 1990), 6.62.

49. See the discussion in Jacqueline Murray, "'The law of sin that is in my members': The Problem of Male Embodiment," in *Gender and Holiness: Men, Women and Saints in Late Medieval Europe*, ed. Samantha J. E. Riches and Sarah Salih (London: Routledge, 2002), 15.

50. Jacquart and Thomasset, *Sexuality and Medicine*, 148.

51. Gregory the Great, *Dialogues*, trans. Odo John Zimmerman (New York: Fathers of the Church, 1959), 1.2, p. 60.

52. Cited in Jacquart and Thomasset, *Sexuality and Medicine*, 148.

53. Murray, "The Problem of Male Embodiment," 15.

54. Hildegard, *Scivias*, 6.54.

55. Cadden, *Meanings of Sex Difference*, 181–82.

56. McNamara and Halborg, *Sainted Women of the Dark Ages*, 212.

57. Indeed, tonsure has been characterized as the ultimate act of gender transformation. McNamara, "Chastity as a Third Gender," 205.

58. Paul Edward Dutton, "Charlemagne's Mustache" in *Charlemagne's Mustache and Other Cultural Clusters of a Dark Age* (New York: Palgrave, 2004), 3–42, at 42.

59. McNamara, "Chastity as a Third Gender," 203.

60. Robert Mills, "The Signification of the Tonsure," in *Holiness and Masculinity in the Middle Ages*, ed. P. H. Cullum and Katherine J. Lewis (Cardiff: University of Wales, 2004), 116–18.

61. Ibid., 116.

62. Jacquart and Thomasset, *Sexuality and Medicine*, 170.

63. Dutton, "Charlemagne's Mustache," 12. McNamara provides multiple examples of the symbolic role of long or sheared hair in her examination of Gregory of Tours ("Chastity as a Third Gender," 205).

64. Walter Daniel, *The Life of Ailred of Rievaulx*, trans. F. M. Powicke (London: Thomas Nelson, 1950), 62.

65. McNamara and Halborg, *Sainted Women of the Dark Ages*, 81.

66. Raymond of Capua, *The Life of St. Catherine of Siena*, trans. George Lamb (London: Harvill Press, 1960), 61.

67. De Vitry, *Life of Marie D'Oignies*, 68.

68. Thomas of Cantimpré, *The Life of Lutgard of Aywières*, trans. Margot H. King (Saskatoon: Peregrina Publishing, 1987), 1.13.

69. Cantimpré, *Life of Lutgard*, 2.21.

70. *The Book of Margery Kempe*, ed. Barry Windeatt (Harlow: Longman, 2000), 274–78.

71. Gregory the Great, *Dialogues*, 4.14.

72. For a discussion of bearded saints, see Vern L. Bullough and Bonnie Bullough, *Cross Dressing, Sex, and Gender* (Philadelphia: University of Pennsylvania Press, 1993), 54–55.

73. The belief that the womb was composed of multiple chambers and the positioning of the fetus could result in the development of a hermaphrodite or a person who would transgress gender norms is discussed in Cadden, *Meanings of Sex Difference*, 201–4.

74. Cited in Moriarty, "'Playing the Man,'" 8.

75. Raymond of Capua, *Life of St. Catherine*, 77.

76. Hildegard, *Scivias*, 5.28, p. 217.

77. Ibid., 217–18.

78. Albertus Magnus, *De animalibus* quoted in Cadden, *Meanings of Sex Difference*, 212.

79. Ibid., 170, 202.

80. McNamara and Halborg, *Sainted Women of the Dark Ages*, 285.

81. Ibid., 165.

82. Herdt, "Introduction," 19.

83. Ibid., 79.

84. *The Letters of Abelard and Heloise*, trans. Betty Radice (Harmondsworth: Penguin, 1975), 184.

85. Herdt, "Introduction," 44.

86. Karras, *Sexuality in Medieval Europe*, 40, 56.

87. Gregory of Tours, *History of the Franks*, 7.1.

88. McNamara and Halborg, *Sainted Women of the Dark Ages*, 141.

89. Hildegard, *Scivias*, 2.11.

90. Ibid., 78.

Chapter 3. Thomas Aquinas's Chastity Belt

Versions of this chapter were presented at the Medieval Institute, University of Notre Dame, and at the Fortieth International Conference on Medieval Studies, Kalamazoo, Michigan. I thank the audiences, including in particular Remie Constable, Tom Noble, and Mathieu Vander Meer for their comments and suggestions, and John Van Engen for additional advice.

1. The term "emasculine" is from R. N. Swanson, "Angels Incarnate: Clergy and Masculinity from Gregorian Reform to Reformation," in *Masculinity in Medieval Europe*, ed D. M. Hadley (London: Longman, 1999), 160–77. Jo Ann McNamara, "Chastity as a Third Gender in the History and Hagiography of Gregory of Tours," in *The World of Gregory of Tours*, ed. Kathleen Mitchell and Ian Wood (Leiden: Brill, 2002), 199–209, argues not that we should consider the chaste a third gender, but that Gregory so considered them.

2. See Ludwig Schmugge, *Kinder, Kirche, Karrieren: Päpstliche Dispense von der unehelichen Geburt im Spätmittelalter* (Zurich: Artemis & Winkler, 1985), for data and further references.

3. Jennifer Thibodeaux, "Man of the Church, or Man of the Village? Gender and the Parish Clergy in Medieval Normandy," *Gender and History* 18.2 (2006), 380–99; P. H. Cullum, "Clergy, Masculinity, and Transgression in Late Medieval England," in Hadley, *Masculinity in Medieval Europe*, 178–96; Daniel E. Thiery, "Plowshares and Swords: Clerical Involvement in Acts of Violence and Peacemaking in Late Medieval England, c. 1400–1536," *Albion* 36 (2004): 202–22.

4. See Elliott, this volume.

5. See examples in Ruth Mazo Karras, *From Boys to Men: Formations of Masculinity in Late Medieval Europe* (Philadelphia: University of Pennsylvania Press, 2003), 50.

6. Karras, *From Boys to Men*, 21; Leo Braudy, *From Chivalry to Terrorism: War and the Changing Nature of Masculinity* (New York: Alfred A. Knopf, 2003), 63–114.

7. Jacqueline Murray, "Masculinizing Religious Life: Sexual Prowess, the Battle for Chastity, and Monastic Identity," in *Holiness and Masculinity in the Middle Ages*, ed. P. H. Cullum and Katherine J. Lewis (Cardiff: University of Wales Press, 2004), 37; Maureen Miller, "Masculinity, Reform, and Clerical Culture: Narratives of Episcopal Holiness in the Gregorian Era," *Church History* 72 (2003): 25–52.

8. See discussion in Ruth Mazo Karras, *Medieval European Sexualities: Doing Unto Others* (London: Routledge, 2005), 28–58.

9. Michel Foucault, *An Introduction*, Vol. 1, *The History of Sexuality*, trans. Robert Hurley (New York: Vintage, 1990), 43. The best discussion of the "acts/identities" question by a committed Foucauldian is David M. Halperin, "Forgetting Foucault: Acts, Identities, and the History of Sexuality," *Representations* 63 (1998): 93–120, reprinted along with other articles in his *How to Do the History of Homosexuality* (Chicago: University of Chicago Press, 2002).

10. John H. Arnold, "The Labour of Continence: Masculinity and Clerical Virginity," in *Medieval Virginities*, ed. Anke Bernau, Ruth Evans, and Sarah Salih, (Toronto: University of Toronto Press, 2003), 107. See also Kathryn Kelsey Staples and Ruth Mazo Karras, "Christina's Tempting," in *Christina of Markyate: A Twelfth-Century Holy Woman*, ed. Samuel Fanous and Henrietta Leyser (London: Routledge, 2004),

11. *The Life of Christina of Markyate, a Twelfth-Century Recluse*, 43, ed. and trans. C. H. Talbot (Oxford: Clarendon Press, 1959), 114–15.

12. *Life of Christina*, 114–19.

13. *AASS, Ian. II* (January 17) "De S. Antonio Magno Abbate in Thebaide Apophthegmata et Collationes," 3.14.

14. Pelagius, *Verba Seniorum*, 5:5, *PL* 73:875.

15. Pelagius, *Verba Seniorum*, 5:4, *PL* 73:874–75.

16. John Cassian, *Institutionem libri 12*, 6:1, 6:4, ed. Michael Petschenig, Corpus Scriptorum Ecclesiasticorum Latinorum 17 (Vienna: F. Tempsky, 1888), 115–18. See also Cassian, *Collationes* 12:7, *PL* 49:880-883, on the degrees of chastity.

17. Gregory the Great, "Vita de sancto Benedicto," *PL* 66 col. 132.

18. C. Leyser, "Masculinity in Flux: Nocturnal Emission and the Limits of Celibacy in the Early Middle Ages," in Hadley, *Masculinity in Medieval Europe*, 103–20, at 105.

19. Kathryn M. Ringrose, *The Perfect Servant: Eunuchs and the Social Construction of Gender in Byzantium* (Chicago: University of Chicago Press, 2003), 111–27.

20. Ringrose, *The Perfect Servant*, 17–18; see also Mathew Kuefler, *The Manly Eunuch: Masculinity, Gender Ambiguity, and Christian Ideology in Late Antiquity* (Chicago: University of Chicago Press, 2001), 245–82.

21. Albrecht Diem, *Das monastische Experiment: Die Rolle der Keuschheit bei der Entstehung des westlichen Klosterwesens* (Münster: Lit Verlag, 2005).

22. *AASS Iul. V* (July 20), "De S. Vulmaro Abbatis," 85.

23. *AASS, Oct. I* (October 1), "De S. Bavone," 249.

24. Emma Pettit, "Holiness and Masculinity in Aldhelm's *Opus Geminatum De virginitate*," in Cullum and Lewis, *Holiness and Masculinity in the Middle Ages*, 12.

25. Jane Tibbetts Schulenburg, *Forgetful of Their Sex: Female Sanctity and Society ca. 500–1100* (Chicago: University of Chicago Press, 1998), 127–75.

26. Murray, "Masculinizing Religious Life," 24–42; Swanson, "Angels Incarnate," 163,

27. Odo of Cluny, "De S. Geraldo, Comite Auriliacensi Confessore," 4, 2, *AASS Oct. VI* (October 18), 54:304 and 54:315, p. 315. On Odo, see Phyllis Jestice, "Why Celibacy? Odo of Cluny and the Development of a New Sexual Morality," in *Medieval Purity and Piety: Essays on Medieval Clerical Celibacy and Religious Reform*, ed. Michael Frassetto (New York: Garland, 1998), 81–115.

28. Janet L. Nelson, "Monks, Secular Men, and Masculinity, c. 900," in Hadley, *Masculinity in Medieval Europe*, 127–30.

29. See Jean Gaudemet, "Le célibat ecclésiastique," *Zeitschrift der Savigny-Stiftung für Rechtsgeschichte, Kanonistische Abteilung* 68 (1982): 1–31, for a good account of the process.

30. See Elizabeth Makowski and Katharina Wilson, eds., *Wykked Wyves and the Woes of Marriage: Misogamous Literature from Juvenal to Chaucer* (Albany: State University of New York Press, 1990), for an anthology of these writings. As they point out (61–63), after an early medieval hiatus, misogamy reemerged in the twelfth century.

31. By contrast, clerics in the eastern (Orthodox) church were allowed to marry (although monks and bishops could not); indeed, it became customary for them to marry prior to ordination, and if they preferred celibacy they became monks. Sexual activity, or the abstinence from it, did not constitute such an integral part of a person's identity or of the dividing line between lay and cleric. This had repercussions for attitudes toward women and gender relations in the society in general. See Eve Levin, *Sex and Society in the World of the Orthodox Slavs, 900–1700* (Ithaca, N.Y.: Cornell University Press, 1989); Liz James, ed., *Desire and Denial in Byzantium* (Aldershot: Ashgate, 1997).

32. On chaste marriage, see Dyan Elliott, *Spiritual Marriage: Sexual Abstinence in Medieval Wedlock* (Princeton N. J.: Princeton University Press, 1993).

33. See Jo Ann McNamara, "The *Herrenfrage:* The Restructuring of the Gender System, 1050–1150," in *Medieval Masculinities: Regarding Men in the Middle Ages,* ed. Clare A. Lees, (Minneapolis: University of Minnesota Press, 1994), 3–29, for some of the consequences of this process; Dyan Elliott, *Fallen Bodies: Pollution, Sexuality, and Demonology in the Middle Ages* (Philadelphia: University of Pennsylvania Press, 1999), 81–126.

34. Murray, "Masculinizing Religious Life," 37.

35. Adam of Eynsham, *Magna vita sancti Hugonis,* 1:9, ed. and trans. Decima L. Douie and Hugh Farmer, 2nd ed. (Oxford: Clarendon Press, 1985), 28.

36. All seven medieval manuscripts whose provenance is known are Carthusian (Douie and Farmer, *Magna vita sancti Hugonis,* xlix–lii).

37. Caesarius of Heisterbach, *Dialogus miraculorum,* 4:97, ed. Joseph Strange (Cologne: Heberle, 1851), 1:265. On this story, see Jacqueline Murray, "Sexual Mutilation and Castration Anxiety: A Medieval Perspective," in *The Boswell Thesis: Essays on Christianity, Social Tolerance, and Homosexuality,* ed. Mathew Kuefler (Chicago: University of Chicago Press, 2006), 254–72.

38. Caesarius of Heisterbach, 8:42, 2:114.

39. William of Tocco, *Ystoria sancti Thome de Aquino,* 11, ed. Claire le Brun-Gouanvic, Studies and Texts 127 (Toronto: Pontifical Institute of Mediaeval Studies, 1996), 112–13.

40. J. F. Niemeyer and C. van de Kieft, *Mediae Latinitatis Lexicon Minor,* rev. ed. J. W. J. Burgers (Leiden: Brill, 2002), 1:236, s.v. "cingulum."

41. Jocelyn Wogan-Browne, *Saints' Lives and Women's Literary Culture, c. 1150–1300: Virginity and Its Authorizations* (Oxford: Oxford University Press, 2001), 123–50.

42. Arnold, "The Labour of Continence, 111.

43. J. T. Muckle, ed., "Abelard's Letter of Consolation to a Friend (*Historia Calamitatum*)," *Mediaeval Studies* 12 (1950): 205.

44. *Life of Christina,* 44: 114–15.

45. *AASS, Ian. I* (January 4), "De B. Angela de Fulginio," c. 20, 228.

46. *AASS, Iun. IV* (June 22), "De B. Christina Stumbelensi," c. 10, 454. Similarly, *AASS, Nov. II Pars I* (November 3), "De beata Alpaide virgine," 203, fighting "viriliter" against temptation of an unspecified kind.

47. Elliott, *Fallen Bodies,* 14–34; see also James Brundage, "Obscene and Lascivious: Behavioral Obscenity in Canon Law," in *Obscenity: Social Control and Artistic Creation in the European Middle Ages,* ed. Jan Ziolkowski (Leiden: Brill, 1998), 252–59; Leyser, "Masculinity in Flux."

48. Joan Cadden, *Meanings of Sex Difference in the Middle Ages: Medicine, Science, and Culture* (Cambridge: Cambridge University Press, 1993), 141–42.

49. Elliott, *Fallen Bodies,* 14–15.

50. Karras, *From Boys to Men,* 44–47.

51. Megan McLaughlin, "The Bishop as Bridegroom: Marital Imagery and Clerical Celibacy in the Eleventh and Early Twelfth Centuries," in *Medieval Purity and Piety,* 224; for a later medieval example, see Ruth Mazo Karras, "The Latin Vocabulary of Illicit Sex in English Ecclesiastical Court Records," *Journal of Medieval Latin* 2 (1992), 1–17, esp.3 n. 6.

52. Caroline Walker Bynum, *Jesus as Mother: Studies in the Spirituality of the High Middle Ages* (Berkeley: University of California Press, 1982), 110–169.

53. This was especially the case in the interpretation of the Song of Songs. See E. Ann Matter, *The Voice of My Beloved: The Song of Songs in Western Medieval Christianity* (Philadelphia: University of Pennsylvania Press, 1990), 86–150.

54. *Ancrene Wisse* 4:690–92, ed. J. R. R. Tolkien, EETS O.S. 249 (London: Oxford University Press, 1962), 121.

55. Caesarius, 4:93, 1:260.

Chapter 4. Women's Monasteries and Sacred Space

1. Jo Ann McNamara and John E. Halborg, eds. and trans., *Sainted Women of the Dark Ages* (Durham, N.C.: Duke University Press, 1992), 148.

2. P.-A. Sigal, "Reliques, pèlerinage et miracles dans l'église médiévale (XIe–XIIIe siècles)," *Revue d'Histoire de l'Eglise de France*, 76 (1990): 193–211.

3. For relics and miracle cults, see Benedicta Ward, *Miracles and the Medieval Mind: Theory, Record and Event, 1000–1215* (Philadelphia: University of Pennsylvania Press, 1982); Ben Nilson, *Cathedral Shrines of Medieval England* (Rochester, NY: Boydell, 1998); John Crook, *The Architectural Setting of the Cult of Saints in the Early Christian West, c. 300–1200* (Oxford: Oxford University Press, 2000); Alan Thacker and Richard Sharpe, eds., *Local Saints and Local Churches in the Early Medieval West* (Oxford: Oxford University Press, 2002); Bat-Sheva Albert, *Le Pèlerinage à l'époque carolingienne* (Brussels: Nauwelaerts, 1999); Société des historiens médiévistes de l'enseignement supérieur public, ed., *Miracles, prodiges et merveilles au moyen âge: XXVe Congrès de la SHMES, Orléans, juin 1994* (Paris: Publications de la Sorbonne, 1995); David Rollason, *Saints and Relics in Anglo-Saxon England* (Oxford: Blackwell, 1989); Raymond Van Dam, *Saints and Their Miracles in Late Antique Gaul* (Princeton, N.J.: Princeton University Press, 1993); Martin Heinzelmann, Klaus Herbers, and Dieter R. Bauer, eds., *Mirakel im Mittelalter: Konzeptionen, Erscheinungsformen, Deutungen* (Stuttgart: Steiner, 2002); Ronald C. Finucane, *Miracles and Pilgrims: Popular Beliefs in Medieval England* (Totowa, N.J.: Rowman and Littlefield, 1977); P.-A. Sigal, *L'Homme et le miracle dans la France médiévale (XIe–XIIe siècle)* (Paris: Cerf, 1985); Thomas Head, ed., *Medieval Hagiography: An Anthology* (New York: Garland, 2000); Peter Brown, *Society and the Holy in Late Antiquity* (Berkeley: University of California Press, 1982); Peter Brown, *The Cult of the Saints: Its Rise and Function in Latin Christianity* (Chicago: University of Chicago Press, 1981); Susan J. Ridyard, *The Royal Saints of Anglo-Saxon England: A Study of West Saxon and East Anglian Cults* (Cambridge: Cambridge University Press, 1988); Nicole Herrmann-Mascard, *Les reliques des saints: formation coutumière d'un droit* (Paris: Klincksieck, 1975); Marcia Kupfer, *The Art of Healing: Painting for the Sick and the Sinner in a Medieval Town* (University Park. Penn State University Press, 2003); Patrick Geary, *Furta Sacra: Thefts of Relics in the Central Middle Ages*, rev. ed. (Princeton, N.J.: Princeton University Press, 1990); Edina Bozóky and Anne-Marie Helvétius, eds., *Les reliques: Objets, cultes, symboles: actes du colloque international de l'Université du Littoral-Côte d'Opale, Boulogne-sur-Mer, 4–6 septembre 1997* (Turnhout: Brepols, 1999); Jean Chélini, *L'Aube du moyen âge: Naissance de la chrétienté occidentale. La vie religieuse des laïcs dans l'Europe carolingienne (750–900)* (Paris: Picard, 1991); Cynthia Hahn, "Seeing and Believing: The Construction of Sanctity in Early-Medieval Saints' Shrines," *Speculum* 72 (1997): 1079–106; Werner Jacobsen, "Saints' Tombs in Frankish Church Architecture," *Speculum* 72 (1997): 1107–43; Anne-Marie Korte, ed., *Women and Miracle*

Stories: A Multidisciplinary Exploration (Leiden: Brill, 2000); B. Brennan, "St. Radegund and the Early Development of Her Cult at Poitiers," *Journal of Religious History* 13.4 (1985): 340–54; Julia M. H. Smith, "Women at the Tomb: Access to Relic Shrines in the Early Middle Ages," in *The World of Gregory of Tours,* ed. Kathleen Mitchell and Ian Wood (Leiden: Brill, 2002), 163–80.

4. Victoria Tudor, "The Cult of St. Cuthbert in the Twelfth Century," in *Saint Cuthbert, His Cult and His Community to A.D. 1200,* ed. Gerald Bonner, David Rollason, and Clare Stancliffe (Woodbridge: Boydell, 1989), 457–58; Henry Mayr-Harting, "Functions of a Twelfth-Century Shrine: The Miracles of St. Frideswide," in *Studies in Medieval History Presented to R. H. C. Davis,* ed. Henry Mayr-Harting and R. I. Moore (London: Hambledon Press, 1985), 193–206; Kathleen Quirk, "Men, Women and Miracles in Normandy, 1050–1150," in *Medieval Memories: Men, Women and the Past, 700–1300,* ed. Elisabeth M. C. van Houts (Harlow: Longman, 2001), 54; Elisabeth M. C. van Houts, *Memory and Gender in Medieval Europe, 900–1200* (Basingstoke, Hampshire: Macmillan, 1999), 54–56.

5. Jane Tibbetts Schulenburg, "Gender, Celibacy, and Proscriptions of Sacred Space: Symbol and Practice," in *Women's Space: Patronage, Place, and Gender in the Medieval Church* ed. Virginia Chieffo Raguin and Sarah Stanbury (Albany: State University of New York Press, 2005), 185–205.

6. McNamara, *Sainted Women of the Dark Ages,* 94.

7. Ibid., 95–96.

8. Ibid., 96–97.

9. Ibid., 97–99.

10. Ibid., 98.

11. *Vita Sanctae Geretrudis* in Paul Fouracre and Richard A. Gerberding, *Late Merovingian France: History and Hagiography 640–720* (Manchester: University of Manchester Press, 1996), 322.

12. Ibid., 232–33.

13. David Rollason, *The Mildrith Legend: A Study in Early Medieval Hagiography in England* (Leicester: Leicester University Press, 1982), 36, 76, 78, 98, 127–28; St. Mildred, *AASS, Iul. III* (July 13), 490–93.

14. Jean-Pierre LaPorte, "Les reliques de Chelles, un sépulture royale mérovingienne," *Bulletin de la société nationale des antiquaires de France* (1989): 290–303; Yitzhak Hen, "Les authentiques des reliques de la Terre Sainte en Gaule franque," *Le moyen âge: Revue d'histoire et de philologie* 105.1 (1999):74–77, 82.

15. James O'Carroll, "Sainte Fare et les origines," in *Sainte Fare et Faremoutiers: Treize siècles de vie monastique,* ed. Gabriel LeBras (Faremoutiers: Abbaye de Faremoutiers, 1956), 38.

16. Walter Goffart, "Le Mans, St. Scholastica and St. Benedict," *Revue Bénédictine* 77 (1967): 107–41 and no. 1, p. 128; Edina Bozóky, "Le role des reines et princesses dans les translations de reliques," in *Reines et princesses au moyen âge: Actes du cinquième colloque international de Montpellier-Université Paul Valéry,* vol. 1 (November 24–27, 1999), ed., Marcel Faure (Montpellier: Université Paul-Valéry, 2001), 351–52.

17. St. Richardis, *AASS, Sep. V* (Sept. 18), 797–98. There is apparently no historical evidence that she actually made the pilgrimages.

18. *Translatio S. Pusinnae, AASS, Apr. III* (April 23), 171–72.

19. *Vita Sanctae Hathumodae, PL* 137: 1171; Thietmar of Merseburg, *Ottonian Germany: The Chronicon of Thietmar of Merseburg* trans. David A.Warner (Manchester: Manchester University Press, 2001), Bk. 2, ch. 19, pp. 105–6.

20. Bozóky, "Le role des reines et princesses," 352; S. Servais/Servatius, *AASS, Maii III* (May 13), 218–19; Walter Wulf, *Saxe romane* (L'Abbaye Sainte-Marie de la Pierre-Qui-Vire: Zodiaque, 1996), 359–66.

21. Goscelin of St. Bertin,*The Vita of Edith*, c. 14, pp. 44–45, and *The Translatio of Edith*, c. 6, 74, in *Writing the Wilton Women: Goscelin's "Legend of Edith" and "Liber confortatorius,"* ed. Stephanie Hollis with W. R. Barnes, Rebecca Hayward, Kathleen Loncar, and Michael Wright (Turnhout: Brepols, 2004); Ridyard, *The Royal Saints of Anglo-Saxon England*, 145–46.

22. J. Guerout, "La Période Carolingienne," in Yves Chaussy, J. Dupâquier, G. Goetz et al., eds., *L'Abbaye royale Notre-Dame de Jouarre*, vol. 1 (Paris: G. Victor, 1961), p. 71.

23. Ibid., 72–73.

24. *Catalogus codicum hagiographicorum latinorum antiquiorum saeculo XVI qui asservantur in Bibliotheca nationali Parisiensi*, Vol. 2 (Brussels: Société des Bollandistes, 1890), 349.

25. Chaussy, *L'Abbaye royale Notre-Dame de Jouarre*, 76–77.

26. Geary, *Furta Sacra*, 111–12, 115.

27. Médard Barth, "Die Legende und Verehrung der hl. Attala, die ersten Aebtissin von St. Stephan in Strassburg," *Archiv für Elsässische Kirchengeschichte* 2 (1927): 123–25; Jane T. Schulenburg, *Forgetful of Their Sex: Female Sanctity and Society, ca. 500–1100* (Chicago: University of Chicago Press, 1998), 361.

28. Jane T. Schulenburg, "Strict Active Enclosure and Its Effects on the Female Monastic Experience (ca. 500–1100), in *Distant Echoes*, Vol. 1, *Medieval Religious Women*, ed. John Nichols and Lillian Thomas Shank (Kalamazoo, Mich.: Cistercian Publications, 1984), 51–86.

29. Caesarius of Arles, *The Rule for Nuns of St. Caesarius of Arles: A Translation with a Critical Introduction*, trans. with an introduction by Maria Caritas McCarthy (Washington, D.C.: Catholic University Press, 1960), ch. 36, pp. 182–83, 150.

30. McNamara and Halborg, *Sainted Women of the Dark Ages*, 103; Raymond Van Dam, trans. *Gregory of Tours, Glory of the Confessors* (Liverpool: Liverpool University Press, 1988), ch. 104, p. 107.

31. McNamara and Halborg, *Sainted Women of the Dark Ages*, 135; Caesarius of Arles, *Oeuvres monastiques: Oeuvres pour les moniales. Sources Chrétiennes*, no. 345, intro. and trans. Adalbert de Vogüé and Joël Courreau (Paris: Cerf, 1988), 98–111. See also William E. Klingshirn, "Caesarius's Monastery for Women in Arles and the Composition and Function of the '*Vita Caesarii*'" *Revue Bénédictine* 100 (1990): 441–81, and William E. Klingshirn, *Caesarius of Arles: The Making of a Christian Community* (Cambridge: Cambridge University Press, 1994).

32. Barbara Rosenwein, "Inaccessible Cloisters: Gregory of Tours and Episcopal Exemption," in *The World of Gregory of Tours*, 181–97; Smith, "Women at the Tomb."

33. Jean-Jacques Hoebanx, *L'Abbaye de Nivelles des origines au XIVe siècle* (Brussels: Palais des Académies, 1951), 65–66; *AASS, Sept. VI* (Sept. 22), 527; *AASS, Iul. II* (July 4), 50–51; *De virtutibus Sanctae Geretrudis, MGH, SRM* 2:469, c. 10; McNamara and Halborg, *Sainted Women of the Dark Ages,* 314; Geneviève Aliette de Rohan-Chabot, marquise de Maillé, *Les Cryptes de Jouarre* (Paris: Picard, 1971), 41; Edward James, "Archaeology and the Merovingian Monastery," in *Columbanus and Merovingian Monasticism*, ed. H. B. Clarke and Mary Brennan, BAR International Series 113 (Oxford: British Archeological Reports, 1981), 41–44.

34. Robert Favreau, "Le culte de Sainte Radegonde à Poitiers au Moyen Age," in *Les Religieuses dans le cloître et dans le monde des origines à nos jours (Actes du deuxième colloque international du CERCOR, Poitiers 29 septembre–2 octobre 1988)*

(Saint-Etienne: Publications de l'Université de Saint-Etienne, 1994), 91–93; McCarthy, *The Rule for Nuns of St. Caesarius of Arles*, 19–25; Klingshirn, *Caesarius of Arles*, 104–6, 117–24; McNamara and Halborg, *Sainted Women of the Dark Ages*, 135.

35. McNamara and Halborg, *Sainted Women of the Dark Ages*, 231, 234.

36. Raymond Van Dam, trans., *Gregory of Tours, Glory of the Martyrs* (Liverpool: Liverpool University Press, 1988) ch. 5, pp. 22–23; ch. 15, p. 96.

37. Rosenwein, "Inaccessible Cloisters," 192–93; McNamara and Halborg, *Sainted Women of the Dark Ages*, 99; Van Dam, *Gregory of Tours, Glory of the Martyrs* ch. 5, p. 24.

38. Klingshirn, *Caesarius of Arles*, 122.

39. McNamara and Halbourg, *Sainted Women of the Dark Ages*, 146.

40. "If some pilgrim or guest comes in need they cannot join the sisters at meal-time but afterwards they may be given a space for their refreshment with the cook or the servants," and "Neither man nor woman is allowed to eat or drink within the monastery walls or gate. But they shall minister to all comers outside in the hospice." (Jo Ann McNamara and John Halborg, trans., *The Rule of a Certain Father to the Virgins*, 2nd ed. [Toronto: Peregrina Publishing, 1993], ch. 3, p. 80).

41. McNamara and Halbourg, *Sainted Women of the Dark Ages*, 301.

42. Ibid., 301–2.

43. Ibid., miracles that occurred at Saint Anstrude's chair—chs. 32, 35, p. 302; miracles at Saint Gertrude's bed—ch. 4, p. 230; ch. 5, p. 231; ch. 9, p. 232.

44. Ibid., 318–25.

45. Ibid., 299–303.

46. Albert, *Le Pèlerinage à l'époque carolingienne*, 100–127; Herrmann-Mascard, *Les Reliques des saints*, 82–87; Chélini, *L'Aube du moyen âge*, 319–22.

47. Chélini, *L'Aube du moyen age*, 272; Suzanne Fonay Wemple, *Women in Frankish Society: Marriage and the Cloister, 500 to 900* (Philadelphia: University of Pennsylvania Press, 1981), 143–48.

48. Schulenburg, *Forgetful of Their Sex*, 308–21; Schulenburg, "Gender, Celibacy and Proscriptions of Sacred Space."

49. Schulenburg, "Strict Active Enclosure," 56–60.

50. *MGH Capitularia* I:76.

51. Crook, *The Architectural Setting of the Cult of Saints*; Jacobsen, "Saints' Tombs in Frankish Church Architecture"; Charles B. McClendon, *The Origins of Medieval Architecture: Building in Europe, A.D. 600–900*, (New Haven, Conn.: Yale University Press, 2005), esp. ch. 2, 7–9; Smith, "Women at the Tomb;" Sigal, "Reliques, pèlerinage et miracles."

52. Crook, *The Architectural Setting of the Cult of Saints*; Jacobsen, "Saints' Tombs in Frankish Church Architecture"; Alain Dierkens, "Réflexions sur le miracle au haut moyen âge," in *Miracles, prodiges et merveilles au moyen âge: XXVe congrès de la S.H.M.E.S., Orleans, Juin 1994*, ed. SHMES (Paris: Publications de la Sorbonne, 1995), 9–30.

53. Anne-Marie Helvétius, "Hagiographie et architecture en Basse-Lotharingie médievale," in *Productions et échanges artistiques en Lotharingie médiévale: Actes des 7es Journées Lotharingiennes*, ed. Jean Schroeder (Luxembourg: CLUDEM, 1994), 27–45.

54. Schulenburg, "Gender, Celibacy and Proscriptions of Sacred Space," 194–99; Dierkens, "Réflexions sur le miracle au haut moyen âge," esp. 26–28; Smith, "Women at the Tomb."

55. McNamara and Halborg, *Sainted Women of the Dark Ages*, 137–41.

56. Ibid., 146.

57. Ibid.

58. Ibid., 146–148.

59. Ibid., 152–53.

60. Ibid., 148–50.

61. Ibid., 148.

62. Ibid., 149.

63. Ibid., 154.

64. Andreas Bauch, ed. *Ein bayerisches Mirakelbuch aus der Karolingerzeit: Die monheimer Walpurgis—Wunder des Priesters Wolfhard* (*Quellen zur Geschichte der Diözese Eichstätt,* Vol. 2) (Regensburg: Friedrich Pustet, 1979), bk. I, 5–8, p. 112.

65. Ibid., 73–78. A total of sixty illnesses were described, with fourteen of the forty-six listed as being cured of several ailments.

66. Ibid., 75–77.

67. Ibid., 125–26.

68. Ibid., 54–55.

69. Ibid., 126.

70. Ibid., bk. IV, 1; bk. III, 1, p. 54; "Kurkarte Fernbezirke."

71. Ibid., bk. III, 2; bk. IV, 5b, p. 115.

72. Ibid., bk. I, 10; bk. I, 14; bk. I, 15; bk. I, 17–19, p. 85.

73. Ibid., 116.

74. Ibid., bk. II, 5; bk. III, 8; bk. III, 9, p. 114.

75. Ibid., bk. IV, 12c, pp. 118–19.

76. Ibid., bk. IV, 7, pp. 118–19.

77. Ibid., 64–66; e.g., bk. IV, 11.

78. Ibid., bk. I, 19, p. 115.

79. Ibid., 27–28; bk. III, 9, pp. 114–15.

80. D. W. Rollason, "Lists of Saints' Resting-Places in Anglo-Saxon England," *Anglo-Saxon England* (1978): 61–93; Barbara Yorke, *Nunneries and the Anglo-Saxon Royal Houses* (London: Continuum, 2003), esp. 129.

81. Ridyard, *The Royal Saints of Anglo-Saxon England,* 16–17, 96–103, 104, no. 30. See also Laurel Braswell, "Saint Edburga of Winchester: A Study of Her Cult, A.D. 950–1500, with an Edition of the Fourteenth-Century Middle English and Latin Lives," *Mediaeval Studies* 33 (1971): 292–333, esp. 292–96.

82. Ridyard, *The Royal Saints of Anglo-Saxon England,* 15–17, 286–89.

83. Ibid., 105; ch. 17, pp. 288–89.

84. Ibid., ch. 17, p. 288.

85. Ibid., 113–14.

86. Ibid., ch. 21, pp. 114, 294–95.

87. Ibid., ch. 18, pp. 113, 291.

88. Ibid., ch. 21–25, p. 119.

89. Ibid., 120. Alan Thacker has argued for a more important role for royalty in the establishment and promotion of the cult of Saint Edburga in the light of the contemporary veneration for Edith and Elfgifu and the establishment of the royal nunneries at Winchester, Shaftesbury, and Polesworth; see Alan Thacker, "Dynastic Monasteries and Family Cults: Edward the Elder's Sainted Kindred," in *Edward the Elder 899–924,* ed. N. J. Higham and D. H. Hill (London: Routledge, 2001), esp. 259–60.

90. Yorke, *Nunneries and the Anglo-Saxon Royal Houses,* esp. 129; see also Graham Scobie and Ken Qualmann, *Nunnaminster: A Saxon and Medieval Community of Nuns* (Winchester: Winchester Museums Service, 1993).

91. Madelyn Bergen Dick, *Mater Spiritualis: The Life of Adelheid of Vilich* (Toronto: Peregrina, 1994).

92. Ibid., ch. 9, p. 36.

93. Ibid., ch. 8, pp. 35–36.
94. Ibid., ch. 9, p. 36.
95. Ibid., ch. 9, pp. 36–37.
96. Ibid., 94.
97. Ibid., ch. 10, p. 37.
98. Ibid., ch. 10–13, pp. 37–40.
99. Ibid., ch. 10, p. 37.
100. McNamara and Halborg, *Sainted Women of the Dark Ages*, 151.
101. Dick, *Mater Spiritualis*, ch. 11, p. 38.
102. Ibid.
103. McNamara and Halborg, *Sainted Women of the Dark Ages*, 96.
104. *Virtutum sanctae Geretrudis continuatio, MGH, SRM,* II: 473–74; see also Hoebanx, *L'Abbaye de Nivelles*, 69, 123.
105 Dick, *Mater Spiritualis*, ch. 13, p. 40.
106. Bauch, *Ein bayerisches Mirakelbuch*, 29, 63, 87, 111, 114, 118 ff., 371 (I, 11; I, 12; I, 16; II, 1; II, 4; II, 8; IV, 3; IV, 12b).
107. Ibid., 88 (I, 11; II, 2; IV, 2; IV, 3; IV, 5; IV, 12).
108. See, for example, the extensive list of relics collected by Angilbert for Saint Riquier (Angilbert, *De ecclesia Centulensi Libellus, MGH*, 55, XV, 1, 176, cited by Chélini, *L'Aube du moyen âge*, 324–25).
109. Michael Lapidge, with contributions by John Crook, Robert Deshman, and Susan Rankin, *The Cult of St. Swithun* (Oxford: Clarendon Press, 2003), 147.
110. Ibid., 252–333, esp. 298–99, 306–7.
111. Ibid., 328–31.
112. Flodoard, *PL:*135, bk. 4, ch. 47, col. 321D.
113. E. M. C. Van Houts, "Orality in Norman Hagiography of the Eleventh and Twelfth Centuries: The Value of Female Testimonies," in *History and Family Traditions in England and the Continent, 1000–1200,* ed. E. M. C. van Houts (Aldershot, Hampshire: Ashgate, 1999), XV, 1–13.

Chapter 5. Priestly Women, Virginal Men

Research for the litanies portion of this chapter was financially supported by the Deutscher Akademischer Austauschdient during the fall semester 1997. For every other kind of support, I gratefully acknowledge the academic and professional staffs of the University of Freiburg (particularly the manuscript reading room and the Abteilung Landesgeschichte). For insisting on the need to consider Aldhelm in connection with the litanies, I thank Clare Stancliffe. A first attempt to articulate the bipartite argument of this chapter was made in a presentation at the University of South Florida in November 2005. I thank James D'Emilio and other members of the University of South Florida community for the invitation and for their vigorous questioning after the talk. Finally, this chapter has benefited from the critiques of the two anonymous readers for the press.

1. Marcel Metzger, *Les Sacramentaires* (Turnhout: Brepols, 1994), 70, 138.
2. Felice Lifshitz, *The Name of the Saint: The Martyrology of Jerome and Access to the Sacred in Francia, 627–827* (Notre Dame, Ind.: University of Notre Dame Press, 2005), 24–25.
3. Felice Lifshitz, "Gender Trouble in Paradise: The Case of the Liturgical *Virgo*" in *Images of Medieval Sanctity: Essays in Honour of Gary Dickson,* ed. Debra Higgs Strickland (Leiden: Brill, 2007), 25–39.

4. Dante Gemmiti, *La Donna in Origene (con testimonianzi dei primi tre secoli)* (Naples: Libreria Editrice Redenzione, 1996), 250–51.

5. Maurice Zufferey, "Der Mauritiuskult im Früh– und Hochmittelalter," *Historisches Jahrbuch* 106 (1986), 23–58, at 33.

6. Jo Ann McNamara, *A New Song: Celibate Women in the First Three Christian Centuries* (Binghamton, N.Y.: Harrington Park Press, 1983), 108–109, 123.

7. Kathleen Coyne Kelly, *Performing Virginity and Testing Chastity in the Middle Ages* (London: Routledge, 2000), 141. For the term *virginologist*, see vi–vii.

8. Kelly, *Performing Virginity*, 15.

9. For instance, in the Freising litany of approximately 800, edited by Maurice Coens, from Munich, Bayerische Staatsbibliothek, MS Clm. 1086, in "Anciennes litanies des saints" in *Recueil d'études bollandiennes*, ed. M. Coens (Brussels: Société des Bollandistes, 1963), 129–322, at 173.

10. Katherine Ludwig Jansen, *The Making of the Magdalen: Preaching and Popular Devotion in the Later Middle Ages* (Princeton, N.J.: Princeton University Press, 2000), esp. 168–96.

11. Jansen, *Making of the Magdalen*, 287–93, esp. 288.

12. Anne-Marie Helvétius, "*Virgo* et *virago*: réflexions sur le pouvoir du voile consacré d'après les sources hagiographiques de la Gaule de nord," in *Femmes et pouvoirs des femmes à Byzance et en Occident (VIᵉ – XIᵉ siècles)*, ed. Stéphane Lebecq, Alain Dierkens, Régine Le Jan, and Jean-Marie Sansterre (Villeneuve d'Ascq: Centre de recherche sur l'histoire de l'Europe du Nord-Ouest, Université Charles de Gaulle-Lille 3, 1999), 189–204, esp. 192.

13. Helvétius, "*Virgo* et *virago*," 195.

14. Ibid., 195.

15. Ibid., 190.

16. Katrien Heene, *The Legacy of Paradise: Marriage, Motherhood and Woman in Carolingian Edifying Literature* (Frankfurt am Main: Peter Lang, 1997), 248–54.

17. Jansen, *Making of the Magdalen,* 243.

18. For Mary as an exemplary figure in Christian spirituality, see Barbara Newman, *From Virile Woman to WomanChrist: Studies in Medieval Religion and Literature* (Philadelphia: University of Pennsylvania Press, 1995).

19. The phrase, which can mean both that Mary is a virgin who is not a virgin and that Mary is a virgin who is not a simplex person, alludes to Luce Irigaray, *Ce sexe qui n'en est pas un* (Paris: Editions de Minuit, 1977), an early classic of feminist theory available in English translation as *This Sex Which Is Not One*, trans. Catherine Porter (Ithaca, N.J.: Cornell University Press, 1985).

20. The details that follow are all taken from Mary Clayton, *The Cult of the Virgin Mary in Anglo-Saxon England* (Cambridge: Cambridge University Press, 1990); for additional information, see Mary Clayton, *The Apocryphal Gospels of Mary in Anglo-Saxon England* (Cambridge: Cambridge University Press, 1998).

21. Clayton, *Cult of the Virgin*, 6.

22. Ibid., 7.

23. Ibid., 39.

24. Ibid., 221.

25. Paris, Bibliothèque Nationale, MS latin 12048 fol. 1v. See *Liber Sacramentorum Gellonensis*, introduced by J. Deshusses (vol. 1) and edited by A. Dumas (vol. 2) (Turnhout: Brepols, 1981).

26. Clayton, *Cult of the Virgin*, 152–53. For further discussion of gender in the visual arts around 800, see Felice Lifshitz, "The Persistence of Late Antiquity: Christ

as Man and Woman in an Eighth-Century Miniature," *Medieval Feminist Forum* 38 (2004), 18–27.

27. Clayton, *Cult of the Virgin*, 144–46.

28. "seo aeþele cwen þara uplica cesterwara, seo stondeþ on þa swyþran healfe daes Heahfaeder ond daes Heahkyninges," from *Das Altenglische Martyrologium*, Vol. 2, ed. Günter Kotzor (Munich: C. H. Beck, 1981), 2.

29. See Clayton, *Cult of the Virgin*, 55–61, 221–39, and 253–54, for these quotes and for additional fervent claims about Mary.

30. For this and for what follows, see Clayton, *Cult of the Virgin*, 95–104.

31. The Book of Nunnaminster is now London, British Library, MS Harley 2965, written around 800.

32. The Book of Cerne is now Cambridge, University Library, MS Ll.I.10, a Mercian manuscript of the early ninth century.

33. The poem is attested uniquely in the Exeter Book (now Exeter, Cathedral Library, MS 3501), a manuscript of the latter part of the tenth century; nevertheless, Clayton and others date its composition to the early part of the ninth century in Mercia.

34. The manuscript is now London, British Library, MS Royal 2.A.XX; the litany appears on folios 26rv of the manuscript and as no. xxvi in Michael Lapidge, ed., *Anglo-Saxon Litanies of the Saints* (Woodbridge, Suffolk: Boydell, 1991), 212–13.

35. The other names on the list are Agnes, Agatha, Juliana, Caecilia, Anastasia, Lucia, Eugenia, Eulalia, and Eufemia.

36. The manuscript is now Orléans, Bibliothèque Municipale, MS 184. The litany is edited and discussed in Coens, "Anciennes litanies des saints," 185–204.

37. Freiburg im Breisgau, Universitätsbibliothek, MS 363. For a detailed description, see *Die lateinischen mittelalterlichen Handschriften der Universitätsbibliothek Freiburg im Breisgau*, vol. 2, ed. Winfried Hagenmaier (Wiesbaden: Harrassowitz, 1974–1980), 363.

38. For instance, "Intercessionibus et meritis sanctae N. virginis ab universis periculis protegat et custodeat nos dominus" ("May the lord protect and guard us from all dangers through the intercession and merits of the holy virgin [fill in the blank with a name]"). See folios 46v–47r.

39. Heene, *Legacy of Paradise*, 112–35.

40. William of Tocco, *Ystoria sancti Thome de Aquino*, vol. 11, ed. Claire le Brun-Gouanvic, Studies and Texts 127 (Toronto: Pontifical Institute of Medieval Studies, 1996), 112–13, cited by Karras, note 39, above.

41. Jo Ann McNamara, "The *Herrenfrage*: The Restructuring of the Gender System, 1050–1150," in *Medieval Masculinities: Regarding Men in the Middle Ages*, ed. Clare A. Lees (Minneapolis: University of Minnesota Press, 1994), 3–29, at 3.

42. Paris, Bibliothèque nationale, MS latin 12048 fol. 184r.

43. Carl R. Baldwin, "The Scriptorium of the Sacramentary of Gellone," *Scriptorium* 25 (1971): 3–17; Carl R. Baldwin, "The Scribes of the Sacramentary of Gellone," *Scriptorium* 27 (1973): 16–20.

44. *Aldhelmi Malmesbiriensis Prosa de Virginitate cum Glosa Latina atque Anglosaxonica*, ed. and int. Scottus Gwara (Turnhout: Brepols, 2001). The text is known as the "Prosa de Virginitate" (abbreviated *Pdv*) to distinguish it from Aldhelm's verse treatise on the same subject. The text is available in English translation as Aldhelm, *The Prose Works*, trans. Michael Lapidge and Michael Herren (Ipswich: D. S. Brewer, 1979).

45. For instance, Gwara, *Pdv*, 70*.

46. Aldhelm, *Prose Works*, 96–99; Gwara, *Pdv*, 455–91. The story of Julian and Basilissa, the other virgin couple, is similar (Aldhelm, *Prose Works*, 99–102; Gwara, *Pdv*, 491–531).

47. Aldhelm, *Prose Works*, 106–7; Gwara, *Pdv*, 581–89.

48. Ibid., 11.

49. "nurus patris, genetrix et germana filii simulque sponsa . . . sanctarum socrus animarum, supernorum regina civium . . ." (Aldhelm, *Prose Works*, 106; Gwara, *Pdv*, 583).

50. Gwara, *Pdv*, 23*–63*, esp. 24*, 41*–46*; G. T. Dempsey, "Aldhelm of Malmesbury's Social Theology: The Barbaric Heroic Ideal Christianized," *Peritia* 15 (2001), 58–80, esp. 77.

51. Gwara, *Pdv*, 55*; Sinéad O'Sullivan, "The Image of Adornment in Aldhelm's *De Virginitate*: Cyprian and His Influence," *Peritia*, 15 (2001), 48–57; Sinéad O'Sullivan, "Aldhelm's *De Virginitate* — Patristic Pastiche or Innovative Exposition?" *Peritia* 12 (1998), 271–95; Clare A. Lees and Gillian R. Overing, "Before History, Before Difference: Bodies, Metaphors and the Church in Anglo-Saxon England," *Yale Journal of Criticism* 11 (1998), 315–34, esp. 318–19. Even Dempsey, who situates Aldhelm's project in the context of a warrior ethos, discusses the treatise as if its audience were entirely female. His argument is not that Aldhelm constructed an ideal of virginity suitable to men because it was heroic, but rather that Aldhelm constructed an ideal of virginity suitable to a barbaric society because it involved violent struggle ("Aldhelm's Social Theology," 77–80).

52. Gwara, *Pdv*, 51*–54*. For a reasoned rejection of Gwara's hypothesis, see the review of Gwara by Gernot R. Wieland in *The Medieval Review* 04.01.04, http://name.umdl.umich.edu/baj9928.0401.001. In response to Wieland, I would note that the fact that Hildelith is named first and alone is called a *magistra* does not necessarily mean that she is the only abbess addressed, only that she was the only abbess possessed of a reputation for special pedagogical abilities. The position of abbess in Anglo-Saxon aristocratic monasteries generally came to a woman because of her family connections, not because of her formidable intellect. The majority of abbesses were run-of-the-mill noble girls. Gwara's arguments have also been accepted by Emma Pettit, "Holiness and Masculinity in Aldhelm's *Opus Geminatum de Virginitate*," in *Holiness and Masculinity in the Middle Ages*, ed. P. H. Cullum and Katherine J. Lewis (Cardiff: University of Wales Press, 2004), 8–23, at 10. Accordingly, Pettit analyzes the text from the perspective of an intended male audience; however, she concentrates on Aldhelm's use of a warrior idiom and a military ethos as key to his text's appeal to men, with no mention of virginity.

53. Catherine Rosanna Peyroux, "Abbess and Cloister: Double Monasteries in the Early Medieval West" (Ph.D. diss. Princeton University, 1991), 219–44.

54. Only one extant copy of the treatise has any chance of having ever been associated with a women's community (although no one has ever positively suggested that it was): Cambridge, University Library, MS Additional 4219, an eighth- or ninth-century fragment from the area of the Anglo-Saxon missions in Germany. For the manuscript, see E. A. Lowe, ed., *Codices latini antiquiores: A Paleographical Guide to Latin Manuscripts Prior to the Ninth Century*, vol. 2 (Oxford: Clarendon Press, 1935), 135, and Gwara, *Pdv*, 83*–85*. It may be significant that this copy, unlike the many known to have been copied and used by men, has no glosses.

55. Würzburg, Universitätsbibliothek, MS M.p.th.f. 21. Gwara (*Pdv*, 77*–78* and 83*) raises the possibility that it was produced at Fulda, because of the use

by one of the scribes of a typically Fulda script. However, one such contribution is not enough to remove this codex from the Gozbald group of manuscripts. It is likely that the cathedral clergy of Würzburg simply included men educated at the major school in Fulda.

56. Gwara, *Pdv*, 9 (the *conspectus siglorum*), 85*–94* ("The Yale Fragment"), 94*–101* (Brussels, Bibliothèque Royale, MS 1650), 101*–106* (London, British Library, MS Royal 5 F.iii), 106*–108* (London, Lambeth Palace Library, MS 200 *pars* ii), 109*–113* (Cambridge, Corpus Christi College, MS 326), 113*–122* (London, British Library, MS Royal 6 B.vii), 122*–147* (London, British Library, MS Royal 7 D.xxiv *pars* ii), 147*–156* (Oxford, Bodleian Library, MS Digby 146), 163*–170* (Salisbury, Cathedral Library, MS 38), 170*–177* (London, British Library, MS Royal 5 E.xi), 177*–80* (London, British Library, MS Royal 6 A.vi), 180*–184* (Oxford, Bodleian Library, MS Bodley 97).

57. Gwara, *Pdv*, 217*; for graphic illustrations of the fever pitch of interest in Aldhelm during the late tenth century, as part of the reform movement, see Gwara's *stemma* and his compact list of the manuscripts with their dates of production and glossing (Gwara, *Pdv*, 187* and 189*–190*).

58. Gwara, *Pdv*, 157*–162* (Hereford, Cathedral Library, MS P.I.17) and 184*–187* (London, British Library, MS Harley 3013).

59. Gwara notes that "concern for virginity would seem to have been apposite in a time of renewed monasticism" but concludes that interest in Aldhelm in fact only derived from the latter's extraordinary style (Gwara, *Pdv*, 69*–70*).

60. Gwara (*Pdv*, 274*–308*) attributes the compilation of the common core of glosses to Aldhelm's own school at Malmesbury and rejects the argument that the Old English glosses were first added in the tenth century in the Winchester circle around Archbishop Æthelwold, the view taken by Mechthild Gretsch, *The Intellectual Foundations of the English Benedictine Reform* (Cambridge: Cambridge University Press, 1999). The most compelling aspect of Gwara's argument concerns the presence of some of the standard *scholia* in the ninth-century Würzburg manuscript; there the Latin glosses appear in their original form and the Old English ones appear in Old High German (Gwara, *Pdv*, 296*–303*).

61. Gwara CCSL 124, 71*–72*.

62. In the opening theoretical section, in which all discussion is gendered in the masculine, there are normally 5–9 lines of Latin text per page, with the majority of pages running at 6 or 7 lines of Latin text (Gwara, *Pdv*, 27–225). In the section discussing exemplary virgin males, there is normally a range of 5 to 8 lines of Latin text per page, with 6 or 7 again being the most common (225–577). In the transitional section concerning Mary, Cecilia, and their husbands, there are normally 6 to 8 lines of Latin text per page (577–89). In the section discussing female virgins, there are generally between 6 and 12 lines of Latin text per page, with the overwhelming majority of pages running at 10 to 12 lines of Latin text (589–699). In the final portion of the work in which Aldhelm moves into dogmatic warnings against lapses and condemnation of luxurious practices, there are generally 9 to 15 lines of Latin text per page, with 12 to 14 lines being the most common (699–761).

63. D. H. Farmer, "The Progress of the Monastic Revival," in *Tenth-Century Studies: Essays in Commemoration of the Millennium of the Council of Winchester and Regularis Concordia*, ed. David Parsons (London: Phillimore, 1975), 10–19, at 11; Dom Thomas Symons, "*Regularis Concordia*: History and Derivation," in Parsons, *Tenth-Century Studies*, 37–59, at 39.

64. H. R. Loyn, "Church and State in England in the Tenth and Eleventh Centuries," in Parsons, *Tenth-Century Studies*, 94–102, at 98–99.

65. The codex is London, British Library, MS Royal 7 D.xxiv *pars* ii (Gwara, *Pdv*, 122*–147*, esp. 142*).

66. Symons, *"Regularis Concordia,"* 37–38.

67. P. H. Sawyer, "Charters of the Reform Movement: The Worcester Archive," in Parsons, *Tenth-Century Studies*, 84–93, at 85.

68. Farmer, "Progress of the Monastic Revival," 13.

69. Loyn, "Church and State," 98.

70. Conrad Leyser, "Masculinity in Flux: Nocturnal Emission and the Limits of Celibacy in the Early Middle Ages," in *Masculinity in Medieval Europe*, D. M. Hadley (London: Longman, 1999), 103–120; Conrad Leyser, *Authority and Asceticism from Augustine to Gregory the Great* (Oxford: Oxford University Press, 2000); Kate Cooper and Conrad Leyser, "The Gender of Grace: Impotence, Servitude and Manliness in the Fifth-Century West," in *Gendering the Middle Ages*, ed. Pauline Stafford and Anneke E. Mulder-Bakker (Oxford: Blackwell, 2001), 5–21, esp. 9.

71. Leyser, "Masculinity in Flux," 105–6.

72. Leyser, *Authority and Asceticism*, vii and 186.

73. One of the first texts produced at Glastonbury, to initiate the reform movement, was a copy of Smaragdus's commentary on the Rule of St. Benedict (Donald Bullough, "The Continental Background of the Reform," in Parsons, *Tenth-Century Studies*, 20–36, at 26). At St. Augustine's (Canterbury), the scribe of one copy of Aldhelm's prose *De virginitate* also produced a copy of the works of Cassian; the Aldhelm manuscript is London, Lambeth Palace Library, MS 200 *pars* ii, and the Cassian manuscript is Oxford, Bodleian Library, MS Auct D. Inf. 2.9 (Gwara, *Pdv*, 106*–108*).

74. They cited Aldhelm in the Proem to the *Regularis Concordia* (ca. 970), the document that pulled together all the ideological strands of the reform movement and legislated for its future (Symons, *"Regularis Concordia,"* 47). For more examples of the reading of Aldhelm's *Pdv* by the tenth- and eleventh-century reformers, see Gareth Mann, "The Development of Wulfstan's Alcuin Manuscript," in *Wulfstan, Archbishop of York: The Proceedings of the Second Alcuin Conference*, ed. Matthew Townend (Turnhout: Brepols, 2004), 235–78, at 253–54; and Michael Lapidge, "Æthelwold as Scholar and Teacher," in *Bishop Æthelwold: His Career and Influence*, ed. Barbara Yorke (Woodbridge: Boydell, 1988), 89–117, esp. 92, 97–100, and 103.

75. For the main adherents of the Benedictine reform and the power they attained, see Patrick Wormald, "Archbishop Wulfstan: Eleventh-Century State-Builder," Joyce Hill, "Archbishop Wulfstan: Refomer?" and Jonathan Wilcox, "Wulfstan's *Sermo Lupi ad Anglos* as Political Performance: 16 February 1014 and Beyond," all in *Wulfstan*, 9–28, 309–24, and 375–96; Barbara Yorke, "Æthelwold and the Politics of the Tenth Century," in Yorke, *Bishop Æthelwold*, 65–88; and N. P. Brooks, "The Career of St. Dunstan," in *St. Dunstan: His Life, Times, and Cult*, ed. Nigel Ramsay, Margaret Sparks, and Tim Tatton-Brown (Woodbridge: Boydell, 1992), 1–24.

76. Emma Mason, *St. Wulfstan of Worcester, c. 1008–1095* (Oxford: Oxford University Press, 1990), 30–31.

77. On the reformers' commitment to sexual renunciation, see Mason, *St. Wulfstan*, 38–40 and 62–64.

78. The manuscript in question is the Leofric Missal (Oxford, Bodleian Library, MS Bodley 579) of the second half of the ninth century. The litanies are

printed in Lapidge, *Anglo-Saxon Litanies*, 225–230. The Leofric Missal is believed by most specialists to have been produced in Flanders or northeast France, but a reasonable argument has also been made in favor of it having been produced in England (C. E. Hohler, "Some Service Books of the Later Saxon Church," in Parsons, *Tenth-Century Studies*, 60–83, at 78–80). Wherever it was originally produced, it was at Glastonbury around 980 (Hohler, "Some Service Books," 69; J. J. G. Alexander, "The Benedictional of St. Æthelwold and Anglo-Saxon Illumination of the Reform Period," in Parsons, *Tenth-Century Studies*, 169–83, at 175). The litany forms part of the original codex, not the Glastonbury appendix.

Bibliography

Abbreviations

AASS—Bollandus, Johannes, et al. *Acta Sanctorum quotquot toto orbe coluntur.* Brussels: Société des Bollandistes, 1643–.
ANF—*The Ante-Nicene Fathers. Translations of the Writings of the Fathers down to A.D. 325.* Ed. Alexander Roberts and James Donaldson, revised by A. Cleveland Coxe. New York: Scribner's, 1988–1900, 10 vols., reprint, Grand Rapids, Mich.: William B. Eerdmans, 1986.
MGH—*Monumenta Germaniae historica.* Hannover: Hahn et al., 1826–.
PL—*Patrologiae cursus completus. Series Latina.* Ed. J.-P. Migne. 221 vols. Paris: Migne, 1844–1865.

Manuscript Sources

Brussels, Bibliothèque Royale
    1650
Cambridge, Corpus Christi College
    326
Cambridge, University Library
    Additional 4219
    Ll.I.10 (The Book of Cerne)
Exeter, Cathedral Library
    3501 (The Exeter Book)
Freiburg im Breisgau, Universitätsbibliothek
    363
Hereford, Cathedral Library
    P.I.17
London, British Library
    Harley 2965 (The Book of Nunnaminster)
    Harley 3013
    Royal 2.A.XX
    Royal 5 E.xi
    Royal 5 F.iii
    Royal 6 A.vi

Royal 6 B.vii
Royal 7 D.xxiv *pars* ii
London, Lambeth Palace Library
200 *pars* ii
Munich, Bayerische Staatsbibliothek
Clm. 1086
Orléans, Bibliothèque Municipale
184
Oxford, Bodleian Library
Auct D. Inf. 2.9
Bodley 97
Bodley 579 (The Leofric Missal)
Digby 146
Paris, Bibliothèque Nationale
Latin 12048 (The Sacramentary of Gellone)
Salisbury, Cathedral Library
MS 38
Würzburg, Universitätsbibliothek
M.p.th.f. 21

Printed Sources

Abelard, Peter. "Abelard's Letter of Consolation to a Friend (*Historia Calamitatum*)." Ed. J. T. Muckle. *Mediaeval Studies* 12 (1950): 163–213.
Abelard, Peter, and Heloise. *The Letters of Abelard and Heloise.* Trans. with an introduction by Betty Radice. Harmondsworth: Penguin Books, 1974.
Acts of the Christian Martyrs. Ed. and trans. Herbert Musurillo. Oxford: Oxford University Press, 1972.
Adam of Eynsham. *Magna vita sancti Hugonis.* 2nd ed. Ed. Decima L. Douie and Hugh Farmer. Oxford: Clarendon Press, 1985.
Adomnan. *Adomnan's Life of Columba.* Ed. and trans. A. O. Anderson and M. O. Anderson. Oxford: Clarendon Press, 1961.
Aldhelm, Saint. *Aldhelmi Malmesbiriensis prosa de virginitate: Cum glosa latina atque anglosaxonica.* Ed. with an introduction by Scott Gwara. Turnhout: Brepols, 2001.
———. *Aldhelm, the Prose Works.* Trans. Michael Lapidge and Michael Herren. Cambridge: D. S. Brewer, 1979.
Ancrene Wisse: The English Text of the Ancrene Riwle. Ed. J. R. R. Tolkien. Early English Text Society, Original Series 249. London: Oxford University Press, 1962.
Apocrypha and Pseudepigrapha of the Old Testament in English. Ed. and trans. R. H. Charles. Oxford: Clarendon Press, 1913. (Available at www.ccel.org/ccel/charles/otpseudepig.html.)
Augustine, Saint. *Quaestionum in heptateuchum libri VII.* Ed. I. Fraipont. Corpus Christianorum Series Latina 33. Turnhout: Brepols, 1958.
Biblia latina cum glossa ordinaria: Facsimile reprint of the editio princeps Adolph Rusch of Strassburg 1480/81. With an introduction by Karlfried Froehlich and Margaret T. Gibson. Turnhout: Brepols, 1992.
Caesarius of Arles. *The Rule for Nuns of St. Caesarius of Arles: A Translation with a Critical Introduction.* Trans. with an introduction by Maria Caritas McCarthy.

Catholic University of America Studies in Medieval History, New Series 16. Washington, D.C.: Catholic University Press, 1960.

———. *Oeuvres monastiques: Oeuvres pour les moniales.* Ed. and trans. Adalbert de Vogüé and Joël Courreau. Sources chrétiennes 345. Paris: Éditions du Cerf, 1988.

Caesarius of Heisterbach. *Dialogus miraculorum.* Ed. Joseph Strange. Cologne: Heberle, 1851.

Cassian, John. *De institutis coenoborium et de octo principalium vitiorum remediis libri XII.* Ed. Michael Petschenig. Corpus Christianorum Series Latina 17. Vienna: F. Tempsky, 1888.

Catalogus codicum hagiographicorum latinorum antiquiorum saeculo XVI qui asservantur in Bibliotheca nationali parisiensi. Subsidia Hagiographica 2. Brussels: Société des Bollandistes, 1880–1893.

Clare of Assisi, Saint. *Clare of Assisi: Early Documents.* Ed. and trans. Regis J. Armstrong. New York: Paulist Press, 1988.

Clement of Alexandria, Stromateis in *ANF* 2.

Conchubranus. "The Life of Saint Monenna by Conchubranus." Ed. and trans. Ulster Society for Medieval Latin Studies. *Seanchas Ardmhacha* 9 (1979): 250–73; 10 (1980–1981): 117–40; 11 (1982): 426–54.

Daniel, Walter. *The Life of Ailred of Rievaulx.* Trans. with notes by F. M. Powicke. London: Nelson, 1950.

Ethelwerd. *The Chronicle of Ætheweard.* Ed. A. Campbell. London: Nelson, 1962.

Goscelin of St. Bertin. "Vita" and "Translatio" of Edith. In *Writing the Wilton Women: Goscelin's "Legend of Edith" and "Liber Confortatorius."* Ed. Stephanie Hollis, with W.R. Baines, Rebecca Hayward, Kathleen Loncar, and Michael Wright. Turnhout: Brepols, 2004.

Gregory the Great. *Dialogues.* Trans. Odo John Zimmerman. New York: Fathers of the Church, 1959.

Gregory of Tours. *Glory of the Confessors.* Trans. Raymond Van Dam. Translated Texts for Historians, Latin Series 4. Liverpool: Liverpool University Press, 1988.

———. *Glory of the Martyrs.* Trans. Raymond Van Dam. Translated Texts for Historians, Latin Series 3. Liverpool: Liverpool University Press, 1988.

———. *History of the Franks.* Trans. Lewis Thorpe. Harmonds Worth: Penguin, 1974.

Hagenmaier, Winfried, ed. *Die lateinischen mittelalterlichen Handschriften der Universitätsbibliothek Freiburg im Breisgau.* 2 vols. Wiesbaden: Harrassowitz, 1974–1980.

Hildegard of Bingen. *Scivias.* Trans. Columba Hart and Jane Bishop. The Classics of Western Spirituality. New York: Paulist Press, 1990.

Jacobus de Voragine. *Legenda aurea.* Ed. Theodor Grässe. Dresden: Libraria Arnoldiana, 1846.

Jacques de Vitry. *The Life of Marie D'Oignies.* Trans. Margot H. King. Toronto: Peregrina, 1993.

Kempe, Margery. *The Book of Margery Kempe.* Ed. Barry Windeatt. New York: Longman, 2000.

Kotzor, Günter, ed. *Das Altenglische Martyrologium.* 2 vols. Munich: Verlag der Bayerischen Akademie der Wissenschaften, C. H. Beck, 1981.

Lapidge, Michael, ed. *Anglo-Saxon Litanies of the Saints.* Woodbridge, Suffolk: Published for the Henry Bradshaw Society by the Boydell Press, 1991.

Liber Sacramentorum Gellonensis (Bibliothèque Nationale MS. Latin 12048) Vol. 1: Text. Ed. A. Dumas Vol. 2: Introduction by J. Deshusses Corpus Christianorum Series Latina 159–159A. Turnhout: Brepols, 1981.

Life of Christina of Markyate, a Twelfth-Century Recluse. Ed. and trans. C. H. Talbot. Oxford: Clarendon Press, 1959.

Mater Spiritualis: The Life of Adelheid of Vilich. Ed. and trans. Madelyn Bergen Dick. Peregrina Translation Series 19. Toronto: Peregrina, 1994.

Methodius of Olympus, Saint. *The Writings of Methodius, Alexander of Lycopolis, Peter of Alexandria, and Several Fragments.* Ante-Nicene Christian Library 14. Ed. Rev. Alexander Roberts, and James Donaldson. Edinburgh: T. & T. Clark, 1869.

Nag Hammadi Library in English. Ed. James M. Robinson. Trans. by members of the Coptic Gnostic Library Project of the Institute for Antiquity and Christianity. New York: Harper and Row, 1977.

Raymond of Capua. *The Life of St. Catherine of Siena.* Trans. George Lamb. London: Harvill Press, 1960

Rule of a Certain Father to the Virgins. 2nd ed. Trans. Jo Ann McNamara and John E. Halborg. Peregrina Translation Series 5. Toronto: Peregrina Publishing, 1993.

Sainted Women of the Dark Ages. Ed. and trans. Jo Ann McNamara and John E. Halborg with E. Gordon Whatley. Durham, N.C.: Duke University Press, 1992.

Tertullian. *Treatises.* In ANF 3-4. *On the Veiling of Virgins, Against Marcion, Apology on Prayer, On the Apparel of Women, On Prescription Against Heretics, Treatise on the Soul, On Baptism, Against Praxeas, An Answer to the Jews, Soul's Testimony, On the Resurrection of the Flesh, To His Wife, Exhortation to Chastity, On Monogamy, On the Flesh of Christ, On Modesty.*

Thietmar of Merseburg. *Ottonian Germany: The Chronicon of Thietmar of Merseburg.* Trans. with notes by David. A. Warner. Manchester, New York: Manchester University Press;

Thomas of Cantimpré. *The Life of Lutgard of Aywières.* Trans. with notes by Margot H. King. Toronto: Peregrina Publishing, 1987.

Vita Sanctae Geretrudis. In *Late Merovingian France: History and Hagiography 640–720.* Ed. and trans. Paul Fouracre and Richard A. Gerberding. Manchester Medieval Sources Series. Manchester, Manchester University Press; 1996.

William of Tocco. *Ystoria sancti Thome de Aquino.* Ed. Claire le Brun-Gouanvic. Toronto: Pontifical Institute for Mediaeval Studies, 1996.

Literature

Albert, Bat-Sheva. *Le Pèlerinage à l'époque carolingienne.* Bibliothèque de la Revue d'histoire ecclésiastique; fasc. 82. Brussels: Nauwelaerts, 1999.

Alexander, J. J. G. "The Benedictional of St. Æthewold and Anglo-Saxon Illumination of the Reform Period." In Parsons, *Tenth-Century Studies,* 169–83.

Archdall, Mervyn. *Monasticon hibernicum, or, An History of the Abbeys, Priories, and Other Religious Houses in Ireland.* Dublin: G. G. J. and J. Robinson . . . and Luke White, 1786.

Arnold, John H. "The Labour of Continence: Masculinity and Clerical Virginity," In *Medieval Virginities,* ed. Anke Bernau, Ruth Evans, and Sarah Salih, 102–18. Toronto: University of Toronto Press, 2003.

Baldwin, Carl R. "The Scribes of the Sacramentary of Gellone." *Scriptorium* 27 (1973): 16–20.

————. "The Scriptorium of the Sacramentary of Gellone." *Scriptorium* 25 (1971): 3–17.

Barrière, Bernadette. "The Cistercian Monastery of Coyroux in the Province of Limousin in the XIIth–XIIIth Centuries." *Gesta* 30 (1992): 76–82.

Barth, Médard. "Die Legende und Verehrung del hl. Attala, die ersten Aebtissin von St. Stephan in Strassburg," *Archiv für Elsässische Kirchengeschichte* 2 (1927): 123–25.

Bateson, Mary. "Origin and Early History of Double Monasteries." *Transactions of the Royal Historical Society* 13 (1899): 137–98.

Bauch, Andreas. ed. *Ein bayerisches Mirakelbuch aus der Karolingerzeit: Die Monheimer Walpurgis—Wunder des Priesters Wolfhard.* Vol. 2, *Quellen zur Geschichte der Diözese Eichstätt.* Regensburg: Friedrich Pustet, 1979.

Beach, Alison I. *Women as Scribes: Book Production and Monastic Reform in Twelfth-Century Bavaria.* Cambridge: Cambridge University Press, 2004.

Bennett, Judith. "History That Stands Still: Women's Work in the European Past." *Feminist Studies* 14 (1988): 269–83.

Berman, Constance H. "Cistercian Women and Tithes." *Cîteaux: Commentarii cistercienses* 49 (1998): 95–128.

Biddick, Kathleen. *The Shock of Medievalism.* Durham, N.C.: Duke University Press, 1998.

Bolton, Brenda. "*Mulieres Sanctae.*" *Studies in Church History* 10 (1973): 77–85.

Bozóky, Edina. "Le role des reines et princesses dans les translations de reliques." In *Reines et princesses au moyen âge: Actes du cinquième colloque international de Montpellier Université Paul-Valéry* (November 24–27, 1999), ed. Marcel Faure, 349–60. Montpellier: Association C.R.I.S.I.M.A., Université Paul-Valéry, 2001.

Bozóky, Edina, and Anne-Marie Helvétius, eds. *Les reliques: Objets, cultes, symboles.* Turnhout: Brepols, 1999.

Braswell, Laurel. "Saint Edburga of Winchester: A Study of Her Cult, A.D. 950–1500, with an Edition of the Fourteenth-Century Middle English and Latin Lives." *Mediaeval Studies* 33 (1971): 292–333.

Brakke, David. *Athanasius and Asceticism.* Baltimore: Johns Hopkins University Press, 1995.

————. "Self-Differentiation Among Christian Groups: The Gnostics and Their Opponents." In *Origins to Constantine.* Vol. 1, *The Cambridge History of Christianity,* ed. Margaret M. Mitchell and Frances Young, 245–60. Cambridge: Cambridge University Press, 2006.

Braudy, Leo. *From Chivalry to Terrorism: War and the Changing Nature of Masculinity.* New York: Alfred A. Knopf, 2003.

Brennan, B. "St. Radegund and the Early Development of Her Cult at Poitiers." *Journal of Religious History* 13.4 (1985): 340–54.

Brooks, N. P. "The Career of St. Dunstan." In *St. Dunstan: His Life, Times, and Cult,* ed. Nigel Ramsay, Margaret Sparks, and Tim Tatton-Brown, 1–24. Woodbridge: Boydell, 1992.

Brown, Peter. *The Body and Society: Men, Women, and Sexual Renunciation in Early Christianity.* New York: Columbia University Press, 1988.

————. *The Cult of the Saints: Its Rise and Function in Latin Christianity.* Chicago: University of Chicago Press, 1981.

————. *Society and the Holy in Late Antiquity.* Berkeley: University of California Press, 1982.

Brubaker, Leslie, and Julia M. H. Smith, eds. *Gender in the Early Medieval World: East and West, 300–900.* Cambridge: Cambridge University Press, 2004.

Brundage, James. "Obscene and Lascivious: Behavioral Obscenity in Canon Law." In *Obscenity: Social Control and Artistic Creation in the European Middle Ages*, ed. Jan Ziolkowski, 252–59. Leiden: Brill, 1998.

Buckley, Jorunn Jacobsen. *Female Fault and Fulfillment in Gnosticism*. Chapel Hill, N.C.: University of North Carolina Press, 1986.

Bugge, John. *Virginitas: An Essay in the History of a Medieval Idea*. The Hague: Martinus Nijhoff, 1975.

Bullough, Donald. "The Continental Background of the Reform." In Parsons, *Tenth-Century Studies*, 20–36.

Bullough, Vern L. "On Being a Male in the Middle Ages." In Lees, *Medieval Masculinities*, 31–45.

Bullough, Vern L., and Bonnie Bullough. *Cross Dressing, Sex and Gender*. Philadelphia: University of Pennsylvania Press, 1993.

Bynum, Caroline Walker. "'. . . And Woman His Humanity': Female Imagery in the Religious Writings of the Later Middle Ages." In *Gender and Religion: On the Complexity of Symbols*, ed. C. W. Bynum, S. Harrell and P. Richman, 257–88. Boston: Beacon Press, 1986.

———. *Holy Feast and Holy Fast: The Religious Significance of Food to Medieval Women*. Berkeley: University of California Press, 1987.

———. *Jesus as Mother: Studies in the Spirituality of the High Middle Ages*. Berkeley: University of California Press, 1982.

———. *The Resurrection of the Body in Western Christianity, 200–1336*. New York: Columbia University Press, 1995.

Cadden, Joan. *Meanings of Sex Difference in the Middle Ages: Medicine, Science, and Culture*. Cambridge: Cambridge University Press, 1993.

Castelli, Elizabeth. "Virginity and Its Meaning for Women's Sexuality in Early Christianity." *Journal of Feminist Studies in Religion* 2 (1986): 61–88.

Chélini, Jean. *L'Aube du moyen âge: Naissance de la chrétienté occidentale. La vie religieuse des laics dans l'Europe carolingienne (750–900)*. Paris: Picard, 1991.

Cherewatuk, Karen, and Ulrike Wiethaus, eds. *Dear Sister: Medieval Women and the Epistolary Genre*. Philadelphia: University of Pennsylvania Press, 1993.

Church, F. Forrester. "Sex and Salvation in Tertullian." *Harvard Theological Review* 68 (1975): 85–101.

Clayton, Mary. *The Apocryphal Gospels of Mary in Anglo-Saxon England*. Cambridge: Cambridge University Press, 1998.

———. *The Cult of the Virgin Mary in Anglo-Saxon England*. Cambridge: Cambridge University Press, 1990.

Coens, Maurice. "Anciennes litanies des saints." In *Recueil d'études bollandiennes*, ed. Maurice Coens, 129–322. Subsidia Hagiographica 37. Brussels: Société des Bollandistes, 1963.

Cooper, Kate, and Conrad Leyser. "The Gender of Grace: Impotence, Servitude, and Manliness in the Fifth-Century West." In Stafford and Mulder-Bakker, *Gendering the Middle Ages*, 5–21.

Crook, John. *The Architectural Setting of the Cult of Saints in the Early Christian West c. 300–1200*. Oxford: Clarendon Press, 2000.

Cullum, P. H. "Clergy, Masculinity and Transgression in Late Medieval England." In Hadley, *Masculinity*, 178–96.

Cullum, P. H., and Katherine J. Lewis, eds. *Holiness and Masculinity in the Middle Ages*. Cardiff: University of Wales Press, 2004.

Dawson, Christopher. *The Making of Europe: An Introduction to the History of European Unity*. London: Sheed & Ward, 1932.

Dempsey, G. T. "Aldhelm of Malmesbury's Social Theology: The Barbaric Heroic Ideal Christianized." *Peritia* 15 (2001): 58–80.

Diem, Albrecht. *"Das monastische Experiment. Die Rolle der Keuschheit bei der Entstehung des westlichen Klosterwesens.* Münster: Lit Verlag, 2005.

Dierkens, Alain. "Réflexions sur le miracle au haut moyen âge." In Société des historiens médiévistes de l'enseignement supériur public, *Miracles, prodiges,* 9–30.

Dutton, Paul Edward. "Charlemagne's Mustache." In *Charlemagne's Mustache and Other Cultural Clusters of a Dark Age,* 3–42. New York: Palgrave, 2004.

Eckenstein, Lina. *Women Under Monasticism: Chapters on Saint-Lore and Convent Life Between A.D. 500 and A.D. 1500.* Cambridge: Cambridge University Press, 1896.

Elliott, Dyan. *Fallen Bodies: Pollution, Sexuality, and Demonology in the Middle Ages.* Philadelphia: University of Pennsylvania Press, 1999.

———. "Flesh and Spirit: Women and the Body." In *The Yale Companion to Medieval Religious Women,* ed. Alastair Minnis and Rosalynn Voaden. New Haven, Conn.: Yale University Press, forthcoming.

———. *Proving Woman: Female Spirituality and Inquisitional Culture in the Later Middle Ages.* Princeton, N.J.: Princeton University Press, 2004.

———. *Spiritual Marriage: Sexual Abstinence in Medieval Wedlock.* Princeton, N.J.: Princeton University Press, 1993.

Elm, Susanna. *Virgins of God: The Making of Asceticism in Late Antiquity.* Oxford: Clarendon Press, 1994.

Erler, Mary, and Maryanne Kowaleski, eds. *Gendering the Master Narrative: Gender and Power in the Middle Ages.* Ithaca, N.Y.: Cornell University Press, 2003.

———. *Women and Power in the Middle Ages.* Athens: University of Georgia Press, 1988.

Farmer, D. H. "The Progress of the Monastic Revival." In Parsons, *Tenth-Century Studies,* 10–19.

Favreau, Robert. "Le culte de Sainte Radegonde à Poitiers au moyen âge." In *Les Religieuses dans le cloître et dans le monde des origins à nos jours. (Actes du deuxième colloque international du CERCOR, Poitiers 29 Septembre-2 Octobre 1988)* 91–93. Saint-Etienne: Publications de l'Université de Saint-Etienne, 1994.

Ferrante, Joan M. *Woman as Image in Medieval Literature: From the Twelfth Century to Dante.* New York: Columbia University Press, 1975.

Finucane, Ronald C. *Miracles and Pilgrims: Popular Beliefs in Medieval England.* Totowa, N.J.: Rowman and Littlefield, 1977.

Foot, Sarah. *Veiled Women.* 2 vols. Aldershot: Ashgate, 2000.

Foucault, Michel. *An Introduction.* Vol. 1, *The History of Sexuality.* Trans. Robert Hurley. New York: Vintage, 1990.

Frassetto, Michael, ed. *Medieval Purity and Piety: Essays on Medieval Clerical Celibacy and Religious Reform.* New York: Garland, 1998.

Gaudemet, Jean. "Le célibat ecclésiastique." *Zeitschrift der Savigny-Stiftung für Rechtsgeschichte, Kanonistische Abteilung* 68 (1982): 1–31.

———. "Note Sur le symbolisme médiévale: Le mariage de l'evêque." *L'année canonique* 22 (1978): 71–80.

Geary, Patrick. *Furta Sacra: Thefts of Relics in the Central Middle Ages.* Rev. ed. Princeton, N.J.: Princeton University Press, 1990.

Gemmiti, Dante. *La Donna in Origene (con testimonianzi dei primi tre secoli).* Naples: Libreria Editrice Redenzione, 1996.

Gilchrist, Roberta. *Contemplation and Action: The Other Monasticism.* London: Leicester University Press, 1995.

Gilchrist, Roberta. *Gender and Material Culture: The Archaeology of Religious Women.* London: Routledge, 1994.

Goffart, Walter "Le Mans, St. Scholastica and St. Benedict." *Revue Bénédictine* 77 (1967): 107–41.

Green, Monica. "Bodies, Gender, Health, Disease: Recent Work on Medieval Women's Medicine." *Studies in Medieval and Renaissance History,* 3rd ser., 2 (2005): 6–9.

Gretsch, Mechthild. *The Intellectual Foundations of the English Benedictine Reform.* Cambridge: Cambridge University Press, 1999.

Griffiths, Fiona. *The Garden of Delights: Reform and Renaissance for Women in the Twelfth Century.* Philadelphia: University of Pennsylvania Press, 2007.

Grundmann, H. *Religiöse Bewegungen im Mittelalter.* Berlin: E. Ebering, 1935.

Guerout, J. "La Période Carolingienne." *L'Abbaye royale Notre-Dame de Jouarre,* ed. Yues Chaussy, J. Dupâquie, G. Goetz, et al. 2 vols. (in vol.1) Paris: G. Victor, 1961.

Hadley, D. M., ed. *Masculinity in Medieval Europe.* London: Longman, 1999.

Hahn, Cynthia. "Seeing and Believing: The Construction of Sanctity in Early-Medieval Saints' Shrines." *Speculum* 72 (1997): 1079–106.

Hall, Dianne. *Women and the Church in Medieval Ireland, c. 1140–1540.* Dublin: Four Courts Press, 2003.

Halperin, David M. "Forgetting Foucault: Acts, Identities, and the History of Sexuality." *Representations* 63 (1998): 93–120.

Head, Thomas, ed. *Medieval Hagiography: An Anthology.* New York: Garland, 2000

Heene, Katrien. *The Legacy of Paradise: Marriage, Motherhood and Woman in Carolingian Edifying Literature.* Frankfurt am Main: Peter Lang, 1997.

Hefele, Karl Joseph von, and Henri Leclerq, eds. and trans. *Histoire des conciles d'après les documents originaux.* Paris: Letouzey, 1907–52.

Heinzelmann, Martin, Klaus Herbers, and Dieter R. Bauer, eds. *Mirakel im Mittelalter: Konzeptionen, Erscheinungsformen, Deutungen.* Stuttgart: Steiner, 2002.

Helvétius, Anne-Marie. "Hagiographie et architecture en Basse-Lotharingie médievale." In *Productions et échanges artistiques en Lotharingie médiévale: Actes des 7es Journées Lotharingiennes,* ed. Jean Schroeder, 27–45. Luxembourg: CLUDEM, 1994.

———. "*Virgo* et *virago*: Réflexions sur le pouvoir du voile consacré d'après les sources hagiographiques de la Gaule de nord." In *Femmes et pouvoirs des femmes à Byzance et en Occident (VIᵉ – XIᵉ siècles),* ed. Stéphane Lebecq, Alain Dierkens, Régine Le Jan, and Jean-Marie Sansterre, 189–204. Villeneuve d'Ascq: Centre de recherche sur l'histoire de l'Europe du Nord-Ouest, Université Charles de Gaulle-Lille 3, 1999.

Hen, Yitzhak. "Les authentiques des reliques de la Terre Sainte en Gaule franque." *Le moyen âge: Revue d'histoire et de philologie* 105.1 (1999): 74–77, 82.

Herdt, Gilbert. "Introduction: Third Sexes and Third Genders." In Herdt, *Third Sex,* 21–83.

Herdt, Gilbert, ed. *Third Sex, Third Gender: Beyond Sexual Dimorphism in Culture and History.* New York: Zone Books, 1994.

Herlihy, David. "Land, Family and Women in Continental Europe, 701–1200." *Traditio* 18 (1962): 89–120.

———. *Opera Muliebria: Women and Work in Medieval Europe.* Philadelphia: University of Pennsylvania Press, 1990.

———. *Pistoia nel Medioevo e nel Rinascimento, 1200–1430.* Florence: Olschki, 1972.

Herlihy, David, and Christiane Klapisch-Zuber. *Les Toscans et leurs familles: Une étude du "catasto" florentin de 1427.* Paris: Fondation nationale des sciences politiques, EESS, 1978.

Herrmann-Mascard, Nicole. *Les reliques des saints: Formation coutumière d'un droit.* Paris: Klincksieck, 1975.

Hill, Joyce. "Archbishop Wulfstan: Reformer?" In Townend, *Wulfstan,* 309–24.

Hoebanx, Jean-Jacques. *L'Abbaye de Nivelles des origines au XIVe siècle.* Brussels: Palais des Académies, 1951.

Hohler, C. E. "Some Service Books of the Later Saxon Church." In Parsons, *Tenth-Century Studies,* 60–83.

Howell, Martha C. *Women, Production, and Patriarchy in Late Medieval Cities.* Chicago: University of Chicago Press, 1986.

Hunter, David. "The Virgin, the Bride, and the Church: Reading Psalm 45 in Ambrose, Jerome, and Augustine." *Church History* 69.2 (June 2000): 281–303.

Irigaray, Luce. *Ce sexe qui n'en est pas un.* Paris: Editions de Minuit, 1977.

Jacobsen, Werner. "Saints' Tombs in Frankish Church Architecture." *Speculum* 72 (1997): 1107–43.

Jacobs, Ellen. "Eileen Power (1889–1940)." In *Medieval Scholarship: Biographical Studies on the Formation of a Discipline.* Vol. 1, *History,* ed. Helen Damico and Joseph B. Zavadil, 219–31. New York: Routledge, 1995.

Jacquart, Danielle, and Claude Thomasset. *Sexuality and Medicine in the Middle Ages.* Trans. Matthew Adamson. Princeton, N.J.: Princeton University Press, 1988.

James, Edward. "Archaeology and the Merovingian Monastery." In *Columbanus and Merovingian Monasticism,* BAR International Series 113, ed. H. B. Clarke and Mary Brennan, 33–55. Oxford: British Archeological Reports, 1981.

James, Liz, ed. *Desire and Denial in Byzantium.* Aldershot: Ashgate, 1997.

Jansen, Katherine Ludwig. *The Making of the Magdalen: Preaching and Popular Devotion in the Later Middle Ages.* Princeton, N.J.: Princeton University Press, 2000.

Jestice, Phyllis. "Why Celibacy? Odo of Cluny and the Development of a New Sexual Morality." In Frassetto, *Medieval Purity,* 81–115.

Johnson, Willis. "The Myth of Jewish Male Menses." *Journal of Medieval History* 24 (1998): 273–95.

Karras, Ruth Mazo. *From Boys to Men: Formations of Masculinity in Late Medieval Europe.* Philadelphia: University of Pennsylvania Press, 2003.

———. "The Latin Vocabulary of Illicit Sex in English Ecclesiastical Court Records." *Journal of Medieval Latin* 2 (1992): 1–17.

———. *Sexuality in Medieval Europe: Doing Unto Others.* London: Routledge, 2005.

Kelly, Kathleen Coyne. *Performing Virginity and Testing Chastity in the Middle Ages.* London: Routledge, 2000.

King, Margaret L. "Book-Lined Cells: Women and Humanism in the Early Italian Renaissance." In *Beyond Their Sex: Learned Women of the European Past,* ed. Patricia H. LaBalme, 66–90. New York: New York University Press, 1980.

Klingshirn, William E. *Caesarius of Arles: The Making of a Christian Community.* Cambridge: Cambridge University Press, 1994.

———. "Caesarius's Monastery for Women in Arles and the Composition and Function of the 'Vita Caesarii.'" *Revue Bénédictine* 100 (1990): 441–81.

Korte, Anne-Marie, ed. *Women and Miracle Stories: A Multidisciplinary Exploration.* Leiden: Brill, 2000.

Kraemer, Ross. "The Conversion of Women to Ascetic Forms of Christianity." *Signs* 6 (1980): 298–307.

Kuefler, Mathew. *The Manly Eunuch: Masculinity, Gender Ambiguity, and Christian Ideology in Late Antiquity.* Chicago: University of Chicago Press, 2001.

Kuefler, Mathew, ed. *The Boswell Thesis: Essays on Christianity, Social Tolerance, and Homosexuality.* Chicago: University of Chicago Press, 2006.

Kupfer, Marcia. *The Art of Healing: Painting for the Sick and the Sinner in a Medieval Town.* University Park: Pennsylvania State University Press, 2003.

Lapidge, Michael. "Æthelwold as Scholar and Teacher." In Yorke, *Bishop Æthelwold,* 89–117.

———. *The Cult of St. Swithun.* Winchester Studies, 4; The Anglo-Saxon Minsters of Winchester, 2. Oxford: Clarendon Press, 2003.

LaPorte, Jean-Pierre. "Les reliques de Chelles, un sépulture royale mérovingienne." *Bulletin de la société nationale des antiquaires de France* [n.v.] (1989): 290–303.

Laqueur, Thomas. *Making Sex: Body and Gender from the Greeks to Freud.* Cambridge, Mass.: Harvard University Press, 1990.

Laslett, Peter. *Household and Family in Past Time: Comparative Studies in the Size and Structure of the Domestic Group over the Last Three Centuries in England, France Serbia, Japan and Colonial North America, with Further Materials from Western Europe.* Cambridge: Cambridge University Press, 1972.

Lassner, Jacob. *Demonizing the Queen of Sheba: Boundaries of Gender and Culture in Postbiblical Judaism and Medieval Islam.* Chicago: University of Chicago Press, 1993.

Le Bras, Gabriel, ed. *Sainte Fare et Faremoutiers: Treize siècles de vie monastique.* Paris: Abbaye de Faremoutiers, 1956.

Lees, Clare A., ed. *Medieval Masculinities: Regarding Men in the Middle Ages.* Minneapolis: University of Minnesota Press, 1994.

Lees, Clare A., and Gillian R. Overing. "Before History, Before Difference: Bodies, Metaphors, and the Church in Anglo-Saxon England." *Yale Journal of Criticism* 11 (1998): 315–34.

LeRoy Ladurie, Emmanuel. *Montaillou: The Promised Land of Error* (New York: G. Braziller, 1978) trans. Barbara Bray, from the French original *Montaillou, village occitan de 1294 à 1324.* Paris: Gallimard, 1975.

Lesne, Emile. *Historie de la propriété ecclésiastique en France.* 6 vols. Lille, R. Giard; Paris: H. Champion, 1910–1943.

Levin, Eve. *Sex and Society in the World of the Orthodox Slavs, 900–1700.* Ithaca, N.Y.: Cornell University Press, 1989.

Leyser, C. *Authority and Asceticism from Augustine to Gregory the Great.* Oxford: Oxford University Press, 2000.

———. "Masculinity in Flux: Nocturnal Emission and the Limits of Celibacy in the Early Middle Ages." In Hadley, *Masculinity,* 103–20.

Lifshitz, Felice. "Gender Trouble in Paradise: The Case of the Liturgical *Virgo.*" In *Images of Medieval Sanctity: Essays in Honour of Gary Dickson,* ed. Debra Higgs Strickland, 25–39. Leiden: Brill, 2007.

———. *The Name of the Saint: The Martyrology of Jerome and Access to the Sacred in Francia, 627–827.* Notre Dame, Ind.: University of Notre Dame Press, 2005.

———. "The Persistence of Late Antiquity: Christ as Man and Woman in an Eighth-Century Miniature." *Medieval Feminist Forum* 38 (2004): 18–27.

Llewellyn-Jones, Lloyd. *Aphrodite's Tortoise: The Veiled Women of Ancient Greece.* Swansea: Classical Press of Wales, 2002.

Lowe, E. A., ed. *Codices latini antiquiores: A Paleographical Guide to Latin Manuscripts Prior to the Ninth Century.* 11 vols. plus supplement. Oxford: Clarendon Press, 1934–1966.

Loyn, H. R. "Church and State in England in the Tenth and Eleventh Centuries." In Parsons, *Tenth-Century Studies*, 94–102.

Maillé, Geneviève Aliette de Rohan-Chabot. *Les Cryptes de Jouarre*. Paris: Picard, 1971.

Makowski, Elizabeth, and Katharina Wilson, eds. *Wykked Wyves and the Woes of Marriage: Misogamous Literature from Juvenal to Chaucer*. Albany: State University of New York Press, 1990.

Mann, Gareth. "The Development of Wulfstan's Alcuin Manuscript." In Townend, *Wulfstan*, 235–78.

Martin, Dale. *The Corinthian Body*. New Haven, Conn.: Yale University Press, 1995.

Mason, Emma. *St. Wulfstan of Worcester, c. 1008–1095*. Oxford: Oxford University Press, 1990.

Matter, E. Ann. *The Voice of My Beloved: The Song of Songs in Western Medieval Christianity*. Philadelphia: University of Pennsylvania Press, 1990.

Mayr-Harting, Henry. "Functions of a Twelfth-Century Shrine: The Miracles of St. Frideswide." In *Studies in Medieval History Presented to R. H. C. Davis,* ed. Henry Mayr-Harting and R. I. Moore, 193–206. London: Hambledon Press, 1985.

McLaughlin, Mary L. "Creating and Recreating Communities of Women: The Case of Corpus Domini, Ferrara, 1406–1452." *Signs* 14.2 (1989): 293–320.

McLaughlin, Megan. "The Bishop as Bridegroom: Marital Imagery and Clerical Celibacy in the Eleventh and Early Twelfth Centuries." In Frassetto, *Medieval Purity*, 210–37.

McNamara, Jo Ann. "Canossa and the Ungendering of the Public Man." In *Render Unto Caesar: The Religious Sphere in World Politics*, ed. Sabrina Petra Ramet and Donald W. Treadgold, 131–49. Washington, D.C.: American University Press, 1995.

———. "Chastity as a Third Gender in the History and Hagiography of Gregory of Tours." In Mitchell and Wood, *World of Gregory*, 199–209.

———. "City Air Makes Men Free and Women Bound." In *Text and Territory: Geographical Imagination in the European Middle Ages*, ed. S. Tomasch and S. Gilles, 143–59. Philadelphia: University of Pennsylvania Press, 1998.

———. "The *Herrenfrage*: The Restructuring of the Gender System, 1050–1150." In Lees, *Medieval Masculinities*, 3–29.

———. *A New Song: Celibate Women in the First Three Christian Centuries*. Binghamton, N.Y.: Harrington Park Press, 1983.

———. *Sisters in Arms: Catholic Nuns Through Two Millennia*. Cambridge, Mass.: Harvard University Press, 1996.

———. "An Unresolved Syllogism." In Murray, *Conflicted Identities*, 1–24.

———. "Women and Power Through the Family Revisited." In Erler and Kowaleski, *Gendering the Master Narrative*, 17–30.

McNamara, Jo Ann, and Suzanne Fonay Wemple. "The Power of Women Through the Family." *Feminist Studies* 1 (1973): 126–41.

Meeks, Wayne. "The Image of the Androgyne: Some Uses of a Symbol in Earliest Christianity." *History of Religions* 13 (1974): 165–208.

Melammed, Renée Levine. "Castilian 'Conversas' at Work." In *Women at Work in Spain: From the Middle Ages to Early Modern Times*, ed. Marilyn Stone and Carmen Benito-Vessels, 81–100. New York: Peter Lang, 1998.

———. *Heretics or Daughters of Israel? The Crypto-Jewish Women of Castile*. Oxford: Oxford University Press, 1999.

Metzger, Marcel. *Les Sacramentaires*. Turnhout: Brepols, 1994.

Miller, Maureen. "Masculinity, Reform, and Clerical Culture: Narratives of Episcopal Holiness in the Gregorian Era." *Church History* 72 (2003): 25–52.

Mills, Robert. "The Signification of the Tonsure." In Cullum and Lewis, *Holiness*, 109–126.

Mitchell, Kathleen, and Ian Wood, eds. *The World of Gregory of Tours*. Leiden: Brill, 2002.

Mitchell, Linda E. *Portraits of Medieval Women: Family, Marriage, and Politics in England, 1225–1350*. New York: Palgrave, 2003.

Monastic Matrix. http://monasticmatrix.org.

Moriarty, Rachel. "'Playing the Man': The Courage of Christian Martyrs, Translated and Transposed." In Swanson, *Gender*, 1–13.

Murray, Jacqueline, ed. *Conflicted Identities and Multiple Masculinities: Men in the Medieval West*. New York: Garland, 1999.

———. "Sexual Mutilation and Castration Anxiety: A Medieval Perspective," in *The Boswell Thesis: Essays on Christianity, Social Tolerance, and Homosexuality*, ed. Mathew Kuefler, 254–72. Chicago: University of Chicago Press, 2006.

———. "'The law of sin that is in my members': The Problem of Male Embodiment." In *Gender and Holiness: Men, Women and Saints in Late Medieval Europe*, ed. Samantha J. E. Riches and Sarah Salih, 9–22. London: Routledge, 2002.

———. "Masculinizing Religious Life: Sexual Prowess, the Battle for Chastity, and Monastic Identity." In Cullum and Lewis, *Holiness*, 24–42.

Nelson, Janet L. "Monks, Secular Men, and Masculinity, c. 900." In Hadley, *Masculinity*, 127–30.

———. "Queens as Jezebels: The Careers of Brunhild and Balthild in Merovingian History." In *Medieval Women: Essays Dedicated and Presented to Professor Rosalind M. T. Hill*. Studies in Church History: Subsidia 1, ed. D. Baker, 31–77. Oxford: Oxford University Press, 1978. Reprinted in J. L. Nelson, *Politics and Ritual in Early Medieval Europe*, 1–48. London: Hambledon Press, 1986.

Newman, Barbara. *From Virile Woman to WomanChrist: Studies in Medieval Religion and Literature*. Philadelphia: University of Pennsylvania Press, 1995.

Nilson, Ben. *Cathedral Shrines of Medieval England*. Rochester, N.Y.: Boydell Press, 1998.

Nirenberg, David. "Conversion, Sex, and Segregation: Jews and Christians in Medieval Spain." *American Historical Review* 107 (2002): 1065–93.

———. *Communities of Violence: Persecution of Minorities in the Middle Ages*. Princeton, N.J.: Princeton University Press, 1996.

O'Carroll, James. "Sainte Fare et les origines." In *Sainte Fare et Faremoutiers: Treize siècles de vie monastique*, ed. Gabriel LeBras, 3–45. Faremoutiers: Abbaye de Faremoutiers, 1956.

O'Sullivan, Sinéad. "Adelhelm's *De Virginitate*—Patristic Pastiche or Innovative Exposition?" *Peritia* 12 (1998): 271–95.

———. "The Image of Adornment in Adelhelm's *De Virginitate*: Cyprian and His Influence." *Peritia* 15 (2001): 48–57.

Pagels, Elaine. *The Gnostic Paul: Gnostic Exegesis of the Pauline Letters*. Philadelphia: Fortress Press, 1975.

Park, Katharine, and Robert A. Nye. "Destiny Is Anatomy." Review of *Making Sex: Body and Gender from the Greeks to Freud* by Thomas Laqueur. *New Republic*, February 18 (1991): 3–57.

Parsons, David, ed. *Tenth-Century Studies: Essays in Commemoration of the Millennium of the Council of Winchester and Regularis Concordia*. London: Phillimore, 1975.

Partner, Nancy. "No Sex, No Gender." In *Studying Medieval Women: Sex, Gender, Feminism*, ed. Nancy Partner, 117–41. Cambridge, Mass.: Medieval Academy of America, 1993.

Pettit, Emma. "Holiness and Masculinity in Adelhelm's *Opus Geminatum de virginitate*." In Cullum and Lewis, *Holiness*, 8–24.

Peyroux, Catherine Rosanna. "Abbess and Cloister: Double Monasteries in the Early Medieval West." PhD diss. Princeton University, 1991.

Power, Eileen. *Medieval English Nunneries, c. 1275 to 1535*. Cambridge: Cambridge University Press, 1922.

———. *Medieval People*. London: Methuen, 1924.

———. *Medieval Women*. ed. M. M. Postan. Cambridge: Cambridge University Press, 1975.

Quirk, Kathleen. "Men, Women and Miracles in Normandy, 1050–1150," in *Medieval Memories: Men, Women and the Past, 700–1300*, ed. Elisabeth van Houts, 53–71. Harlow: Longman, 2001.

Rambaux, Claude. *Tertullian face aux morales des trois premiers siècles*. Paris: Société d'Edition "Les Belles Lettres," 1979.

Ridyard, Susan J. *The Royal Saints of Anglo-Saxon England: A Study of West Saxon and East Anglian Cults*. Cambridge Studies in Medieval Life and Thought, 4th ser., 9. Cambridge: Cambridge University Press, 1988.

Ringrose, Kathryn M. *The Perfect Servant: Eunuchs and the Social Construction of Gender in Byzantium*. Chicago: University of Chicago Press, 2003.

———. "Living in the Shadows: Eunuchs and Gender in Byzantium." In Herdt, *Third Sex*, 85–109.

Rollason, David. "Lists of Saints' Resting-Places in Anglo-Saxon England." *Anglo-Saxon England* 7 (1978): 61–93.

———. *The Mildrith Legend: A Study in Early Medieval Hagiography in England*. Leicester: Leicester University Press, 1982.

———. *Saints and Relics in Anglo-Saxon England*. Oxford: Blackwell, 1989.

Rosenwein, Barbara. "Inaccessible Cloisters: Gregory of Tours and Episcopal Exemption." In Mitchell and Wood, *World of Gregory*, 181–97.

Ross, James Bruce, ed. *The Portable Medieval Reader*. With an introduction by James Bruce Ross and Mary Martin McLaughlin. New York: Viking, 1949.

Russell, Josiah Cox. *Late Ancient and Medieval Population Control* (Philadelphia: American Philosophical Society, 1985).

Salisbury, Joyce. *Perpetua's Passion: The Death and Memory of a Young Roman Woman*. New York: Routledge, 1997.

Sawyer, P. H. "Charters of the Reform Movement: The Worcester Archive." In Parsons, *Tenth-Century Studies*, 84–93.

Schirrmacher, Thomas. *Paul in Conflict with the Veil*. Nuremberg: Verlag für Theologie und Religionswissenschaft, 2002.

Schmugge, Ludwig. *Kinder, Kirche, Karrieren: Päpstliche Dispense von der unehelichen Geburt im Spätmittelalter*. Zurich: Artemis & Winkler, 1985.

Schulenburg, Jane Tibbetts. *Forgetful of Their Sex: Female Sanctity and Society ca. 500–1100*. Chicago: University of Chicago Press, 1998.

———. "Gender, Celibacy, and Proscriptions of Sacred Space: Symbol and Practice." In *Women's Space: Patronage, Place, and Gender in the Medieval Church*, eds. Virginia Chieffo Raguin and Sarah Stanbury, 185–205. Albany: State University of New York Press, 2005.

———. "Sexism and the Celestial Gynaeceum—from 500 to 1200." *Journal of Medieval History* 4 (1978): 117–33.

———. "Strict Active Enclosure and Its Effects on the Female Monastic Experience (ca. 500–1100)." In *Distant Echoes*. Vol. 1, *Medieval Religious Women*, ed. John Nichols and Lillian Thomas Shank, 51–86. Kalamazoo, Mich.: Cistercian Publications, 1984.

Scobie, Graham, and Ken Qualmann. *Nunnaminster: A Saxon and Medieval Community of Nuns*. Winchester: Winchester Museums Service, 1993.

Scott, Joan Wallach. "Gender: A Useful Category of Analysis." *American Historical Review* 91 (1986): 1053–75.

Sigal, P.-A. *L'Homme et le miracle dans la France médiévale (XIe–XIIe siècle)*. Paris: Cerf, 1985.

———. "Reliques, pèlerinage et miracles dans l'église médiévale (XIe–XIIIe siècles)." *Revue d'Histoire de l'Eglise de France* 76 (1990): 193–211.

Smith, Julia M. H. "Women at the Tomb: Access to Relic Shrines in the Early Middle Ages." In Mitchell and Wood, *World of Gregory*, 163–80.

Société des historiens médiévistes de l'enseignement supérieur public (SHMES) ed. *Miracles, prodiges et merveilles au moyen âge: XXVe Congrès de la SHMES, Orléans, juin 1994*. Paris: Publications de la Sorbonne, 1995.

Stafford, Pauline, and Anneke E. Mulder-Bakker, eds. *Gendering the Middle Ages*. Oxford: Blackwell, 2001.

Staples, Kathryn Kelsey, and Ruth Mazo Karras. "Christina's Tempting." In *Christina of Marykate: A Twelfth-Century Holy Woman*, ed. Samuel Fanous and Henrietta Leyser, 184–96. London: Routledge, 2004.

Stark, Rodney. *The Victory of Reason: How Christianity Led to Freedom, Capitalism and Western Success* (New York: Random, 2005).

Swanson, R. N. "Angels Incarnate: Clergy and Masculinity from Gregorian Reform to Reformation." In Hadley, *Masculinity*, 160–77.

———, ed. *Gender and Christian Religion*. Studies in Church History 4. Woodbridge: Boydell, 1998.

Symons, Dom Thomas. "*Regularis Concordia*: History and Derivation." In Parsons, *Tenth-Century Studies*, 37–59.

Thacker, Alan. "Dynastic Monasteries and Family Cults: Edward the Elder's Sainted Kindred." In *Edward the Elder 899–924*, ed. N. J. Higham and D. H. Hill, 248–63. London: Routledge, 2001.

Thacker, Alan, and Richard Sharpe. *Local Saints and Local Churches in the Early Medieval West*. Oxford: Oxford University Press, 2002.

Thibodeaux, Jennifer. "Man of the Church, or Man of the Village? Gender and the Parish Clergy in Medieval Normandy." *Gender and History* 18.2 (2006): 380–99.

Thiery, Daniel E. "Plowshares and Swords: Clerical Involvement in Acts of Violence and Peacemaking in Late Medieval England, c. 1400–1536." *Albion* 36 (2004): 202–22.

Tougher, Shaun. "Social Transformation, Gender Transformation: The Court Eunuch, 300–900." In *Gender in the Early Medieval World: East and West, 300–900*, ed. Leslie Brubaker and Julia M. H. Smith, 70–82. Cambridge: Cambridge University Press, 2004.

Townend, Matthew, ed. *Wulfstan, Archbishop of York: The Proceedings of the Second Alcuin Conference*. Turnhout: Brepols, 2004.

Trevett, Christine. *Montanism: Gender, Authority, and the New Prophecy*. Cambridge: Cambridge University Press, 1996.

Tudor, Victoria. "The Cult of St. Cuthbert in the Twelfth Century." In *Saint Cuthbert, His Cult and His Community to A.D. 1200*, ed. Gerald Bonner, David Rollason, and Clare Stancliffe, 457–58. Woodbridge: Boydell, 1989.

Van Dam, Raymond. *Saints and Their Miracles in Late Antique Gaul*. Princeton, N.J.: Princeton University Press, 1993.

Van Eijk, Ton H. C. "Marriage and Virginity, Death and Immortality." In *Epektasis: Mélanges patristiques offerts au Cardinal Jean Daniélou*, ed. Jacques Fontaine and Charles Kannengiesser, 209–35. Paris: Beauchesne, 1972.

Van Houts, Elisabeth M. C. *Memory and Gender in Medieval Europe, 900–1200*. Basingstoke, Hampshire: Macmillan, 1999.

————. "Orality in Norman Hagiography of the Eleventh and Twelfth Centuries: The Value of Female Testimonies." In *History and Family Traditions in England and the Continent*, ed. Elisabeth M. C. Van Houts, 1–13. Aldershot, Hampshire: 1999.

Venarde, Bruce. *Women's Monasticism and Medieval Society: Nunneries in France and England, 890–1215*. Ithaca, N.Y.: Cornell University Press, 1997.

Viller, Marcel, et al., eds. *Dictionnaire de la spiritualité ascétique et mystique, doctrine et histoire*. Paris: G. Beauchesne, 1937–1967.

Ward, Benedicta. *Miracles and the Medieval Mind: Theory, Record and Event, 1000–1215*. Philadelphia: University of Pennsylvania Press, 1982.

Weber, Max. *The Protestant Ethic and the Sprit of Capitalism*, trans. Talcott Parsons. New York: Scribner, 1930.

Wieland, Gernot R. Review of Gwara, *The Medieval Review* 4.01.01. http://name.umdl.umich.edu/baj9928.04041.001.

Wemple, Suzanne Fonay. *Women in Frankish Society: Marriage and the Cloister, 500–900*. Philadelphia: University of Pennsylvania Press, 1981.

Wilcox, Jonathan. "Wulfstan's *Sermo Lupi ad Anglos* as Political Performance: 16 February 1014 and Beyond." In Townend, *Wulfstan*, 375–96.

Williams, N. P. *The Ideas of the Fall and of Original Sin*. London: Longman's, Green and Company, 1927.

Wogan-Browne, Jocelyn. *Saints' Lives and Women's Literary Culture, c. 1150–1300: Virginity and Its Authorizations*. Oxford: Oxford University Press, 2001.

Wormald, Patrick. "Archbishop Wulfstan: Eleventh–Century State-Builder." In Townend, *Wulfstan*, 9–28.

Wulf, Walter. *Saxe roman*. L'Abbaye Sainte-Marie de la Pierre-Qui-Vire: Zodiaque, 1996.

Yorke, Barbara. "Æthelwold and the Politics of the Tenth Century." In Yorke, *Bishop Æthewold*, 65–88.

————, ed. *Bishop Æthewold: His Career and Influence*. Woodbridge: Boydell, 1988.

————. *Nunneries and the Anglo-Saxon Royal Houses*. London: Continuum, 2003.

Zufferey, Maurice. "Der Mauritiuskult im Früh– und Hochmittelalter." *Historisches Jahrbuch* 106 (1986): 23–58.

Contributors

Lisa M. Bitel is professor of history, gender studies, and religion at the University of Southern California, and is director of Monastic Matrix (http://monasticmatrix.org). She is the author of *Women in Early Medieval Europe, 300-1100* (2002), *Land of Women: Tales of Sex and Gender from Early Ireland* (1996), *Isle of the Saints: Monastic Settlement and Christian Community in Early Ireland* (1990), and *Landscape with Two Saints: How Genovefa of Paris and Brigit of Kildare Christianized Barbarian Europe* (forthcoming).

Dyan Elliott is John Evans Professor of History at Northwestern University. She is the author of *Proving Woman: Female Spirituality and Inquisitional Culture in the Later Middle Ages* (2004), *Fallen Bodies: Pollution, Sexuality, and Demonology in the Middle Ages* (1999), and *Spiritual Marriage: Sexual Abstinence in Medieval Wedlock* (1993).

Ruth Mazo Karras is professor of history at the University of Minnesota, and the general editor of The Middle Ages Series for the University of Pennsylvania Press. She is the author of *Sexuality in Medieval Europe: Doing Unto Others* (2005), *From Boys to Men: Formations of Masculinity in Late Medieval Europe* (2003), *Common Women: Prostitution and Sexuality in Medieval England* (1996), and *Slavery and Society in Medieval Scandinavia* (1988).

Felice Lifshitz is professor of history at Florida International University and Medieval Europe editor for History Compass (www.blackwell-compass.com). She is the author of *The Norman Conquest of Pious Neustria: Historiographic Discourse and Saintly Relics, 684–1090* (1995) and *The Name of the Saint: The Martyrology of Jerome and Access to the Sacred in Francia, 627–827* (2005), and coeditor (with Celia Chazelle) of *Paradigms and Methods in Early Medieval Studies* (2007).

Jacqueline Murray is dean of arts and professor of history at the University of Guelph. She is the editor of *Love, Marriage, and Family in the Middle Ages: A Reader* (2001), *Conflicted Identities and Multiple Masculinities: Men in the Medieval West* (1999), *Desire and Discipline: Sex and Sexuality in the Premodern West* (1996), and *Technology and Culture* (1994).

Jane Tibbetts Schulenburg is professor of history at the University of Wisconsin—Madison. She is the author of *Forgetful of Their Sex: Female Sanctity and Society, ca. 500–1100* (1998).

Index

Acknowledgments

The editors wish to thank the following for their help with this project: Constance Berman, Sarah Blake, Thelma Fenster, Janet Loengard, Karl Morrison, Joel T. Rosenthal, James D. Ryan, Pete Schermerhorn, and Bonnie Wheeler. The editors and contributors all acknowledge the helpful comments of the anonymous readers for the University of Pennsylvania Press. We are also grateful to the Bibliothèque Nationale de France and the County Clare Library for permission to reproduce images used in this book.